The
Magic
of the
Elements

ABOUT DEBORAH LIPP

Deborah has been teaching Wicca, magic, and the occult for over 30 years. She became a Witch and High Priestess in the 1980s, as an initiate of the Gardnerian tradition of Wicca. She's been published in many Pagan publications, including newWitch, The Llewellyn Magical Almanac, Pangaia, and Green Egg, and has lectured on Pagan and occult topics on three continents.

As an active "out of the closet" member of the Pagan community, Deborah has appeared in various media discussing Wicca, including Coast-to-Coast radio, an A&E documentary *(Ancient Mysteries: Witchcraft in America)*, television talk shows, and the New York Times.

In "real life" Deborah is a systems specialist in legal technology. She lives with her spouse Melissa and an assortment of cats in Jersey City, NJ, three blocks from a really great view of Freedom Tower. Deborah reads and teaches Tarot, solves and designs puzzles, watches old movies, hand-paints furniture, and dabbles in numerous handcrafts.

The Magic of the Elements

Deborah Lipp

Chicago, Illinois

The Magic of the Elements copyright © 2023 by Deborah Lipp. All rights reserved. No part of this book may be reproduced in any manner whatsoever without written permission from Crossed Crow Books, except in the case of brief quotations embodied in critical articles and reviews.

Paperback ISBN: 978-1-959883-16-6
Library of Congress Control Number on file.

Cover design by Wycke Malliway.
Typesetting by Gianna Rini.
Edited by Becca Fleming.

Disclaimer: Crossed Crow Books, LLC does not participate in, endorse, or have any authority or responsibility concerning private business transactions between our authors and the public. Any internet references contained in this work were found to be valid during the time of publication, however, the publisher cannot guarantee that a specific reference will continue to be maintained. This book's material is not intended to diagnose, treat, cure, or prevent any disease, disorder, ailment, or any physical or psychological condition. The author, publisher, and its associates shall not be held liable for the reader's choices when approaching this book's material. The views and opinions expressed within this book are those of the author alone and do not necessarily reflect the views and opinions of the publisher.

Published by:
Crossed Crow Books, LLC
6934 N Glenwood Ave, Suite C
Chicago, IL 60626
www.crossedcrowbooks.com

Printed in the United States of America.

OTHER TITLES BY DEBORAH LIPP

CROSSED CROW BOOKS

The Way of Four

OTHER PUBLISHERS

Bending the Binary: Polarity Magic in a Nonbinary World

*The Beginner's Guide to the Occult:
Understanding the History, Key Concepts, and Practices of the Supernatural*

*The Complete Book of Spells:
Wiccan Spells for Healing, Protection, and Celebration*

*Magical Power for Beginners:
How to Raise & Send Energy for Spells That Work*

*Tarot Interactions:
Become More Intuitive, Psychic & Skilled at Reading Cards*

*The Study of Witchcraft:
A Guidebook to Advanced Wicca*

*Elements of Ritual:
Air, Fire, Water and Earth in the Wiccan Circle*

This book is dedicated to the Wicked Witch of the West, to the Witch of Endor, to Snow White's stepmother, and to every other woman who ever got a bad reputation for casting a spell.

Contents

Acknowledgements XII

Introduction to the New Edition   1

Introduction   3
Magical Expertise 5
Spell Construction. 6

Chapter One: What Are the Elements?   8
The Qualities of the Elements 9
Is There a Fifth Element?. 18
Elementals. 20
Elemental Overload. 23

Chapter Two: What Is Spellcasting?   25
What Is Magic?. 26
How Does Magic Work? 26
Should You Do Magic? 42
What Is a Spell?. 48
Working with the Magic of the Elements 63

Chapter Three: Preparing for Magic   65
Preparing Your Space. 65
Preparing Yourself 67
Preparing Your Tools and Ingredients. 71

Chapter Four: Magic that Brings the Elements to You 86
Balancing Spells.................................. 87

Chapter Five: Using the Elements in Spells 110
Using All Four Elements in a Spell 110
Using a Particular Element in a Spell............... 115

Chapter Six: Using Air in Spells
Using Air... 120
Aromatherapy and Scent 121
Magical Writing and Speaking...................... 127

Chapter Seven: Using Fire in Spells 144
Using Fire 144
Candle Magic 145
Spells That Burn Things 160
Sex Magic 175

Chapter Eight: Using Water in Spells 188
Using Water...................................... 188
Washing, Soaking, Sprinkling 189
Painting with Water............................... 196
Drinking and the Cup 201
Divination Magic.................................. 217

Chapter Nine: Using Earth in Spells 223
Using Earth...................................... 223
Food Magic 224
Burial and Planting Magic.......................... 233
Stone and Gem Magic............................. 243
Magic in Clay and Sculpture 247

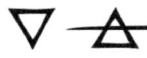

APPENDIX A: THE SPELLS   253

APPENDIX B: GOING SHOPPING   255
Candles 256
Craft Store. 256
Grocery Store/Supermarket 256
Hardware/Garden Store. 257
Herbs and Incenses 257
Housewares Store 259
Oils 260
Recipes 260
Specialty Stores 261
Stationery Store/Office Supply Store 262

APPENDIX C: GODS AND GODDESSES   263

APPENDIX D: INVOKING AND BANISHING PENTAGRAMS   266

APPENDIX E: CORRESPONDENCE CHARTS   268
Elemental Herbs, Flowers, and Other Plants 268
Elemental Gems and Stones 270

BIBLIOGRAPHY. *272*
INDEX *273*

ACKNOWLEDGMENTS FOR THE NEW EDITION

I could not have written this new edition without support and inspiration from the wonderful people in my life. Christine LaPlante inspired me to believe this was even possible. Jack Chanek threw stellar research at me—with great force—which helped me transform my thoughts and writing on elemental tools. Elysia Gallo and Andrea Neff at Llewellyn helped me pull together material from the original manuscript. I owe thanks to them all.

ACKNOWLEDGMENTS

I would sort of like to acknowledge everyone I've ever met. Ever. Because it's scary to sit down and think about how good I feel about people, how grateful I am for the knowledge freely shared, the help generously offered, the comfort readily available, and to think that I have somehow left out one of those wonderful people. Some gratitude!

While it would be safer to just thank everyone, I would very much like to thank people by name, so if I've left you out, please know I meant to thank you. Like the Oscar winner who forgot to thank her spouse, the moment just got away from me. Most of what I know about magic I learned from two people: Susan Carberry and Isaac Bonewits. I thank them, their teachers, and their teachers' teachers way on down the line. I also thank the people I learned with in the Jersey Shore Pagan Way, in Stormcircle, and in ADF; people who were there with me sharing my experiments, participating in group spells, and lending their energy to the work of Witchcraft and magic. As ever, I thank my daughter, Ursula, for giving me the space to write, and for letting me experiment on her (in a nice way). Donald Michael Kraig gave me wonderful feedback for the section on sex magic. If I didn't take his good advice, the fault is entirely mine and not his. Andrea Neff at Llewellyn makes me a better writer. Good editors are an author's joy, and Andrea is better than good.

Introduction to the New Edition

When I wrote the original introduction to this book, it opened with, "About a year ago…" Now it's been over fifteen years. I've learned a lot in those years, large things and small, and this book reflects that.

Throughout every page of *Magic of the Elements*, there's new material, starting with a new title that more accurately reflects the contents. I was quite taken with the original title, *The Way of Four Spellbook*, but the truth is, the book was never and is not a spellbook. It's *about* spells, and the relatively small number of spells (thirty-two) are present to teach spellcraft, whereas a true spellbook is a reference book with hundreds of spells or more.

There's new material on the elements, expanded correspondences, and a lot more material on elemental tools. I've added new research on the Golden Dawn and their elemental correspondences. Speaking of tools, there's also new material on directing power with tools and updated tool instructions throughout, including more options in virtually every spell.

The section on invocations is brand new.

I added information on the "Maharishi Effect" that I learned while researching another book.

I like to think I'm a better writer than I was fifteen years ago and small edits, just to make it all sound better, appear in every section.

Factual information has been revised so that anything that was current in 2006 but is obsolete in today is newly up to date. This is good, and also sad. Three of the people thanked in the original acknowledgements, Susan Carberry, Isaac Bonewits, and Donald Michael Kraig, are no longer living. I have made sure any references to living and formerly living people are accurate.

I've gotten a little smarter about gender since 2006—a lot of us have. I have carefully reviewed language, including pronouns, and have removed language that, looking back, seems gender essentialist. For one, I've replaced "he or she" (and its variations) with "them" throughout. It was my thought upon originally writing this book that "he or she" removed the sexism of assuming "he," but now I look at it and see the assumption that everyone is one or the other. If I missed something, I hope you will forgive me.

I hope this new edition is enjoyable, useful, and interesting. The reward of writing is knowing that somewhere, a reader is touched in some way. I hope you are that reader.

Jersey City, New Jersey, January 2022

Introduction

It was about fifteen years ago that I finished working on my book, *The Way of Four*. That book was very special to me, as it came from a passion about the four elements that has been with me most of my life. To me, the elements are how I shape my occult knowledge. Some people are Kabbalists and view the whole world through the perceptual lens of paths and sephirot, but I have always been drawn to the deceptive simplicity of a universe of four. I coined the term "The Way of Four" to describe a system, and indeed a life, built upon a path balanced in Air, Fire, Water, and Earth.

A writer goes about their business in one of two basic ways. They either write about something they already know, pouring knowledge from their head to the page, or they decide to write about something and then research it. However, these extremes leave out a vast middle ground, because even if you're writing about what you know best, say, an autobiography,[1] a certain amount of research is needed. You don't remember everything offhand; you have to fact-check, and sometimes you want to flesh out the background a bit. As in that example of the autobiography, I might want to write about what I was doing when I was twenty-one, and I might clearly remember an incident that happened while the radio was playing in the background. I might decide

---

1 I've done one of those as well, called *Merry Meet Again*.

to research the hit songs of that year so that I would have a good guess as to what was on the radio. No one knows everything, and even if you know, you check, you double-check, you expand, you elaborate.

So, I wrote *The Way of Four*, and in it, I included a section called "Elemental Spells." Now, I already knew a lot about spells, and I already knew a lot about elemental spells. But writing this section opened up a whole lot of possibilities; it made me explore areas I knew well more deeply, and it made me ask questions about areas I didn't know as well. I was surprised at how much depth there was to uncover. Several times in the course of that half-chapter, I thought, "This could be a whole book." About the third or fourth time I typed that phrase, or one similar, it occurred to me that, by gosh, it could.

As a writer, I had no interest in rehashing material that has been amply covered by others. Nor have I had a great deal of interest, as a Witch, in buying and owning spellbooks, although I do have a few. But each spell in *The Way of Four* was an illustration of a principle. A book *about* spellwork and the elements seemed exciting to me.

Experienced chefs may not need new recipes on their shelves, but they'll passionately enjoy a book *about* cooking and food. Mark Bittman's classic *How to Cook Everything*, for example, talks about the "how to" and "why" and "why it's so much fun" at least as much as it provides cooking instructions.

Magic of the Elements isn't "How to Magic Everything," but it's how, and why, and why it's so much fun.

This book is structured around the elements. After introductory material on the elements and on magic, each chapter is a lesson in the magic of an element. So, you'll learn what an Earth spell is, why to do it, what an Earth purpose is, what Earth ingredients are, and what kinds of spells best fall into this category. Then a spell is provided as an object lesson for each spell type. Spells are laid out for easy reference and listed together in an appendix, but you may enjoy the "not recipe" stuff as much, or more, than the spells themselves.

Magic of the Elements does not omit balance spells, which combine all four elements. Because of my own philosophy of the Way of Four, balance spells are used where other teachers might advise "Spirit" spells (see Chapter 1 for a discussion of Spirit as an element).

Of necessity, I will first introduce you to exactly what the four elements are, what they symbolize, and how they can be understood.

Because this section was already written for my previous works and because I think I did a bang-up good job at the time, that section will be very similar to the one in *The Way of Four*.

After that, we'll go into magic: what spells are, how they work, how to build them in a way that makes them effective, and how to manage your own energies so that they are most effective for spellcasting. I've written an entire book on how to do magic,[2] so consider this the condensed version.

We'll build a little spell resource center for you in your home. You'll learn about spell preparation, ingredients, and tools.

At this point, we're ready to begin the juicy part—the magic itself. For each type of spell, I'll reveal the principles behind it and exactly how the spell is created so that you can modify the spell for your particular use or create your own. I will lay out the spells like good recipes with ingredients and preparation up-front, because I personally hate to be in the middle of baking a cake and only when my hands are coated in batter discover that I need the walnuts crushed, not chopped.

I have an unavoidable bias here. I'm a Wiccan, and have been since 1981. There are lots of different sorts of people who use spells, and Wiccans are only one of those sorts. I have made every effort throughout this work to make it accessible for any kind of spellcasting, but I think a certain slant is always present. Just know that these spells were written for *you*, whatever your magical style, and you can adapt them as needed.

MAGICAL EXPERTISE

As I believe I already mentioned, I don't know everything. I keep trying, but…

I am very good at certain forms of magic, and I am a little-to-very knowledgeable about more forms than I typically practice. That said, there were areas I felt belonged in this book but in which I was not an adept. Even after a furious period of research and practice I cannot say I am an expert. I have offered, for example, solid information on dream magic, but in all honesty, the dream

---

2 *Magical Power for Beginners: How to Raise & Send Energy for Spells That Work.*

magic section was the most difficult part of the book for me to write, as I'll describe in more detail later.

In the course of writing this book, I did a lot of reading and got a lot of advice, and I also did a heck of a lot of spells. In the end, there are all sorts of things that I am not. I am not an astrologer, yet I am comfortable using astrological sigils in my spells. I am not a Kabbalist,[3] yet I find it appropriate to apply Kabbalistic correspondences to my magic. I am not a singer (I would be, but people throw things), but I feel confident in telling you that you can use singing magically. In short, I decided to give myself permission to go ahead and write a book about magic *before* I reached that state of knowing everything. (If I get there, I'll let you know.)

SPELL CONSTRUCTION

There's a toolkit that a skilled magician has, of course, from the simple knowledge of power-raising (see Chapter 2) to ritual tools to things like herbs, symbols, numerology, and the phases of the moon. When deciding how to do a spell, I think about these things: what kind of spell I could do, what kind of spell suits the purpose, and what kind of spell I feel like doing. I think lazily about what ingredients I have in the house already, and I think adventurously of what sort of working I've never had a reason to do before but have always wanted to try. I think of any culture, era, or style of which the purpose of the work reminds me.

While writing this book, I spent most of my time sitting in the midst of a pile of reference materials. I was surrounded by books on herbs, gems, symbols, and magical systems, but I carefully avoided so much as *looking* at spellbooks. It's possible I've written the same spell, in more or less the same way, as some other author. Rather than second-guessing myself, which paralyzes me, I decided to just avoid other spells. After all, I couldn't possibly read *all* spellbooks, so it was best to not worry myself with thoughts of being influenced or unoriginal. That said, if I had been writing a spell and not a book, spellbooks would certainly have been in the stack with my other resources.

---

3 To be perfectly honest, I wasn't a Kabbalist when I wrote this book, but it is a recent passion.

Introduction

Usually, I set my resources aside at some point and just imagine, "If I were this spell, how would I come into being?" If something is stuck, I might imagine movement and then build a spell around the idea that somewhere in it, something or someone has to move. If I was lonely, I might think of being held and experiment with wrapping myself tightly in a blanket as part of a spell. Sometimes I think about what's interesting about the spell. In Chapter 8, you'll find an invisibility spell. I began constructing it using various herbs and gems and quickly became bored. How many herbs was I going to use, for goodness' sake? Any darn fool can write a spell with herbs! (Do you ever have nights like that? Sometimes I think I just need a break.) A spell that bores you is likely to be an ineffectual spell, so I started casting my mind about for something unusual (for a spell, that is) that could function to preserve secrecy and came up with *keys*. I am very pleased with the result.

Sometimes I go in the opposite direction. I flip through books and think: How would this be in a spell? Do I have a need for this herb? How would I use this gem in a spell if I had it? Do I need to do a spell of that sort? This type of reflection can be really helpful in opening the mind along magical pathways. Sometimes we don't even realize that a problem we face can be addressed magically; in fact, sometimes we don't even realize it's a problem at all! So just looking at magical resources and imagining I'll have a use for them can open a lot of doors.

So those are my secrets. A toolkit, a resource library, experience, imagination, a willingness to overcome boredom, and a sense of exploration. I offer a whole slew of lessons and spells in this book, and it is my hope that by reading them and using them, you can figure out for yourself how I write spells and how you can write your own.

Chapter 1

What Are the Elements?

In much of Western occultism (including Wicca and many forms of Paganism), the four elements of Air, Fire, Water, and Earth describe the universe and everything in it. Everything can be understood as taking part in one or more element. Everything that is whole contains all four and can be understood more deeply by dividing it into four and viewing it through that lens. The elements are the building blocks of creation; they are the beginning of *things*. The undifferentiated void that preceded creation had no elements; or, to put it another way, all elements were One. But creation—things, reality—consists of the elements.

From a scientific point of view, the periodic table of the elements describes the building blocks of the universe, and the modern magician doesn't reject science. But from a magical point of view, both simplicity and symbolism call for only four elements.

The four elements give us a way of thinking about the world. They give us a structured approach to knowing the unknowable. They provide us with a system of interrelations, and magic is all about interrelations. Have you ever heard of "sympathetic magic"? If you've heard of a Voodoo doll or poppet you have. Sympathetic magic means that something that is *like* a thing (has sympathy with a thing) *is* the thing. A doll is like the person it represents; therefore, it *is* that person. That's interrelationship—sympathy. A doll is an obvious, direct representation, like drawing a picture. Other sympathetic objects are *parts* of the original. The well-known stereotype of Witches using fingernail clippings in a spell is an example of sympathetic magic; the part (the clippings) has sympathy with the whole (the person). There are all manners of direct and indirect sympathies that interconnect us. Elemental things have an indirect sympathy with each other. A candle is not the same as a lion, but both represent Fire and therefore have sympathy with each other. These interrelationships add to our understanding of the universe around us.

THE QUALITIES OF THE ELEMENTS

Understanding the qualities of each element helps us understand what elements are present and absent in a given situation. When we move on in the following chapters to doing magic with the elements, knowing these qualities will be essential to knowing what kinds of magical purpose belongs to each.

AIR

In the natural world, Air is associated most closely with the sky, wind, and clouds. Mountain peaks, which seem to touch the sky, are Air. Birds of all kinds belong to this element, and hawks and eagles are especially associated with Air because they fly so very high and make their nests at such high altitudes. A stork or duck, by contrast, is a less powerful symbol of Air because although they are birds and they fly, they live in and near the water.

In a person, Air is associated with thought and with the intellect, corresponding with the Witches' Pyramid to "To Know."[4] Ideas are said to come from Air, as is inspiration, a word that also means "to breathe in." Logic and scholarship are Air functions, which is perhaps why academics are said to live in ivory towers as opposed to ivory basements. People who spend all their time thinking "have their heads in the clouds," and if they are "airheads," they mistake

---

4   The Witches' Pyramid is the Wiccan name for a magical saying and philosophy that originated with the Golden Dawn. It goes: "To Know, To Will, To Dare, and To Be Silent, these are the four tools of the Magician."

imagination for real life and are impractical (because practicality is an Earth quality, which they lack).

The direction of Air is the east, and since the sun rises in the east, Air is associated with the morning, with the spring (the beginning of the agricultural and astrological year), and with beginnings of all kinds. Anything that "dawns" is a thing of Air. The things in our lives that dawn, be they projects, creations, or careers, begin with an idea. Often, inspiration feels like the sunrise, a bright beginning full of promise and possibility. Since seeds are beginnings and are associated with the spring, seeds, too, belong to Air.

Western occultism sees the elements as inherently polar and assigns gender labels to them. Air's gender is traditionally seen as male. Rather than thinking of this as "men," it should be considered yang, or outward-moving, in terms of magical energy. Airy people can be any gender.

For magic, we need to look at Air's symbolic associations. The alchemical color of Air is yellow, and the Golden Dawn uses the alchemical colors. Other systems will give Air sky colors—white and sky blue. The magical entity of Air (its *elemental*) is known as a *sylph*. The astrological Air signs are Gemini, Libra, and Aquarius. The Tarot suit of Air is Swords.

Let's jump into an interesting aside. For decades, the following story has been told in the occult:

In 1910, Arthur Edward Waite published his book *The Pictorial Key to the Tarot* and his "Rider-Waite" Tarot deck (nowadays more often called Waite-Smith or Rider-Waite-Smith, crediting the illustrator, Pamela Coleman Smith, for her enormous contribution). Waite was a Kabbalist and a member of the Golden Dawn magical lodge. His was the first deck to give all seventy-eight cards unique illustrations and the first to draw associations between the Tarot and the Kabbalah. The Rider-Waite deck became the most popular and influential Tarot ever created, and its influences are seen in the vast majority of decks available today.

However, Waite's membership in the Golden Dawn included an oath of secrecy, so he hesitated to reveal too much in his deck or accompanying book. He decided to switch two of the elemental correspondences in order to preserve his oath. He couldn't very well change the association of Cups to Water, since that's a pretty obvious one, and Pentacles are mostly depicted as coin—and again, the association between money and Earth is straightforward and obvious. But Swords and Wands are abstract tools, which were not in common usage at the turn of the last century. The Golden Dawn associated Air with Wands and Fire with Swords, so Waite reversed these two and filled his deck with Fiery Wands and Airy Swords.

Here's the thing about this interesting story—it is almost certainly not true. The source for it is Francis X. King, a well-regarded occult writer. Janet and Stewart Farrar[5] insist that King is such a good source that he should be believed, even though they also offer evidence that he's wrong. It's frankly a little odd since he had a somewhat complicated relationship with the truth. King is known for another utterly false yarn—that Gerald Gardner paid Aleister Crowley to write the Gardnerian Book of Shadows.

We can point to every published reference to tools in the Golden Dawn and say, "well, they're preserving their secrets," but can we dig deeper?[6] Renowned poet William Butler Yeats (1865–1939) was a Golden Dawn member. His magical journal and tools are on display in the National Library of Ireland.[7] Here we can't argue that the flame-tipped wand (Fire) and the yellow dagger (Air) are blinds for the uninitiated; these were private possessions.

Israel Regardie[8] quotes the "General Orders," an interior document of the Golden Dawn that prescribed the curriculum for the various degrees of study. That document says that the instructions for creating and consecrating the elemental weapons (reproduced elsewhere in the book) were available to initiates of the Adeptus

---

5   *The Witches Way*, pp. 252-253.

6   I owe the entire following section on the Golden Dawn and its tools to discussion with, and research by, my friend Jack Chanek, who has generously allowed me to use his research here.

7   The National Library of Ireland has unfortunately removed the photographs of the journal and tools from their website so I can no longer provide a url to the evidence.

8   *The Golden Dawn* page 42.

Minor grade only: they were allowed to borrow and copy them into their own magical diaries, but then they had to return the originals. Despite the fact that Israel Regardie chose to publish this material (and therefore, it could be argued as another blind), we should at least pay attention to what it says about the magical tools, and combined with Yeats' private materials, it is persuasive.

And yet, somehow, the story of "fake" elemental attributions became commonplace. Everyone I know in the occult community knows the story, and I never heard it refuted until fairly recently. As a result, decades later, many occultists were taught that the "real" correspondence for Air is wands. You'll now find the magical community split almost down the middle.

The vast majority of Tarot decks on the market are influenced by Waite-Smith, and so use Air for swords/Fire for wands, although a significant minority reverse these attributions.

If you're a Tarot reader who has used Waite-Smith or a Waite-Smith-derived deck, it's hard to break the mental pictures of Air/Sword and Fire/Wand. Every Wand in Waite-Smith has little flames, salamanders, and orange colors, and every Sword has prominent clouds, sylphs, and a lot of light blue. Perhaps because most Witches read the Tarot, most associate the sword, or athame, with Air.

On the other hand, the association of wands with Air makes a good deal of sense. The Sword is the stronger and more destructive tool, and Fire is more destructive than Air. The Wand is the tool of the intellectual magician, but the Sword is the tool of the willful warrior (Fire is associated with will). Once you get to know the tools, it's hard to escape the conclusion that a person wielding a Sword means business (has will), but a person holding a Wand might still be just thinking it over.

Other magical tools that are associated with Air are incense, feathers, bells, rattles, and fans.

Philosophers have been exploring the elements for centuries. Aristotle said the "quality" of Air is wet and hot (wet because it has no solid shape, but takes the shape of whatever space it fills, hot because of how it interacts with its environment). Hippocrates associated the elements with "humors"—Air is sanguine, and therefore, red like blood. Jung assigned personal strengths to the elements: *Intuition* is the strength of Air.

Fire

In nature, Fire is *itself*, first and foremost. Fire has always been set apart from the other elements because Fire alone has no natural home on the earth; Air has the sky, Water the sea, and Earth the land, but only Fire stands apart from geography. In nature, Fire is the outsider; it is out of control, and it conforms to no known rules.

The places to which Fire is most connected are the desert and volcanoes. The Fiery animals, lions and tigers, are distinguished by their fiery color and disposition. Salamanders are also associated with Fire, both because of their bright orange color and because of the way that licks and curls of a fire can come to resemble salamanders (which is how the elemental of Fire got its name). Other lizards, such as iguanas and Gila monsters, are also Fiery. Other natural things associated with fire either burn—like chilis and cumin—or are red or (especially) orange-colored, like fire opals.

Fire is male and outward-focused. The personal quality of Fire is *will*, and in the Witches' Pyramid, Fire is "To Will." Willfulness burns hot, and the will to get things done is a spark that ignites. Temper is also associated with Fire; a fiery person is a "hothead," and lust is Fiery—you *burn* with desire. All of these things are closely associated with the life force itself, the spark within that fills us with life. For that reason, healing is a thing of Fire; a person who is losing their spark needs Fire magic to reignite them.

Fire resides in the south. It is associated with noon, the hottest and brightest time of day, and summer, the hottest and brightest time of year. In terms of endeavors, just as beginnings and ideas are Air, things that are "on fire" are Fire. As Air is the seed, Fire is the sprout, emerging. Fire takes the original seed and gets it going, gives it force. Lots of creativity gets stuck in Air; it needs an application of Fiery will to turn on the power.

Fire can be a transformative force; in fire, the old is burned away and what comes out is utterly different. Transformation by fire is sudden and total: the blacksmith transforms iron ore into steel, raw meat becomes a delicious meal, and logs become embers, all by using fire.

In occult symbolism, Fire is orange, red, and sometimes yellow. The alchemical color of Fire is red. As already mentioned, its magical entity is the salamander. Fire signs of the Zodiac are Aries,

Leo (another lion association), and Sagittarius. As just discussed in the section on Air, the tool and Tarot suit of Fire can be either Swords or Wands.

The representative of Fire on a Wiccan altar is one of those things that people like to debate. The obvious choice is a candle, or perhaps an oil lamp. A flame on the altar is a pretty intuitive way to represent Fire—can't argue with that! Others (including me) prefer to use burning incense to represent both Fire and Air. In a typical Wiccan ritual, the yin elements Earth and Water are combined, and the saltwater is used to represent them both. So, I think it makes sense and is more balanced to represent the two yang elements by combining them as well. So, the incense (Air) is put onto the censor (Fire) to make smoke (Air) rise from a burning ember (Fire)—an elegant arrangement.

In terms of philosophy, Aristotle has Fire as dry and hot, and Hippocrates says it's choleric, and therefore yellow. Jung gives Fire the strength of *feeling*.

WATER

There are myriad natural forms of water, including not just the sea but every body of water, from a little creek to the Great Lakes. Water is also found in our bodies: in the clichéd "blood, sweat, and tears," in breast milk, and, perhaps most importantly, in amniotic fluid. Just as life first evolved in the sea, the fetus swims in saltwater as it "evolves" and develops. Since all bodies of water have tides, the moon is also associated with Water, and many lunar qualities are also Water qualities.

Sea creatures, both plant and animal, are connected to Water. Fish, eels, shells, coral, seaweed, sponges, and driftwood all partake of this element. Dolphins and whales are the creatures most commonly associated with Water, although I suspect this has more to do with our affection for them than with any natural or symbolic imperative.

The personal quality of Water is *feeling*. Emotion flows, following its own path, which may meander. Emotion runs deep with mysteries not visible on the surface. Emotions can be like sunken treasure, hiding secrets at the bottom of the waters of memory or the subconscious.

Emotionality and mood swings are, of course, associated with the moon, as are secrets—those things that are just barely visible, lit by moonlight, and not exposed to the sun. In the Tarot, the Moon card is full of watery images, such as crustaceans crawling out of the water, and the card's meaning is rooted in secrets, mysteries, and hidden knowledge. Water is female and looks within.

The moon and Water are the menstrual cycle, and Water is childbirth as well, making Water perhaps the most uterine of elements. Since moon phases are cyclic, ending where they begin and beginning where they end, it makes sense that Water is also associated with death, and it's not surprising that many people's folklore depicts death as a passage over water (for example, crossing the River Styx). To make the cycle complete, Hindus refer to rebirth as an ocean.

All of these things—the moon, feeling, depth, birth-death-rebirth, and mystery—combine to associate Water with dreams and the subconscious, and from there to altered states in general—trance, vision, and transformation coming from these things. (Note that the slow, dreamy transformation of Water is different from the sudden, shapeshifting Fire transformation.) Transformation by Water is visionary and may take the quality of a journey, which is probably why the Hero's Journey, as described by Joseph Campbell,[9] generally begins with a passage over water.

Watery people are weepy and overflowing with feeling. They are dramatic, sensual, and otherworldly. They can be draining to be around—wet rags. They can also be the opposite—joyful and full of love; their cup runneth over. The generosity of Water flows forth abundantly; people in love feel love toward everyone, and Water is love.

Water's direction is west. Sunset in the west is associated also with death, with the end of things, and with transition. Twilight is an in-between and mysterious time, as is autumn. Neither seed nor sprout, Water is the sap flowing through flora, just as blood flows through fauna.

In our creative/becoming process, we used Air to gain inspiration and Fire to provide the get-up-and-go. Now we need to let creativity

---

9 In *The Hero with a Thousand Faces*.

flow through us. If you've ever written, played music, or painted, you know there's a time to let go and let it happen. That's the Water time. Intuition has to play a part in any endeavor, and a "go with the flow" attitude has to allow us to take advantage of opportunities we never could have predicted in advance. Because this is daring, in the way that closing your eyes and letting yourself fall is daring, Water corresponds in the Witches' Pyramid to "To Dare."

For magical symbolism, Water has ocean and lunar colors—deep blue, sea green, and silver. Its alchemical color is blue. In Western occultism, green is the color most typically used. The magical *undine* is Water's entity. Water signs are Cancer, Scorpio, and Pisces (Cancer's crab and Scorpio's scorpion both appear on the Moon card in the Tarot). The magical tool of Water is the cup which is the Holy Grail. On a Wiccan altar, Water is always represented by a simple dish of water—some people add a seashell, generally a conch. A conch can even double as a water dish.

The quality of Water, according to Aristotle, is wet and cold, its humor is phlegmatic and clear, and its Jungian strength (in contrast to most occult thought on the subject) is *thinking*.

Earth

Finally, we reach Earth. In nature, well, Earth *is* nature. Earth is the substance of the body of our Mother Gaia, the Earth Herself. Earth is manifest in all things that are solid, fertile, or both, including rocks, green fields, rolling hills, and soil. Caves and other buried places are quintessentially Earthy. Most people consider the bear the animal of Earth, although pigs, boar, and cattle also belong to this element. Bulls are an important Earth symbol, both because of their Earthy nature and because they are associated with the astrological sign Taurus. So, astrologically, goats are Earth as well since they are associated with Capricorn. Also, humans drink milk from both cows and goats. Although all beverages are associated with Water, if one was to choose an Earth beverage, it would surely be milk.

A human being's Earth is their *body*. From Earth comes solidity, stability, and commitment. We call Earth our home, both the home of all life that is Mother Earth, and the house or apartment we live in. By extension, Earth is hearth and family and all those qualities that make us feel "at home." To be an earthy person is to be pragmatic, realistic, and tactile. Good Earth qualities in a person make them "the salt of the earth," but an excess of negative Earth qualities make them a "stick-in-the-mud." Earth is that deep, solid, immobile place, both in the negative sense of stubbornness and in the positive sense of patience. The Witches' Pyramid describes this quality in the attribute "To Be Silent."

Earth is located in the north and is associated with midnight—because north is opposite the noon of south and because subterranean places are dark. Winter is in the north—the coldness of midnight, the coldness of deep soil, and the stillness and silence of waiting for spring. To be solid is to be patient and to hold still. Contrarily, Earth is also fertility—pregnancy, fruit, the physical manifestation of our labors. In endeavors, Earth is completion—the finished project—the *thing* that results. Earth is female and inward-focused.

The colors of Earth are brown and black for soil, and deep green for fertility—the alchemist uses green. *Gnomes* are the magical creatures said to inhabit the earth, and the Zodiac signs associated with Earth are Taurus, Virgo, and Capricorn. The Tarot suit of Earth is Pentacles or Disks which represent money, that most physical of possessions (since it provides all other physical possessions). Wealth and *buried* treasure are things of Earth. The elemental tool of Earth is also the pentacle, which, in Wicca, is a disk or plate with a pentagram inscribed on it. (Some traditions inscribe other symbols as well.) Since a plate also holds food and since food is also of Earth (the physical product that is the outcome of farming; the sustenance of the body), the pentacle is a doubly good symbol (triply good, really, since the pentagram on it represents wholeness).

The representation of Earth on a magical altar is usually salt. Salt is considered an exceptionally magical symbol. It was once used as money and is also used as a food preservative—preserving the body through winter and driving away harm.

Philosophically, Aristotle says Earth is cold and dry, and Hippocrates ascribes to it a *melancholic* humor (which is black). Jung gives Earth the strength of *sensation*.

Air-Fire-Water-Earth

By now you've noticed how the four elements combine to make cycles, like circling the compass (east-south-west-north), the seasons, or the time of day. They can make abstract cycles, like the cycle of an endeavor or creation that we described in this chapter: idea, then empowerment, then intuition, and then manifestation/outcome.

A romance, too, can begin with an idea—an observation, a crush, a hope. Next comes Fiery lust, then Watery love, and finally Earthy commitment. In Paganism, we know that every cycle ends at the beginning: midnight is followed by dawn, winter is followed by spring, and the manifestation of a creative process gives birth to the inspiration for the next process.

The alchemists placed the elements in the order Fire, Water, Air, Earth, but most Western occultism (including Wicca and most Neopagan traditions) use the order we have here: Air, Fire, Water, Earth. This order describes a circle that starts in the East and ends in the North—returning, at last, to the East.

Figure 1: Alchemical Symbols of the Elements

Is There a Fifth Element?

The Hindus have five elements—Air, Fire, Water, Earth, and Spirit (*akasha*). Most Western occultists (Wiccans, Neopagans, magicians, Theosophists, etc.) go along with this view. In fact, the pentagram—the major symbol of Paganism and Witchcraft—is said to represent the five elements. According to this view, each of the points of the pentagram represents one of the elements, with Spirit on top (Figure 2).

I was taught that Wiccans place Spirit on top of the pentagram, while Satanists place Spirit on the bottom of their inverted pentagram. The idea is that Spirit is either above or below matter. For me, as a Wiccan, I see a contradiction between a religion focused on the

Earth Mother and a mystical separation of Spirit from matter—how can either be above the other without them being forever separate? In a religion that venerates the earth as a Goddess, sacred spirit is inseparable from sacred matter.

Instead of looking at the four elements as being apart from Spirit, I chose to look to my own rituals to find a more meaningful philosophy.

Figure 2: Pentagram

A Wiccan circle is set up with a candle or torch at each of the cardinal points (east, south, west, and north), representing the elements around the perimeter. Traditions vary as to where the altar is placed, but I was taught to place it in the center. I began to see the mystical value of the altar's placement: the ritual is a "squared circle" (Figure 3), marked at the quarters, and the altar is the meeting point of the elemental points.

The mystical sigil that depicts a magic circle, then, is the squared circle—not the pentagram (which has mystical significance in its own right). At the center of the circle is the altar, drawing exactly balanced energies from each of the four quarters.

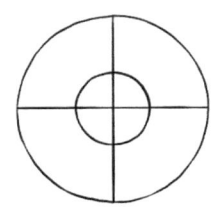

Figure 3: Squared Circle

What's on the altar? Why, the altar is where the representations of the *gods*, the idols, are placed. Doesn't that make the altar the place of *Spirit*?

The answer that I discovered, what I now believe, and what I teach is this: Spirit is what happens when all four elements meet and combine. Spirit is the *quintessence*, the "fifth essence," the original elemental whole from which the other elements emerged. Elementals have only their individual qualities. For example, gnomes will only be Earth and are incapable of acting in any way but an Earthy way; they won't feel or be willful. Salamanders will only and forever be Fire; we cannot ask them to be stable or exercise self-control. But *people* and other beings with Spirit have the capacities of all four elements, and the freedom to grow and explore in any direction.

Squaring the circle also represents wholeness, balance. Just as nature is balanced, every person should be balanced in the elements—neither an airhead nor a stick-in-the-mud, not a hothead or a sob sister. Rituals should represent that balance and any ideas, projects, or theories that don't reflect wholeness are probably missing the boat.

ELEMENTALS

Elements, as we have seen, are raw materials—building blocks, if you will. They aren't sentient and don't have personalities. There are, however, elemental beings known as *elementals*, whose nature is defined by and limited to the elements. Elementals are not gods; they are beings of a nonphysical plane (although they sometimes take on a physical appearance) who each partake of the nature of their specific element.

Elementals were identified, named, and described in the sixteenth century by the noted German physician and alchemist Paracelsus. He coined the words *sylph* for the elemental of Air and *undine* for the elemental of Water and gave the names *gnome* and *salamander* to the elementals of Earth and Fire, respectively. Paracelsus remains an influential force today in medicine (he is considered the father of homeopathy) and the occult.

Elementals are often called *lesser beings*. I think this is true, but I don't think this means they are *inferior* beings. They have fewer components than we do; they are less complex, more basic.

Elementals are conscious, sentient beings who have been called the *spirits of the elements*. Each is composed entirely of its own element and partakes only of that element's nature. Each is able to manipulate the forces of its element; for example, undines can influence both rain and matters of the heart. Although they are *called* spirits, they don't *have* Spirit, in the sense that Spirit is the combination of all four elements and so they cannot change themselves; they don't have the capacity to become more than the single nature that they are.

It takes an imaginative leap to understand what an elemental is. We are used to seeing the attributes of elements in combination, both in ourselves and all around us, so it is hard for us to picture beings of just one element.

Sylphs

Sylphs are composed of Air. They think and they float. They are rarified and elusive. They do not respond to feeling and they do not feel. They cannot be praised, fed, or excited. They are exclusively beings of wind, thought, and flight. You cannot persuade a sylph to care because caring is emotion—Water. Do not expect deep connections with sylphs, because depth is not in the nature of Air.

Renaissance art depicts sylphs as winged with human forms, often appearing to be tiny cherubs. I believe that the modern idea of fairies, such as seen in Victorian illustration, has more to do with sylphs than with the fey folk. Like wind, sylphs move quickly and suddenly and can travel great distances. Like the element of Air, sylphs are masters of thought and speech—they are intelligent and persuasive. Remember, though, that the gift of gab is a double-edged sword. Sylphs are not known for their honesty or concern. Although no person is made purely of intellect, if you think of people who are mostly intellectual, you'll realize that sylphs can be superior, disdainful, and dismissive.

Salamanders

Paracelsus viewed salamanders as great, radiant, godlike beings. Woodcuts show them to be dragon-like, some winged, some not, and some with human faces. Some say that the shapes you see when staring into a fire, which sometimes appear to be creatures, actually *are* beings—salamanders—and that is how they should be visualized. Of course, just as a fire is constantly changing its shape, salamanders can be shapeshifters, but they will always look Fiery, especially in coloration.

Salamanders are Fire. They burn and explode; they smolder and burst and consume. They are temperamental, impulsive, quick, and willful. They have no caution, no concern, no restraint; none of those are in the nature of Fire. Magicians who invoke Fire elementals must always be careful and cautious because salamanders are incapable of these qualities. It's very hard to get a salamander to do your will because salamanders *are* will. Usually, if they cooperate, they still leave their own stamp somehow.

Undines

Undines are Water. They feel and flow. They fulfill themselves in desire, intuition, and love. Do not expect them to be sensible or to hold still for very long. Sense is for Air, stillness is for Earth, and undines have none of either. You can't reason with an undine, although you can *attract* one.

Undines can appear to be quite human as they share many qualities with humans—we can often be irrationally emotional and often seek love above all other things. Folklore around the world is full of tales of lovely female creatures of the sea who attract men with their infinite sensuality—mermaids, selkies, sirens, etc. are all manifestations of undines. Like the current, they pull you in, and like the tide, they are quite changeable. Undines are graceful, their movements are fluid, and if they speak, their voices have a liquid, melodic quality.

Gnomes

Gnomes are Earth. Because we live on the earth and we are solid, we can often relate to gnomes, but we can also be mistaken about their nature. Remember that gnomes are slow, if they move at all, and are both infinitely patient and immensely stubborn. Trying to talk a gnome into something is like trying to persuade a rock. They cannot be persuaded or enticed, although they do respond to sensory stimulation and respect.

In appearance, gnomes are solid and squarish of shape and have craggy brown, gray, or black skin. They blend into their environment and disappear into shadows. Gnomes live in caves and caverns and can be sensed in dark, inaccessible crevices, whence a compelling stillness can seem almost to be calling you.

Elementals can sometimes be encountered in day-to-day life, for good or ill. The first time I met a salamander was way back in the early 1980s when my roommate accidentally set fire to the kitchen curtains. I don't think that salamanders caused that fire—I think my roomie's drinking was the real problem. But a big fire (this one destroyed a corner of the kitchen) can certainly *attract* salamanders, and for months thereafter, small fires burst out all over the apartment—incense dishes fell over, ashtrays got too close to paper, and so on. I was fairly new to Wicca at the time, but eventually, it penetrated my thick head that salamanders were living in my apartment. So, I did the nicest, most polite banishing spell I could come up with. The salamanders left—but they took the hot water with them for the next four days!

That encounter probably opened my eyes to the world of elements and elementals more than any magical text or lecture by my High Priestess. I learned that elementals follow their own nature—my salamander wasn't vindictive or evil; it was just Fiery. I learned that I could sense and commune with elementals in their own environments—the whisper of a gnome in the back of a cave, the lure of an undine in the deepest part of a pool, or the hypnotic compulsion to watch the match burn down all the way to the end that can mark the presence of a salamander. Elementals should be respected because of their power, but one should be wary because of their lack of balance. If you, the magical practitioner, stay balanced, elementals can open your eyes and empower your work.

ELEMENTAL OVERLOAD

During spellcasting, you may sense or call upon elementals to aid spells that follow after their nature, but you must always carefully balance and control a spell that calls upon them. It is also important to note that heavy work in a single element—such as several Earth spells over a period of time unbalanced by other elemental work—might call forth the presence of the corresponding elemental. It is important to pay attention to signs of excessive elemental activity in your life. Any of the following signs are notable, especially if they're unusual—dishonesty if you're already an inveterate liar, for example, can't be seen as a symptom of something new entering your life.

Sylphs can be very welcome, provided they exist in balance. They bring ideas and verbal skills. Writers like me would be at a loss without them. If there is a problematic sylph presence in your home, you may have an excess of restlessness and perhaps insomnia characterized by racing thoughts. You have many good ideas but cannot seem to implement any of them. You may experience drafts in the home and cannot seem to get warm. You may become disinterested in your body and lose interest in sex and food. You may lose interest in honesty and find yourself telling untrue tales for no reason. Symptoms are similar to amphetamine use.

We already discussed salamanders. You normally have a few living in your heating system or fireplace, but when they break free of those confines, trouble can ensue. The house is too warm, and people in the house have an unhealthy interest in fire. Be sure to keep fire extinguishers handy in every room because fires can start spontaneously in the oddest places and short circuits can happen. Salamanders want fire to be loose and wild and will cause "safe" fires to burst their boundaries, tipping over candles and splattering grease onto the stovetop. Personal symptoms can include intense passions and overwhelming anger.

Leaks and dampness in the home are typically the first signs of undines. A wet basement, a leaky faucet, and a cold, damp feeling throughout the house are common manifestations. Intense emotionalism, obsession, moodiness, and depression are the human manifestations of an undine problem. Heartbroken people often attract enormous amounts of undine energy as they weep, brood, mourn, and obsess. Both Fire and Earth can help heal a Water overload, as the heartbroken person needs will and/or stability. (Try Fire first.)

Homes normally have gnomes living in their dark or silent places, often under the floor. These elementals keep the home pleasant, solid, and safe. The cross-cultural legends of pleasant household spirits (such as brownies) who make a home feel good, help with small chores, and find lost objects are probably stories of gnomes. Gnomes are also probably behind legends of *unpleasant* household spirits who steal objects and make messes. If your home is a welcoming place with a well-stocked larder (a good rule of thumb is to always have enough in the house to serve something to an unexpected guest) and in relatively good order (gnomes are forgiving about cleanliness but draw the line at squalor), household spirits are helpful, handling small messes, finding lost objects, and creating good vibes. If your home is squalid and dirty, if there's never enough to eat, and if you are neglecting domesticity, the same spirits will hide your keys and jewelry, knock things over (especially the salt shaker), and in general, punish you for forsaking them.

Chapter 2

What is Spellcasting?

Before we get down and dirty with the business of casting spells, we should have a clear idea of what we're talking about. The use of magic is widespread among practitioners of a great variety of occult paths—Witches and Pagans as well as magicians—but it often goes undefined or loosely defined. People sometimes leap into casting spells because it is the sexiest, most exciting part of a magical life before they know what they're about.

Most fictional depictions of the use of magic go one of two ways: either only "special" people can do it because it is an inborn power or gift, or anyone can do it by reciting the proper words in the proper order while waving the proper tools about. *Buffy the Vampire Slayer*, oddly, worked both ways at once. Only some special people are Witches (although granted, they get there only through study and practice), yet anyone can do spells from old books (I particularly recall the character Spike reciting a spell in a flat, uninterested voice). Several characters on that show who were not Witches were called upon to recite spells that succeeded.

Fiction isn't real life. We need to know what magic is about in *our* world, not the one on television. So, let's pause, take a deep breath, and go over the basics.[10]

---

[10] This chapter offers a brief introduction to the topic. For a book-length discussion with lessons, see my book *Magical Power for Beginners*.

WHAT IS MAGIC?

The most-circulated definition of magic these days is Dion Fortune's, "the art of changing consciousness at will." The advantage of this definition is that it places the responsibility securely within the self ("consciousness"). The disadvantage is that it seems to place the *results* in the same location, and it isn't all that magical, at least not for those of us who believe and know that magic can effect tangible changes in the physical world. A better definition is Aleister Crowley's, "the Science and Art of causing Change to occur in conformity with Will," from which Fortune's was adapted. The "science and art" part (without all that capitalization) is especially apt, as it conveys a sense of both the rigorous and quantifiable (science), with the freeform, flowing, unpredictable (art) nature of the beast. Where Crowley's definition fails is that it can be read to refer to *any* change. I cause change in accordance with my will every time I drink a cup of coffee—in fact, *both* of these definitions apply, as I am changing my own consciousness.

Crowley slyly wanted people to understand that the magical and mundane are not so far apart as we might think, that drinking coffee *is* magical, just as casting a spell *is* real. But for linguistic purposes, it's a shaky definition at best. I would say that magic is *the science and art of using occult and/or mystical and/or spiritual forces to cause change in accordance with will*. That occult/mystical/spiritual fudge is purposely meant to cover all bases. Some people call magical energies natural, and some call them supernatural. All I really want here is a definition of magic that leaves caffeine off the list.

Magic is the science and art of using occult and/or mystical and/or spiritual forces to cause change in accordance with will.

HOW DOES MAGIC WORK?

If you decide to work magic, you will hear that you are to follow particular steps to "cast a spell," to "raise power," and/or to "focus your will." These various words and phrases can be baffling for beginners. Even for the experienced magician, the underlying meaning can be opaque. What exactly is being done? What makes magic work? Is it the spell, the focused will, or the "power"—whatever *that* is?

It turns out that everything that makes magic work can be said to reside in one of three basic areas:

- The web of interconnection
- The illusion of time and space
- Power and intention

Let's address these one at a time.

THE WEB OF INTERCONNECTION

The premise that drives magic is that all of life, all of reality actually, is a vast web of interconnections. Everything is a part of everything else. This is a spiritual concept, and as such, it is quite abstract. We can deepen our self-actualization, our sense of love and our contentment by knowing this and by meditating on the Oneness of the Universe. But this face of interconnection lacks practical application. In order to see interconnectedness in practical terms, we must look at the *way* we are connected to the rest of life.

Some of our connections are practical and obvious, and others obscure. There are physical, spiritual, symbolic, and synchronous connections. Obviously, you're connected to all of your relatives, by blood or marriage, and the closer the relation, the closer the connection. Similar DNA is a potent connecting thread. We are obviously connected to everyone we know as well; and as in the famous Kevin Bacon game, we are indirectly connected to an expanding web of people.

Less personally, we are connected to people from our own culture and to people in our hometown. You have a connection, however circumstantial, to all the babies born in the same maternity ward as you, on the same day as you, or both. You have a space-time connection to everyone who was in the Super Stop & Shop at the same time as you last Thursday.

As a Taurus, I am connected to other Tauruses, and the more astrological similarities we share, the more deeply we are connected. I am connected to other writers by my work, to other Gardnerians by my initiatory lineage, to other mothers by the singular experience of motherhood, and to those unique and special people who, like me, withstand the mockery and distaste of friends and proudly declare our love of sardines.

These are all human connections. We have all experienced some of them, and the funny thing is that we can feel that wave of connection at times when we know the facts don't support it. Have you ever been far from home and met someone from your hometown? There's this sense of being drawn toward each other, even if you have nothing in common and know none of the same people. We feel it because it speaks of the larger truth, that all connections are just strands in a vast web and each strand can be a valid way of touching another person. Or place, or thing. We are not just connected to other people but to all manner of things. Most significantly, from a magical point of view, a person is connected to that which they own, touch, do, and that which resembles them.

Sympathetic Magic

Sympathetic magic was discussed briefly in the introduction. "Sympathy" describes a connection of a certain resonance. Things in sympathy have, in some way, a similar "vibration," a feeling of commonality. The underlying principle of sympathetic magic—and it is a powerful one—is that anything *like* a thing, *is* that thing. When we do sympathetic magic, we use an object that is in sympathy with a part of the spell, and the object *becomes* that part of the spell. To cast a spell on me (let's be nice and say you're sending me great wealth), you would use something that has a connection to me—a photograph, a lock of hair, or a copy of my book *The Elements of Ritual*—and for the purpose of your spell, that item would *be* me. The more intimate the connection, the deeper the sympathy and the better the likeness. In fact, powerful magic can use layers of sympathy, multiple strands of connection.

In sum, sympathy is a way of accessing the web of interconnection of which we all are a part. The connecting objects are tools that allow us to travel along that web. Visualize a vast spider-web with yourself at one end and me at the other. There are probably dozens of strands that travel between you and me, and you could simply imagine those strands and traverse them in order to work your magic. Many people say you can do magic with your mind alone, and this is true—objects aren't strictly necessary. But they help: they deepen the connection, they deepen your knowledge of and confidence in the connection, and they have their own energy.

Symbolic Sympathy

All of the examples of sympathy given so far have been direct. Clearly, I *am* like a picture of me, and I am directly connected to a lock of my own hair. But connections can also be symbolic. I am directly connected to my date of birth, and hence to my astrological sign, Taurus. Symbolically, then, I am connected to bulls because the bull is the symbol of Taurus.

Symbolic sympathy isn't much needed to connect to people since there are myriad direct connections, as we've seen. Symbols are most useful when connecting to ideas. Strands of the web can carry us to abstracts as well as to people, places, and things, but finding such strands requires greater creativity and/or occult knowledge. That's where symbolism comes in.

To connect to "love," for example, we might use colors associated with love (pink and red), or we might use the element of Water, which is associated with love. Elemental symbolism and connections will, obviously, figure prominently in this book.

THE ILLUSION OF TIME AND SPACE

What is timelessness, and why does it matter? Let's start with the understanding that time is an illusion. Time is merely a construct by which we organize our experience of events in a linear fashion.

Let's compare time to space. Space is experienced all at once—when you look at a room, you visually take in all of the space of that room simultaneously. But a blind person who cannot see the room takes the space in linearly, one piece at a time. As the blind person enters the room, they experience first the doorway, then the coffee table, then the couch. Their brain organizes these items in a linear fashion—if they were born blind and cannot cross-reference the experience with a memory of sight, they will not come up with a mental concept of the room "happening" all at once. In blind people whose sight has been surgically restored, this turns out to be a huge, often insurmountable problem. The newly-sighted person simply cannot accept, cannot get their brain around the idea that space is happening all at once. Yet, to the sighted, the simultaneity of space is a given.

Imagine, now, that there's a "sight" by which *time* can be perceived as simultaneous. We lack that sight, but it exists. We cannot quite wrap our brains around the imaginative task of picturing time as simultaneous, but let's just postulate that only a form of time-blindness prevents it. Time is like the room; all the moments are there, like the couch and the coffee table. We think the moments are linear only because we reach them in a linear way. If time *is* simultaneous, it certainly explains a lot of the occult arts, doesn't it? Clairvoyance is perceiving something that is actually happening *now*. It's in the *linear* future, but it's part of the simultaneous now. Past life recollection is actually *simultaneous* life *perception*. And magic is effecting a change in a future that *doesn't really exist*.

Many people correctly say that changing the present changes the future. Go on a diet today, be thinner next year. Magic also changes the future by being worked in the now that is past-present-future. If we go back to the metaphor of a room, then we see that we can change every part of the room, and giving the whole room a coat of paint will change the entire decor, no matter where each component is in a linear sense. Indeed, I can even change my past, which is how certain psychological experiences work; the Inner Child is the past in the present, and we can heal the past by healing its present-day resonance.

To a certain extent, space is also an illusion, although one even harder to overcome. Magically, we can overcome fixed space in several ways. One of the questions I have heard many beginners ask is: *Is it necessary to cast a circle in order to do magic?* The short answer is no. But a Wiccan circle (the kind with which I am most familiar) is "between the worlds," and thereby supersedes both time and space. This is very useful when, for example, doing distant healing. Sympathetic magic also overcomes space by bringing the distant to you. Say you're doing that wealth spell on my behalf, but I live in New Jersey, and you live in Arizona. You'll use the principle of sympathetic magic—anything *like* a thing, *is* that thing—to declare a picture of me (that you printed from my website) to *be* me. Once you have me in the circle, you have overcome distance.

POWER AND INTENTION

Power and intention are the batteries that spark your magical work. On television and in the movies, all you have to do is say certain magical words and use certain magical objects to achieve powerful results with a spell. But in real life, magic works primarily by what is going on behind the colorful scenery. If you mouth a spell without a focused intention, it will never work. Gathering the recommended tools and appropriate sympathetic objects and then just going through the motions will never get you anywhere. Tools are the car (the motor, the seat, the steering wheel), power is the gasoline, and intention is the driver.

What Is Intention?

To intend something is not merely to want it. We want things all the time, idly, without the energy of desire ever amounting to magic. To intend is to focus fixedly and consciously, with determination and absolute confidence. Intention requires the ability to hold a single idea in your mind, to visualize it clearly, and to imbue it with as much emotion as possible.

To achieve this, you need to practice, practice, practice. The main practice method is meditation.

Meditation

There are several misconceptions about meditation. The first is that if you have a hard time of it, you're "not good at it." While it is true that some people have more natural skill at meditation than others, it is also true that *everyone* has a hard time sometimes, and *everyone* can achieve sufficient mastery for magical purposes.

Secondly, people seem to believe that successful meditation is defined as eliminating all extraneous thoughts. It is possible that this is necessary to achieve nirvana, but our goals, for now, are not so lofty. We can define successful meditation as the ability to ignore extraneous thoughts enough so that our concentration is not interrupted. What does this mean?

In order to write, I need to concentrate. At this very moment, as I write, there is a big black fly buzzing around the windowpane, and my cat is desperately trying to kill it. Attention given to the buzzing or to the hunt is attention taken from my writing. However, I don't need to make the fly and cat go away, nor do I need to concentrate with such ferocity that I forget they are there. I need merely to stay with my writing and allow the cat-and-fly chase to be part of the background—ambient noise and activity.

People can get very circular with meditation; they can follow thoughts down a trail of Away From Focus . It goes like this: I am concentrating on writing. There's the cat. Darn, now I'm thinking about the cat instead of thinking about writing. I shouldn't think about the cat. Darn, now I'm thinking that I shouldn't think about the cat. I shouldn't think about how I shouldn't think about the cat. Darn, now I'm thinking about how I shouldn't think about not thinking about the cat.

And so on. Forever. Note how my writing stopped being a part of my thoughts very early on.

A more effective method is this: I am concentrating on writing. There's the cat. Writing. Writing. Still hear that cat, darn it. Writing, writing. Buzzing. Writing.

Notice that I am still somewhat distracted by the cat and the fly. Notice that I always go *directly* back to the writing, without feeding any more energy to the cat and fly. Notice, too, that I may come away from this experience thinking ill of myself. Darn, I really should concentrate better; I sure did think a lot about that cat and that fly! Nonetheless, despite these self-deprecating thoughts, I still managed to get a significant amount of writing done so I can call my effort at concentration a success.

Remember this: The measure of success is not that there were no other thoughts. The measure of success is not if you "felt successful" and had no thoughts of self-criticism. The measure of success is, *did you concentrate*? If you held a thought, if you let the other thoughts wash away like background noise, then you succeeded.

When you begin training yourself in meditation, start with a cluster of concepts. If, for example, you wish to meditate on writing, then allow yourself to meditate on *any* writing concept. Think about paper or about typing. Visualize yourself writing. Visualize someone else writing. Visualize the finished product. Hear the sounds of the clicking keyboard or the rustling paper. Think about the abstract—what are you writing about, and what does it mean? Your goal is to keep your thoughts within this fairly large range; only thoughts unrelated to writing need to be eliminated.

Once you can successfully meditate on a cluster of concepts, you can narrow the range until you can maintain focus on a single thought. For example, visualize drawing an invoking pentagram (see appendix D). That's a very specific and finite shape. Your mind can't wander around much with an image like that one.

Meditation should be multisensory. Bring in visuals, sounds, aromas, and sensations. This helps you become totally absorbed and therefore able to focus better because more of your brain is engaged. It also helps you discover what kind of meditation works best for you. Most people concentrate and imagine best using visual images, but there are many exceptions. Although visually oriented people make up about 80 percent of the populace, that still leaves a large group that focuses best through other means. Only you can discover your own best areas of concentration and imagination.

Most people will tell you to meditate daily, or twice daily, and that's a very good idea. However, if you do the suggested meditation exercises three or four times a week for fifteen minutes each time, you'll notice an improvement fairly quickly. Of course, meditation is a far more complex subject than I've outlined here, with a wide variety of techniques and goals. Meditation can clear the mind, awaken the spirit, cleanse the chakras, and bring one closer to the gods. But for the purpose of focusing one's intention more successfully, the steps I've provided will do the trick, and the deeper aspects of meditation remain yours to explore.

In sum:

- Meditate to increase your powers of concentration during magic.
- Meditate at least three times a week for fifteen to twenty minutes each time.
- As a beginner, meditate on a variety of related concepts. Later, narrow your focus.
- Use as many of your senses as possible in your meditations.

Focal Points and Focal Objects

One way of improving concentration and the ability to focus your attention is to use a focal object. This is simply any object upon which you concentrate your attention and focus. Ideally, this object will have a connection to the subject of your intention.

You can meditate with focal objects such as a mandala or candle flame. But let's concentrate on how such objects are used in actual magic.

There are basically two ways to focus intention using an object. The first is to use the object to release the mind from extraneous thoughts so that concentration is not impeded. That is, trance is induced and, because the part of the mind that might otherwise generate distractions is kept busy, your ability to focus your intention on a single thought is enhanced. Typically, a null object that alters visual perception is used: a candle flame, a crystal ball, water, a black mirror, a geometric pattern or other symbol—something that allows you to "space out" while you're gazing at it.

This first method of focusing intention moves the mind outward. The second method moves it inward. Here you concentrate your intention on the object itself, an object that draws your attention to it. This is usually a meaningful sympathetic item, such as a photograph, map, or poppet. Here you are not distracting your extraneous thoughts, but rather you are pulling them onboard, making *all* thoughts move in on the object.

Sympathetic objects and symbols help you focus because they contain the idea and energy of the spell upon which you are concentrating. When sending me wealth, you concentrate on my image; should your mind threaten to wander, the reminder is right in front of you.

Where Does Power Come From?

We're not going to ask, "What is power?" Power is *power*—force, drive, energy, oomph. The important question to most people is not what power is, but how to get it. There are several sources of power, any or all of which can be used in a spell.

Power from the Self

You generate a certain amount of power naturally from your own body. This power can be brought forth and heightened by meditation, dance, sexual arousal, orgasm, aesthetic pleasure, singing, yogic postures, and other means.

It is vitally important, before raising power from your own body, that you be firmly grounded (see Chapter 3). Drawing power from your own body without first tapping into a source of greater and renewing power (that is, the earth) can be dangerous. This is especially true when healing since the bodily power most needed for healing is life force itself. You don't wish to drain your own health and well-being. So first ground yourself, drawing power up from the earth. You'll then have a virtually infinite supply of power that can be sent out as needed.

Power from the Gods

In various rituals, power is increased by entreating the gods for assistance. This is essentially prayer in which we ask that our needs be met, our work be empowered, and our wishes be granted. Some people gain power simply by praying while others work a spell as usual, doing the majority of the work themselves, and ask the gods merely to "lend aid" to the spell.

Because this is a book about spells and magic, I have chosen to de-emphasize prayer. For every spell, I have suggested appropriate deities who might be invoked to aid the spell. Depending upon the system you are working—Wiccan, another form of Witchcraft, eclectic Pagan, a Reconstructionist path, or what have you—you may or may not choose to follow these suggestions. None of the spells depend upon the invocations, so you can easily modify that part.

Just because I suggest certain deities doesn't mean you have to use those suggestions. It isn't a good idea to invoke deities you don't know anything about, and the deities themselves don't always take kindly to it. If I present a name with which you are unfamiliar, either don't use it or research it thoroughly before proceeding. Thorough research, I should add, involves more than looking up one web page (see appendix C).

Power from Natural and Supernatural Sources

Life force can come from numerous sources. Nature, nature spirits, and elementals never give us more than they can afford to give. Unlike people, natural and supernatural entities don't tend to disconnect from the source of their own energies and thus don't risk draining them away. Only in the case of sacrifices, such as cut flowers, is life force used up.

Power in this category can come from large natural sources, such as the oceans or mountains; from smaller things, such as stones or trees; and from "invisible" entities, such as nature spirits, elementals, and plant genii.

Accumulated Power; Stored Power

Under the right circumstances, power builds up and is stored over time. All sorts of things store a modicum of energy which partially explains how a psychic can pick up information from someone's possessions. It has long seemed to me that minerals (stones and metals) store more energy than organic matter—your ring contains a bit more of "you" than your wool sweater. (Some magicians whom I respect disagree with me on this, but I can only speak from my own experience.)

Larger amounts of power accumulate over longer periods of time, when the accumulation is intentional, or specifically magical (or all three).

One way that power accumulates is when many people give something (such as a magical tool, a symbol, or an idea) their intention and focus. For example, think about Tarot cards. Many people believe that the power of a Tarot reading is due strictly to the psychic skills of the reader. This is not entirely true, in my experience. A Tarot deck also has accumulated power from multiple sources. First, it has the power of its history—people have been using Tarot for hundreds of years, and they've been feeding into an idea, a system of belief and energy called "Tarot," to which this individual deck is connected sympathetically (it is like all other Tarot decks). Next, it has the power of its various individual symbols, whatever they happen to be—pentacles, Kabbalistic signs, magical glyphs, and so on—and each of these symbols has been accumulating power through belief and use just as the concept

"Tarot" has. Finally, the individual deck has the power that you have been feeding it; it has been the focus of some number of readings, has been concentrated on some number of times by you and the querent, and has been treated with respect and regard for some period of time.

The Tarot gives us an example of power accumulating over time because of belief, of power available because of ancient symbols, and of power accumulated by magical use and intention.[11] Any magical tool will carry at least some of this charge. You can intentionally increase such a charge through consecration and through treating your tools as power reserves. It is common, for example, for a Witch to drain excess power into their athame. After working magic, if you feel hyped up and loaded with energy, pick up your athame and visualize your excess energy draining into it. In this way, your athame will become a reserve and a resource that holds a charge long term.

Accessing Power

Now that we know where power comes from, we still need to know how to get ahold of it. The easiest source to tap into is the one we discussed last—stored power. *That* we can get just by using the tool, object, or symbol in question, which is why these things are so handy to have around.

Of course, that's not enough. Concentration and focus are also required, allowing you to reach into sources of power without interruption or distraction. A mind that you have trained to perceive and access magical energy is irreplaceable.

We can raise power from our bodies and minds through meditation, trance, ecstasy, rhythm, and movement. Anything that alters consciousness, especially rhythmically, will work, including dance, drumming, sex, and chanting. Other rhythmic and repetitive activities, such as weaving and spinning (with a spinning wheel), are quite effective. Intense physical sensation works, although it can be distracting; both pain and pleasure can enable us to access

---

11 A Tarot deck also has aesthetic power—beauty, and the ability of beauty to move us. Along with that, it bears the intentions and energies of the artist(s) who created it. These don't fall into the category of accumulated power being discussed here, but they exist, nonetheless.

power but can also break concentration, which is why both severe austerities and sex magic are considered fairly advanced practices.

Dancing, drumming, clapping, and chanting are all easier methods of raising power. They are inherently less demanding, so trance can be *slipped* into rather than *slammed* into, as with more intense work. These methods can be very effective, and the power raised can be quite deep.

We will soon get to the topic of spells themselves, but for now, it helps to know that one of the things spells do is *organize* the power-raising process. A spell puts the tools, symbols, sympathetic objects, concentration, rhythm, etc. together in a structure that will flow from beginning to end.

Raising and Sending Power

It isn't enough to gain power using any one or several of the techniques just discussed (use of tools, concentrating, inducing trance, moving your body, etc.). You also need to know how to raise and send it effectively. It's important to understand how power flows so you can take advantage of it. This means understanding how to begin, build, peak, and release.

Beginning

Whether working with a high-energy raising, such as drumming or dancing, or with a quieter raising, such as a low "Om" or meditation, it's best to start slowly to allow yourself a chance to get the feel of it and to allow yourself to falter. You're not going to be starting at your optimal level—neither at ecstasy nor at perfect mental focus.

It's natural to take a few minutes to get the feel of things, to relax into the experience. If you're working in a group, you also have to get a feel for each other's pace and mood. It's okay to stop and start over if you feel you've really gotten off on the wrong foot. For example, with drumming, start with a slow, simple beat, and stay at that level until you, as a solitary, or the entire group, if there's a group, are together and comfortable with that beat. Then, if your goal is ecstatic power, you build toward it bit by bit.

The beginning level of raising power should be easy to catch on to. Stick with that until it feels comfortable and natural—until it's no longer work, until there is a certain transparency to the process.

When you first learn to drive a car, you're totally aware of everything: your foot on the gas, the rear-view mirror, the steering wheel in your hands. Eventually, driving becomes somewhat transparent. It is still vitally important that you pay attention to the road, the other drivers, pedestrians, and so on, but the idea and mechanics of driving itself have become invisible to you. It is no longer work, and it is in this sense that I mean power raising should not be work.

Building

For a raising that moves toward an ecstatic peak, let it build and layer itself on top of your easy beginning. Don't push yourself; just move into a higher gear. Give yourself room to really go. Don't assume that once your energy has begun to feel good you've built it up enough. You can almost always go much farther than you think you can. If you allow a surge of energy to be "it" as soon as you feel it, you will almost certainly have sold your power short.

In order to bring the power up to its highest point, you'll often take three steps forward and one step back—catching your breath and letting the power find you again when you begin to feel spent. In a group, it is easy for the energy to take on a life of its own, and one or two people can be slowing down a little without impeding the build-up; but when solitary, you'll find the pauses quite noticeable. Accept and embrace those pauses as a part of the process; you're *spiraling* toward a peak, not shooting off a rocket.

In a quieter power-raising, such as one using low chanting, it's important to maintain your pace and resist letting the energy build too fast. Quiet power is most often used when you need to extend power building over a length of time—a run rather than a sprint (see the section "Releasing," below).

Peaking

It can be tricky to know when to stop building energy. In an ecstatic raising, a lot of people just build to a furious peak, and then drum and dance and dance and drum until they're completely spent. At this point, though, you're too exhausted to focus on sending your energy to the target of the spell; you've gone too far. The perfect moment to release the energy is when you feel absolutely glorious, but also as though there's a place just a little bit higher right around the next bend. When you feel you're a tiny moment away from a true peak, you're *there*—you're at the perfect peak, and it's time to let go. That's because the minute you hit the true peak, the top, you'll start coming down again. It's like having an orgasm—in most cases, the top of the roller coaster is followed instantly by the tumble back down to earth. If you wait until you reach the top before sending the energy, you'll be tumbling down by the time you do. There's a delay between deciding to let go and actually letting go, even if that delay is only a nanosecond. If you *decide* at the peak, then you've already passed it.

Think of it this way (Figure 4). If you decide to let go at *A*, you'll send energy at *B*, or near it. If you decide to let go at *B*, the energy you send will be at the level of *C*, and if you miss *B* by even a moment, you'll be sending at *D*.

You might miss your peak. You might be peaking and feeling great, and the next thing you know, find yourself leveling off, sliding down the slope. When I was younger and less experienced, I'd think, "Oh no!" and send at once, trying to salvage the situation by sending whatever was left. I learned over time, though, that if I let the energy wane to its lowest ebb, it would start to pick up again and head for another peak. It's a tiring and inefficient method, but it will work.

Figure 4: Peaking

Releasing

When it's time to release the energy, throw, push, or shoot it toward the target (more on targets shortly). This is the simple part; all you have to do is maintain focus on a clear picture of the target and just send all the built-up energy to it. Usually you can send most, but not all, of your energy in one wave. Once the majority of power has been "emptied out" of you, there's still more you can get with a little shake, like getting the last few splotches of ketchup out of the bottle. So just as you didn't assume during build-up that your first high was your highest, now you shouldn't assume that the first blast of sending delivers the entire package.

The release on a quiet, extended raising is somewhat different. Isaac Bonewits likened the two kinds of raise-and-release to male versus female orgasm.[12] The male/burst builds steadily in intensity toward a furious peak followed by a rapid decline in energy. The female/wave builds in undulating waves that allow her to gradually peak and gradually come down partway, only to build and peak again. In the "wave" model, you'll raise and peak, raise and peak at a lower level of intensity, which you can sustain for a length of time.[13]

There are several advantages to this wave kind of working. Because such a spell is silent or quiet, it is more neighbor-friendly; a late-night ritual in an apartment with paper-thin walls is not the best place for drumming and hollering. A spell like this is also great when a practitioner doesn't have the physical health needed for dancing, the stamina to tolerate high-intensity drumming, chanting, clapping, etc., or the temperament to enjoy them.

In a large group, it's easier to coordinate a quieter power-raising. If you're doing a ritual with thirty or more people, it's hard to know if everyone's going to be comfortable with, or able to do, a high-energy raising. It can easily degenerate into chaos.

---

12 *Rites of Worship: A Neopagan Approach*, page 207. Isaac was a renowned magician, Druid, and author, as well as my ex-husband.

13 Although this gender analogy seemed fine in 2006 when the first edition of this book was published, I've learned a lot about gender and gender identity since then. I've therefore replaced references to "male" and "female" power-raising with "burst" and "wave" respectively.

There are also situations in which you can use the duration of such power to your advantage. You might have a lot to do, for example, if your spell is broken into many parts or if you're in a group that does several spells in the course of one ritual (I don't think this is as common among solitaries).

One instance of a multipart spell that I recall was on behalf of an injured child. In different "sections," we sent loving energy and prayer, we sent life and vitality, we sent recovery. Finally, after all of these, we sent sustenance to the child's parents, who had been in the hospital with their child for more than twenty-four hours without sleep. The work was exhausting, but 100 percent successful—the child recovered very well (and is now a grown man). We could not have accomplished so much if we had collapsed in exhaustion after the first few minutes.

When coordinating a spell among several groups or solitaries in separate locations, it is helpful to work in a way that can last for fifteen minutes or more. This is more common nowadays with online "covens." If you cannot be absolutely certain of the exact time at which each member will start, you can draw out the power over a period of fifteen to forty-five minutes, so that everyone is together for at least part of the working.

Having brought the power up more slowly and released it more gradually, you will naturally want to come down more gradually as well. Instead of shooting out the power, you'll send it at a peak and then allow it to wane bit by bit, like the fading of a melody.

SHOULD YOU DO MAGIC?

Knowing *how* to do magic is entirely different from deciding *whether* to do magic. The decision involves both practical and ethical issues.

If you are just learning magic, you've probably heard a lot of things about when you *should* and *shouldn't* do it. You may not know what to expect from magic or the conditions under which it works best. You may even have been influenced by its portrayal in popular occult fiction.

The Magical and the Mundane

It's a mistake to think of magic as entirely separate from "real life," or to view casting a spell as a substitute for approaching a problem in a real-world way. The most useful way of looking at magic is as an integrated part of life.

One mistake that many people make is to work for something magically without working for it in mundane ways. They decide to do a magical healing without first seeing a doctor or other medical practitioner. They do a spell to get a job, but they don't update their resume. They work to heal communication in their relationship, but they don't sit down and talk with their partner.

As discussed, when we were defining magic, the distance between the magical and the mundane is not so far as we imagine. In fact, the dividing line between them changes all the time. The things we think of as "magical" are considered such in part because they are unknown. As the unknown becomes known, magic becomes science. Only thirty years ago, herbalism was thought to be New Age quackery; now your doctor tells you to take St. John's Wort. Weather prediction was once considered magic. The "laying on of hands" is still considered magic, unless you call it "therapeutic touch," in which case it's an accepted nursing practice. Ancient practitioners of magical arts were open to doing whatever worked; the result was the key, and they didn't fuss about whether they were doing something that was ordinary or non-ordinary.

This approach—doing what works without regard to the category in which it fits—is the best way to look at casting spells. *Do what works.* A village wise woman of ancient times wouldn't avoid using a healing technique because it wasn't magical, and neither should you. Not only that, but she would know that avoiding doing something that would help would disempower the work, and you must know the same thing.

If you're sick and you cast a healing spell but refuse to take mundane steps to get better, you rob your spell of its potency. Instead, see your healthcare provider, follow their instructions, *and* do a spell. If they say there's nothing they can do, keep seeking answers while continuing to do magic. Don't do magic if you have no intention of treating your illness in any other way—that doesn't mean you shouldn't rely on magic when conventional medical resources are exhausted or when you choose to forgo treatments that you think are harmful. It means when you won't even try.

Similarly, if you need a job, casting a spell should be an adjunct to other job-seeking efforts. Use magic to consecrate resumes, to empower interviews, or to create opportunities. But only do so if you're also making phone calls, sending e-mails, networking, seeking input on improving your resume, and so on. The spell alone won't make your phone ring.

So don't do magic unless you're prepared to work for the goal in mundane ways as well. Don't do magic for others if you don't believe they are willing to also work in the mundane. In fact, this is especially important when someone asks to have a spell done on their behalf. Many such requests are sincerely motivated and come from real need, but there is perhaps nothing lazier in all the world than asking someone else to do magic for you, and some people who make such requests have simply found a new (or very old) way to avoid making an effort.

Ethical Considerations

There is an awful lot of discussion among Pagan folk about what kind of spells are right or wrong to do. Many thousands of words have been written; many heated arguments have been had. For some, the Wiccan Rede— "An it harm none, do as ye will"—is the be-all and end-all of ethical guidelines. Others find the Rede flawed in its vague understanding of harm—is it even possible to "harm none"? If you get a job, don't you "harm" the person(s) with whom you competed for the position? If you fight disease, don't you "harm" the virus you kill? While the virtue of guiding oneself by the Rede's combination of freedom and harmlessness is apparent, it sure is lacking in the specifics.

Some use as their guide a principle of non-manipulation. By doing magic only where explicit permission is granted, they assure themselves that no one's free will has been interfered with by their spellcraft. This makes a certain amount of sense, yet it also ties the magician's hands in situations where much good could be done.

This ethical rule is based on the belief that it is arrogance, even hubris, to think that one can know what is good for another, and there is certainly wisdom to be gained by restraining the tendency to believe you know best. On the other hand, there is a different sort of arrogance in refusing to get one's hands dirty. We must ask the age-old ethics question about the unconscious person bleeding by the side of the road: Save him without permission, or leave him to die? The magician guided by the rule of permission is bound to leave him. Others would find this reprehensible.[14] While it is true that helping this person may incur negative karma, what exactly is ethical or good about avoiding negative consequences to oneself? Isn't part of goodness found in taking a personal risk on behalf of another? It seems that this rule offers some wisdom, but also some limitations that not all magicians would be willing to embrace.

The single best ethical rule for working magic that I ever learned was taught to me by Isaac Bonewits. The simplicity of the rule works in its favor, as does the fact that it also allows for complex, nuanced ethical choices. The rule is this: *Never do something magically that is unethical when done in the mundane.* Likewise, *if something is ethical in the mundane, it is ethical magically.*

As you can see, this rule works hand in hand with the principle discussed previously, that the magical and the mundane should not be treated as separate worlds; they should work together. Let's look at some examples.

Love Spells

It is unethical in the real world to force someone into your bed, whether through violence, drugs, or threats. Therefore, it is unethical to force someone into your bed magically by doing a spell that bends their will. You cannot force someone to love you, and bending someone's mind to your desire, whether with drugs, alcohol, or magic, is force.

How, then, can a love spell work? It is perfectly ethical to make yourself more attractive, interesting, and available to the person you desire or an unknown person whom you hope to meet. It is not only

---

14 Some magical practitioners seek permission telepathically or through spirit contact, something not covered in mundane ethics classes.

ethical, but a good idea to clean and beautify yourself and use perfume, cologne, or essential oils to create an atmosphere of sex appeal about yourself. You might arrange to be places where your beloved will be or go to places where available people whom you might desire will be. People often join clubs or groups, do volunteer work of some sort, or take classes in the hope of meeting someone. You might even study up on topics of interest to the one you desire so that your conversation can be more engaging. It is, therefore, ethical to do a love spell that achieves any or all of these things magically. You can magically make yourself attractive and increase your sex appeal. You can arrange, through a spell, that the paths you walk (metaphorically and literally) will be the paths your beloved or potential beloved walks. You can cast a spell that creates a commonality of interests between you and a known or unknown person.

Job Spells

It is unethical to harm competitors seeking a job you want. You shouldn't damage the car of a competitor so they can't get to the interview, nor should you plant a foul-smelling item in their briefcase so that their resumes have an unpleasant odor. Not only would this be inconvenient (there might be *many* competitors), but it would be wrong. The best job-seeking strategies involve appropriate and appealing presentation, as well as being in the right place at the right time.

Magically, the same thing applies. Focus your magic on timing, appeal, and excellence. Let the competition take care of itself. Since you know it is ethical to concentrate on these areas in the mundane world, it stands to reason that it is ethical to work on them with magic.

Crime-Stopping

Most people find the actions of a lynch mob unethical. Most of us would say it is wrong for a group of private citizens to hunt down a criminal and enforce "mob justice" (which is rarely just). If you agree that this is unethical, then you should not do magic that effects the same result.

On the other hand, many people support things like neighborhood watch committees, and if such a group catches a criminal and calls the police so that justice can be done, all the better. Thus, magic focused on protection and true justice would also be ethical.

I could continue with examples in this vein. The idea is a simple one—come up with a real-world example and carefully examine the ethics of it. Don't place your magic apart from yourself; *keep it real*.

Knowledge Is Power

One of the best pieces of advice I can offer is this: *Don't do magic if you don't know what you're doing.* By this I do not mean that you need to be some sort of super-magician, an extraordinary expert in the magical arts. Rather, I mean that you must know as much as possible about the particulars of the spell. The more you know, the more effective you can be.

For example, say someone has asked you to do a healing spell. What illness does the patient have? What part of the body is affected? Where does it hurt? Do you know the patient? Do you know what the patient looks like when they are healthy? Sending general healing energy toward a person without having answers to at least some of these questions will diminish your ability to accomplish a healing goal.

Remember that you're relying on *focus*, which, in turn, needs clear visualization. You need to visualize *something* with some accuracy. Very often, I hear of people "sending energy" to people they have never seen (not even a photograph) for conditions they do not understand to unspecified locations. Some of the energy might get where it needs to go and some of it might help, but you're totally disempowering your magic when you willingly give energy to something so vague.

Suppose you are painting a house. If you close your eyes and toss a bucket of paint in the direction of the house, it *might* hit the right house, it *might* be enough paint to advance the process, and it *might* be the right color. Or not. The smart house painter knows exactly where the house is, what color it should be, and about how much paint will be needed to finish the job. Finding out the analogous information about a spell is part of your job as a magician. Don't skip the information-gathering step and don't assume you can do a useful spell without that step.

The Health of the Magician

When discussing sources of power, we saw that one place from which power comes is our own bodies. I stressed the importance of being grounded so that you do not drain your body's energy when working magic.

Since you've grounded, theoretically, your life force is completely protected, and you need not concern yourself with your own health or well-being. Theoretically. In practice, you will often involve your bodily energy in the spell to a small degree, either because you were imperfect in your grounding, or because you become emotionally involved and literally throw yourself into the spell.

For this reason, *if you are ill, recovering from an injury, or if you are pregnant, do not cast any spells*. Not only do you not want to risk spending your own life force, even in tiny amounts, but you also do not want to divide your focus. When you are ill or in the process of healing, part of your energy, at least subconsciously, is always devoted to your own recovery. Some pregnant people *do* cast spells, especially in an emergency. Many of us have sensed that the fetus is not at risk. Generally, it is the expectant parent who is of most concern when deciding whether to cast spells during pregnancy. When you are pregnant, part of your mind and heart is always nurturing and growing the baby. Thus, you would only give part of your attention to your spell.

WHAT IS A SPELL?

The careful reader will have noticed that we've gone a long way into the discussion of magic without actually describing or defining spells. Let's start by saying that a spell is a way to *use* magic. It is one thing to know what power is, where it comes from, and how to raise it. It is another thing entirely to know what to do with it once you've got it. If the power we've been talking about, the magic itself, is food, we've learned so far about planting, weeding, and harvesting our crops. Now we must learn how to cook. Spells are our recipes, but before we turn to our recipes, we need to know some basic information about cooking. Your cookbook for food assumes you already know how to work in a kitchen, that you've already got pots and pans, and that you can boil water and use an oven safely. So, let's go into some of the basic "what's what" of spells.

Magic works by focusing your intention, raising power, and then sending that power toward your target. A spell is a series of steps taken to achieve a magical goal. Those steps, in their simplest form, are focus-raise-send. The fine-tuning comes from understanding the goal in detail, deciding specifically how and where to focus, and raising power in a way that moves it toward the goal even before the sending. Spells use sympathy and interconnection so that by the time the power is sent, it is "flavored" with the target and goal and will have a natural movement toward them.

Spells can be thaumaturgic, meaning they have tangible, specific goals such as money, love, or health, or they can be theurgic, meaning they have spiritual goals oriented around our connections with the gods and ourselves.

The Components of a Spell

A spell consists of a set of components, as follows:

- A goal
- A target
- Focused will
- Ingredients gathered beforehand (possibly none)
- Raising power
- Sending power to the target
- Disposing of the spell's remains

The Goal and the Target

Your goal in a spell is the outcome. The spell we've been using as an example, sending me great wealth, has, as its goal, a wealthy Deborah Lipp. The goal of a spell is always visualized as *accomplished*. Remember that magic works, in part, because time is an illusion. The goal should be visualized in the present. So, if you are doing a healing, your goal is not a sick person getting better, your goal is a well person. Don't picture the person sick and then recovering; picture them utterly and completely healthy.

Your target is where you are sending the power in order to accomplish the goal. If your goal is to win an archery contest, your target is, well, *the target*. You aim toward that target in order to win. You visualize winning while firing your arrows, but you don't shoot your arrows toward an image of winning; you shoot the arrows toward the round thing with the concentric circles on it.

When healing, the target is the sick portion of the body, for example, a tumor. You are aiming your power at the tumor, yet you are visualizing the person as already well. Now you know why you practiced meditating and visualizing!

One reason photos and sympathetic objects are very helpful is because of this dual visualization. You might use a photo of the sick person before they became ill to visualize your goal. Your goal is in front of you in the picture—a well person. The target, on the other hand, is a picture in your mind. Or use the opposite approach. Use a picture from an anatomy book to locate the exact point of the tumor or other cause of the illness and mark that picture with a bullseye. Aim at that target while visualizing the well person in your mind's eye.

In general, choosing a goal is easier than choosing a target. One reason that Witches aren't all wealthy is that choosing the right target for a money spell is often a challenge. It is easy to picture the money flowing in, but harder to define the source from which the money should come.

Focused Will

Your focus is important on a number of levels. First, you must be clear about what you're working toward, and this means being honest with yourself. Often, we tell ourselves little lies, and in day-to-day life, they may do no harm; but when working magic, they can spell disaster. It is important to avoid casting a spell if you are ambivalent about the results; that is, if you cannot be honest, clear, and forthright about what you intend to happen. Many people know that it is unethical to cast a love spell that attempts to force a particular person to feel a particular way. So, they cast a general "bring love to me" spell (which is a perfectly ethical thing to do). Yet, all the time, they are visualizing the person they really want, the person on whom they'd be casting a love whammy if only their scruples allowed it.

Ambivalence and dishonesty, like poor health, destroy your focus. This also means you should not agree to work a healing on someone with whom you are angry, as your anger can creep into the energy of the spell.

Ingredients

Recalling our earlier discussion, we know that objects used in a spell might have accumulated power, or they might bring the power of symbolism and sympathy. Most people think of certain objects first when they think of casting a spell—the herbs, a lock of hair, candles, a cauldron, words to say, and so on. These objects are entirely optional, of course—a spell can be cast entirely with the mind—but I think they are hugely empowering, and I encourage their use.

Gathering your ingredients prior to beginning the spell brings a certain caution to the proceedings. After all, with a no-ingredients spell, you can perform the spell the moment you decide you want to, and that's not necessarily a good thing. Magic requires deliberation, time spent making sure the goal is worthy and the target is aptly chosen. That time allows you to examine yourself and your attitude about the spell and lets subconscious problems bubble to the surface. Meanwhile, if the spell is, indeed, a good idea, you'll be building up power toward its performance while you gather ingredients.

Suppose, once again, that you are performing the spell to make me wealthy. You go to the store to buy your green candles, all the while thinking, "Deborah is wealthy. Deborah is wealthy." Then you decide to use cinnamon oil and go to a different store for that, again thinking, "Deborah is wealthy," while waiting for the cashier. With all that concentration, one of two things will happen. Either you'll decide you don't really *want* to work magic for Deborah's wealth (darn you!), or you'll build up a level of concentration and intention that will be a potent resource when you actually cast the spell.

Something will happen over a period of years of performing magic, which is that you'll acquire a lot of stuff. For example, when you buy that green candle, you'd be wise to buy not just the one candle you actually need. Suppose it cracks before you can use it? Suppose the wick is no good? It's really better to buy two or three while you're there, just to be on the safe side. With herbs and essential oils, you will virtually never use up the supply you've acquired for a single spell.

I have found that storing these ingredients in a "magic drawer" of some kind[15] and then, when a spell is at hand, going into that drawer and choosing ingredients has much the same effect as the shopping described previously. In fact, the drawer of spell stuff becomes, to a degree, a source of accumulated power itself.

Raising Power

It is possible, and in fact typical, to raise power more or less the same way for every spell you do. Many people, for example, fire up a candle no matter what they are working on—candle magic is convenient and compact, and the needed ingredients are easy to come by.

One could attribute this to laziness on the part of the practitioner, or more generously, point out the practical advantage of imprinting a response pattern based on repeated behavior. That is, whenever you do something the same way over and over, your mind begins to key into it, and you anticipate its unfolding and move yourself into the appropriate state of mind. Like Pavlov's dogs, who salivated as soon as they heard the dinner bell, your mind begins to enter a focused magical state as soon as it is cued to do so.

As much as this is true, it is also true that when you raise power in a way that's attuned to the desired result, it provides a distinct advantage. In Chapter 3, we'll go over the preparation and setup for spellworking; these steps will provide the Pavlovian cuing that is so helpful. Once into the spell proper, you can then vary your power raising based upon the specifics of the spell because your mind is already in the proper state.

In this book, we are focused on the magic of the elements, and so we will rely heavily on the four elements to attune power to the purpose of our magic. We will use water for Watery goals, raise power in Fiery ways when our aims are Fiery, and so on. Attuning power

---

[15] Except the ones that require refrigeration, although in theory you could have a "magic refrigerator shelf." At one time, I had an entire magic dresser, but that's excessive for most people.

can also be done using sympathetic objects and imitative behavior, but this is a book about elemental magic, so we'll concentrate on that.

Imitative magic involves acting out the results you hope to achieve. One rather famous example is making love in fields in order to make the crops grow—you act out the behavior you expect from the crops. Once, when I was working a spell in a group, one group member got a strong intuition that the subject of the spell was stuck and was unwilling to walk his path out of his problems. So, while we raised power, she walked around the circle, raising and walking at the same time. She used an imitative action to flavor and shape the power being raised.

Sending Power

Your spell has built up power attuned to the goal, and so now you have built up goal-flavored (or goal-colored) power to send.

Remember that you are sending your power toward the target. As the power is being sent, visualize the target before you; you are shooting an arrow of power into it, or, more gently, you are pouring waves of power over it. One way of looking at it is that you are sending the goal (full of power) to the target. That is, you are sending healing to the patient, you are sending wealth to Deborah, you are sending justice to the wronged, etc.

Disposition of the Spell

In some spells, disposing of the ingredients is part of the spell—a candle is allowed to burn all the way down, a parchment is burned, a Witches' Bottle is buried. But in other cases, you'll have to figure out what to do with the ingredients.

Three of the four elements figure prominently in disposing of many spells. The fourth, Air, is rarely used, in part because few of us have access to remote locations for leaving items exposed to open air or to cliffs appropriate for releasing small items. Sometimes you can leave something lightweight to be scattered in the wind. I've known magicians who threw spell remainders out the window, but the downstairs neighbors didn't care for it!

Fire is used to burn the remainders of a spell. Things given to a fire are seen in one of two ways. First, fire can be used to convert something to its spiritual essence. Things burned are sent to the gods; hence you might write a wish and burn it up so that the gods might read it. This is a very common way to finish a spell and prevents you from having little bits of paper imbued with hope lying around. Second, the destructive aspect of fire can be used: to burn is to devour and undo, and this is often a way to release negativity. Many is the spell that involves releasing the past, letting go of something, or getting rid of anger by throwing a symbol or written words into a fire. Anger is particularly appropriate; when you're "burned up," you can "burn it up." It is important to remember, though, that fires can be hard to control. Sending out-of-control energy into fire can be dangerous. It's like throwing a fire into a fire; sometimes there is an explosion.

Water is used for its purifying qualities. For the disposition of a spell, natural running water is desired—a stream or river, typically. Running water cleanses the remainders of a spell from an object. Sometimes all that is left is a simple charge, an energetic buzz. Sometimes, though, there is a magical pollution from the spell; for example, when an object is used as a magical buffer or substitute. In that case, the spell is essentially a diversion; negativity that would otherwise go to a person is diverted into the object. This can be done for some healing and protection spells. The object would be disposed of only after the purpose of the spell is no longer an issue, i.e., the patient is cured. Obviously, you would not throw anything into a body of water that would pollute it, but for the disposition of a magical object that also puts the object through a cleansing process, natural water is ideal. Often, magical pollution has no relationship to environmental pollution, so you can do this harmlessly.

Earth is used in two ways. Offerings are often placed upon the earth; liquid offerings are absorbed by the soil, while food, flowers, and other items are left outdoors under a bush or tree, or some other appropriate spot. If an animal walks off with it, that animal is considered an agent of the deity to whom the item was offered. For spells, the second method—burial—is usually preferred. Burial is viewed in a number of ways: first, as placing the item into the arms of the Earth Mother; second, as giving the item over to the natural decaying processes of Nature, returning it to the components of which it was made; third, as hiding it in a dark and secret place; fourth, as letting the item's power dissipate gradually (as opposed to the instantaneous results achieved with fire); and finally, as letting the item continue to do its work from within the ground—in this case, it is not "disposed of" at all. An item might be dedicated to the task of watching over a piece of land, for example. It isn't gotten rid of; it is set up where it is meant to be.

Local and Specific Spells

Spells work best when they are localized and specific; that is, when they are confined by place and detail. Confining the spell improves your visualization—you can picture a person you know far more easily than "people" in a general way. "A fuzzy spell produces a fuzzy result," as Isaac Bonewits was wont to say.[16] Vague, general pictures don't produce clear targets, which you need. Vague targets dissipate magical energy so that any spot within the target area receives less.

Visualize your spell's power as filling a bucket. Theoretically, there is an infinite amount of power that can fill that bucket, but pragmatically, you're only going to gather a finite amount of power per given spell, even if that amount is quite large. Earlier we talked about painting a house, so let's picture a two-gallon bucket of paint. If you pour that paint over a single square foot, that spot will be very wet and brightly colored. If you pour it over a square mile, that area will be spottily painted at best. If you dissolve the paint into a fine mist and spray it over the entire world, it is doubtful that any part of the world will experience a color change.

There's a bit of data supporting the idea that meditation can change the surrounding environment. As I wrote in *Magical Power for Beginners:*

> *The Maharishi University of Management—founded by Maharishi Mahesh Yogi, who is also the founder of Transcendental Meditation (TM)—has reported a "Maharishi Effect," where crime rates are*

---

[16] I can't give you a citation on that—pretty much every conversation about magic that I ever heard Isaac partake in included that phrase!

reduced in the city where TM is practiced, as compared to cities where practitioners are less prevalent. The first study on this effect was reported in 1976, but was discredited. However, there have been several studies since, including an intriguing one in 1993 in Washington, DC.[17]

It is crucial to note two things: First, these were experienced meditators, not beginners. Second, the results were local; these folks made *their* space more peaceful—not the world, not the nation, but their space and their neighborhoods. "Visualize World Peace" doesn't seem to have produced much, but working for peace, ecological well-being, or what have you, in *your* neighborhood, or one specific, selected area, can and does work.

A "healing" spell might work well, but a spell to "reduce the size of an ovarian tumor" will undoubtedly work even better. A "new job" spell might work, but a "new job in the healthcare industry requiring skills I have, within a thirty-minute commute, and for no less than forty thousand a year" will nail that sucker down but good .

If you re-read the last paragraph, you'll notice something important about being specific: *You have to know what you want.* We talked about knowledge when discussing reasons not to do magic. When working for yourself, you must know what you want. "Be careful what you ask for, because you may get it" is a charming bit of irony for most people, but the literal truth for workers of magic. Knowledge, especially self-knowledge, isn't always cut and dried; situations need to be examined closely, and assumptions should not be made. When I was first learning magic, my teacher told me the story of a Witch who wanted a lover. Because she was studying Native American ways, she did a spell asking for an Indian lover. She didn't specify what *kind* of Indian and ended up falling in love with a man from India.

Here's a mistake that I made. The amusing part is that I was a very experienced Witch and Priestess by this time, but I suppose anyone can be careless. In 1999, I was looking to buy a condo. Because my requirements were quite specific, there were only two condo complexes in the area in which I was interested, and neither

---

[17] *Magical Power for Beginners,* page 165

had any available units. The realtor had been unable to show me anything for days and days.

I drove to each complex and picked up a stone from within its residential area. I used the two stones as focal points for a spell, and the words of the spell were something like this: "A home for me! So mote it be! / A home for me! So mote it be!"

The next morning, the realtor called. A one-bedroom unit had just opened up in one of the complexes. Unfortunately, I was looking for a two-bedroom condo. Since it was an opportunity to see the complex from the inside (and since it was clearly a manifestation of my spell), I looked at the unit, which was lovely but far too small. I spoke with a friend later that day and explained what I had done and the results, and she said, "You left out your kid!" To which I could only reply, "d'OH!"

So that night I started over. This time the words of the spell were: "A home for my child and me! So mote it be! / A home for my child and me! So mote it be!"

The next morning the realtor called. This time a *two*-bedroom unit had just opened up, and I lived in that condo for the next fifteen years.

There is a famous horror story called "The Monkey's Paw," written in 1902 by W. W. Jacobs and reprinted in various collections many times since. The tale tells of a magical charm placed on a monkey's paw that grants the owner three wishes. According to the tale, "It had a spell put on it by an old fakir...He wanted to show that fate ruled people's lives, and that those who interfered with it did so to their sorrow."

The story shows that people's wishes are ill-considered, that just crying out for what you want is dangerous. In the story, the man who comes into possession of the paw asks for a specific amount of money. The next day, his son is killed on the job, and by way of recompense, the company gives the family the exact amount wished for. The man's second wish is to restore the son to life, but the wish is made days after, and when the rotting, decayed body of his son, now alive, stands outside the man's front door, he makes a final wish, for his son to be dead and restored to his grave again.

One could follow the fakir's plan and never work magic, or one can work magic carefully, with respect for the larger forces of the universe. Many people build a protective caveat into their spells, adding

"For the good of all!" or "An it harm none!" to the end of a spell. Of these two, I prefer the positive one. We'll talk later about magical language, but for now, it's important to know that your subconscious mind listens

with great care to what you say, and that affects the spell. If you say "An it harm none" while working magic, a part of you deep down is thinking, "Harm none? You mean this spell could cause harm?" This will create trepidation and draw power away from your magic. "For the good of all" works better because it's like an added bonus. Your mind is not engaged with thoughts of harm, and you're now thinking that, in addition to making Deborah wealthy, by the gods, *all* will benefit. How cool is that?

A caveat statement, though, doesn't release you from the obligation to be as specific and focused as possible.

Group Working: The Battery Method

In the course of this chapter, we've learned that having a bifocal concentration—on both the target and the goal—is important, and I've acknowledged that this can be difficult. One way that a group can bypass this difficulty and deepen the focusing strength of a spell is through a "battery" operation (Figure 5). A group raises power with the goal in mind but sends the power not to the target, but instead to the person in the group with the strongest ability to visualize the target. That person is the "battery." The battery receives power from the group and sends that power to the target. The battery focuses on one thing intently—the target. The rest of the group focuses on the goal. No one is concentrating bifocally; everyone has a single visualization.

This is very useful when not every member of the group is connected to the target. Suppose, for example, that my coven is doing a spell for my sister, Sunny. If none of them have met her, they have an impediment to visualizing the target. Here is a case where they can effectively use me as a battery. (Even if the others *have* met her, it is safe to assume that I have the strongest connection.)

We've also talked about the importance of being specific in one's intention and visualization. When a group visualizes a goal, it is usually fine for there to be slight variations in how that goal is imagined by each person. The group will have discussed it beforehand, of course, but during the power-raising, if one person visualizes my sister in radiant health, and another visualizes me saying, "Sunny is doing great," and yet another sees, in her mind's eye, a photo of my whole family glowing with a healthy light, that is fine. As a *goal*, all of those things can be manifested by the spell. In other words, when the spell is effective, Sunny will be in radiant health, *and* I will say she is doing great, *and* a glow of health will be manifest about my family. So, visualizing diffuse results of the spell (provided they are connected) can be okay. The target, on the other hand, must be visualized as specifically and exactly as possible. In this regard, slight variations from person to person can be problematic.

Figure 5: Battery Working

In an Olympic archery contest, the entire team might cheer the archer on, but only one person shoots the arrow. The team lends energy and visualizes the goal (which might be a gold medal, a cheering crowd, or the arrow in the bullseye), but only one person can see and aim at the target. In a magical working, the "battery" is the archer.

The method of such a working is usually to have the battery sit, stand, or lie down in the center of the circle. The power is raised however the group determines, and the power is then sent to the battery, who immediately sends it on to the target.

The Rest of Ritual

People often ask what other parts of ritual are necessary when working magic. Should a circle be cast? Should the gods be invoked? Must magic be worked in accordance with the tradition of which you are a member, or are spells a separate sort of thing?

A spell can be cast as simply as you'd like or can be included as part of a ritual of your tradition, whatever that may be. Cast circles have advantages that Wiccans (among others) appreciate. They are between the worlds, and hence free of the bounds of space and time. They hold in power until it is released and provide protection. In addition, any ritual, be it Wiccan, Hellenistic, Goetic, Kemetic, or name-your-poison, allows for extra time to shift the mind's consciousness into a more focused and magical state. If you take a while to get to the magic-working portion of your rite, by the time you get there, you're likely to be really primed.

An elaborate lead-in to a spell also gives you time to reconsider the work you are about to do. Sometimes it can push you into more careful thought. If it takes ten minutes to do a spell, what the heck, might as well do it. If it takes an evening, you have to be far more committed. I often work spells simply, without a cast circle, but if I feel my magical work is becoming slack or if my results lately have been less than excellent, I revert to a more involved approach.

You must also follow the dictates of your tradition. It's not a good idea to work two systems that are at odds with each other. If your path has a rule that magic is worked only within a certain context, then even though magic *can* be worked otherwise, you shouldn't do it. Empower your path by walking its ways.

What about invoking one or more deities? This is not strictly necessary when working a spell, and many people don't do it. In fact, magic is often worked by people who don't believe in gods.

As with your tradition, you may be under a prior obligation. If you have a commitment to worship one or more deities, you may wish to ask yourself why you are leaving them out of your spellcasting. This has nothing to do with your spell and everything to do with your worship relationship and hence is an issue of theology, not magic. But it's food for thought.

Sometimes we invoke particular deities for their aid or expertise. Athena is often willing to help a spell of righteous justice. In addition, she knows *how* to work justice. If you are working through a situation that is a tangled legal knot, you may need an expert to untangle it. In the mundane world, that would probably be a lawyer, and in the spiritual world, that would be a goddess or god of justice. You may ask a deity for help in understanding what is right and proper in a particular situation, and you may request a blessing. Many people believe that if you bring a spell to the attention of the gods and they do not wish the spell to work, it creates the opportunity for them to stop it. Most Pagans don't believe in an omniscient deity, so there is no reason to believe the gods will reach in and stop a spell *unless* it's brought to their attention.

A spell is not identical to prayer. You can pray to one or more deities for something you want, and that's a fine thing. To do a spell is to lend *your* power to it. If you consider the many sources of power we discussed in this chapter, you'll recall that one of the sources was the gods. But *only* one. A spell generally weaves together many sources of power, whereas prayer relies on the power of the gods alone.

Following Up

Football coaches get together with their team after a game and review the video of the game. They can see what they did right and what they did wrong. Players might keep making the same mistakes over and over if they don't see the problem and identify what needs to be corrected. As a magician, you need to act as your own coach.

Most people are familiar with the "rule of silence." A spell is not to be spoken about until after it is completed or until it is achieved. I was taught that maintaining silence for twenty-four hours is sufficient—once you've slept on it and let a "cycle" (a night and a day) pass, the spell is on its way, and your words cannot pull it back or weaken it.

In either case, at some point, it'll be okay to discuss your spell. If you're working magic in a group, it's helpful and educational to sit down together and have a coaching session. What happened? What worked and what didn't work? What felt right and what felt awkward? When people work together, learning one another's style is a process; it doesn't happen overnight, and there are kinks to work out before you flow well together.

The most important thing to go over afterward, though, is whether the spell *worked*. I keep a magical diary, and I suggest you do the same. Record the date, the goal of the spell, what you did, and then *follow up*. I find it somewhat appalling when people work healings or other spells designed to help someone and then never trouble to find out if they actually helped. If your doctor didn't check in with you after operating, you'd be offended! Besides, if you don't know your results, you're like the ball player who doesn't watch the video or even know their league standing—you have no way of knowing how you're doing and how to improve.

Your diary should include your results. I continue to jot down notes about spells even years later. A child who suffered a head injury and was not expected to regain consciousness was miraculously healed through magic; some twenty-five years later, he has issues related to Traumatic Brain Injury (TBI) but is a functional adult. Another child with severe health problems is now a healthy young adult. One particular spell seemed to have had no results at all—the sick person took six months to recover!

Only a year later did the patient learn that the normal recovery period for that particular (rare) disease was two years; without follow-up, I'd have thought the spell hadn't worked, when in fact it had worked marvelously. It is true, of course, that I sometimes lose touch with people and cannot follow up. It is also true that not every spell requires long-term follow-up. If I do a spell for you to get a job within two weeks, and you receive an offer on day twelve, that's all I need to know. If you're fired a year later, that's not something I'm going to connect to my magic (unless the spell specified that you would have the job for many years).

The thing is, if you don't care enough about someone to follow up on their situation, why are you working magic for that person?

I think there is a level of discomfort in recording the results of one's magical work. It is one thing to do spells, to feel the power, to have a sense of success, and even to see the tangible results with your own eyes. It is another thing to see those results in black and white. What if your statistics indicate a success rate of just 50 percent? If that's the case, you're doing no better than random chance would have it!

Here's the thing: "I don't want to know" is a form of fear, and fear will rob you of your power. The truth will set you free. Keep the diary, look honestly and fearlessly at your outcomes, and learn from what you find.

Your diary can contain things like moon phases, people present, things you liked and disliked about how the spell turned out, omens that occurred before, during, or after the work, and so on. Your point in the menstrual cycle (if applicable) and other physical or health information can be noted. As you look at your successes, failures, and surprises, you can also look for patterns. If your best results come on an empty stomach, you can decide to fast before working spells. If unsatisfying results seem connected to a particular style of magic or a particular magical tool, then discontinue its use. Over a lifetime of magical working, you will increase your skills by learning from one of your very best teachers—yourself.

WORKING WITH THE MAGIC OF THE ELEMENTS

This book presents spells as lessons or exercises, but also as spells in their own right. As we approach each section, we'll learn about *how* and *why* to do each kind of magic: balancing spells as well as Air, Fire, Water, and Earth spells. Then each section will have a spell that serves to cap that lesson off. For example, candle magic is included (not surprisingly) as a Fire spell. After a section on various ways of performing candle magic, two different candle spells are provided, step-by-step, that serve to illustrate two ways in which candle magic presented in that section can be done.

These spells are like recipes and have both the advantages and the limitations of following recipes in a cookbook.

When you first learn to cook, following recipes closely is a good idea. Even as a beginner, though, you need to be able to change a recipe proportionately for the number of people eating (to halve or double it, for example), and you start, fairly early on, to learn substitutions (soy milk for dairy milk, vegetable shortening for lard, etc.). Right from the beginning, then, you're modifying and adjusting recipes to fit your needs.

No cookbook has every recipe for every dish you might want or need to prepare. Instead, different cookbooks have different focuses and themes—beginner recipes, recipes using only some foods (my ex had a book of 365 pasta recipes), recipes for special dietary needs, recipes for particular occasions, and recipes for particular types of food (Mexican, vegetarian).

All of this is exactly analogous to working with published spells. This book has recipes (spells) and a theme (the elements). But it's not really a recipe book. *The Magic of the Elements* is a book *about* "cooking" with the four elements. Nonetheless, you'll find many spell recipes, which can be looked up conveniently in the list of spells at the end of this book (appendix A)

Spell Structure

Every spell in this book is presented as follows:

- Goal
- Target
- Needed Tools
- Other (Here is where information about working solitary or in a group, indoors or out, and other miscellany are presented.)
- Appropriate Deities (As discussed, no spell requires that deities be invoked, and the names presented here do not exhaust all possibilities.)
- The Spell (Before you begin, be sure to review carefully what will be done.)

Note that each spell repeats certain steps, i.e., every spell will remind you to ground and center, but not every spell will tell you to "raise power." This is because the power is sometimes raised as a result of performing certain steps of a spell. Look over each spell and get a feel for its flow and movement. Notice how power will move when the spell is actually being worked—where it will build, where it will plateau, and where it will be released.

Chapter 3

Preparing for Magic

There are a number of things to do before you actually cast a spell. Some of these are necessary, and some are simply good ideas. For example, you don't technically *have* to ground and center before working magic, but why wouldn't you? It will increase your power, clear your mind, improve your focus, and protect you from becoming drained.

In the previous chapter, I mentioned that some people do magic the same way every time, which has certain advantages. Repetition is undeniably hypnotic, and the hypnotic state of mind is one conducive to magic. In this book, we're using lots of different methods to perform spells. By doing the preliminary steps presented here before each spell, you gain the advantage of repetition while still varying the magic itself.

We can break up spell preparation into three stages:

- Preparing your space
- Preparing yourself
- Preparing your tools and ingredients

PREPARING YOUR SPACE

Your "magic room" (or alcove, or basement, or whatever) needs two things: it needs to *allow* an altered state of consciousness, and it needs to *encourage* such a state. In other words, you need to create a space free of the distractions and disturbances that keep you trapped in mundane experience, and you also need an atmosphere and props that help you reach a magical state.

When possible, work magic in the same place each time. This is practical, as it allows your tools and other necessities to be kept in a convenient place. It also adds to the repetition that is so valuable.

The first order of business is *privacy*. The distraction of wondering if the door will open, if the phone will ring, or if you will otherwise be interrupted is virtually guaranteed to disrupt your focus. The door to your magic room should have a lock (unless you live alone). But a locked door and an unplugged phone are not enough. You should also make sure that the rest of your household is able to allow you the privacy you need. Are the kids in bed? No, *really*? Do the cats have fresh water in their dish? You don't want anyone chasing you down to meet their needs.

You also don't want *you* chasing yourself down. Are there any nagging tasks that simply must be done? I prefer to work my magic later in the evening and not save any chores for afterward. Otherwise, my mind has "after" in it. Your magic is freer when you haven't the thought in the back of your head that you have limited time.

That takes care of the negatives—with these handled, you *allow* spellcraft. Now, how do you encourage it?

The Room

- There should be a comfortable spot for sitting. Although I often do spells standing, you should be able to sit if you want to.
- The room should not be too bright and could be candlelit.
- There is a place (drawer, chest) where your tools and paraphernalia can easily be found. It is more than a little irritating to interrupt a spell because you've run out of matches and can't find more! I haven't always followed my own rule. At one time, I had a large chest of drawers in the basement where my supplies were kept and a small drawer upstairs in the room where I actually worked magic. When I relocated my working area, I wasn't about to carry the

chest upstairs. If you can't keep everything in one place, keep the essentials together and double-check the storage area before you begin.
- The room should be of a comfortable temperature. I like to keep a blanket throw handy, as I sometimes get cold in the middle of things.
- Know your directions! When you move into a new place, use a compass (or compass app) to find north, east, south, and west, and remember which is which.

PREPARING YOURSELF

Preparing yourself or yourselves involves body and mind. It can involve a solitary practitioner or a group.

Preparing Your Body

The use of *a ritual bath, symbolic cleansing*, or *anointing* is more common to full-blown ritual than to simple spellwork. The choice depends upon how elaborate you want your spellcraft to be.

A bath is just that—a soak in a tub. A symbolic cleansing is when a bath is not desired, not available, or too inconvenient. A basin is used, and the face and hands, and perhaps some or all of the chakras, are splashed or touched with the water. Anointing doesn't involve washing at all; rather, the water, oil, or whatever is touched to the third eye and/or other chakras (the heart and throat chakras being the most common).

The primary purpose of these pre-spell activities is to clear away the day, relax the body, and focus the mind. The water in either the bath or the basin can have added ingredients—consecrated salt, special herbs, or perhaps an essential oil. These ingredients can have a ritual or a practical significance; they can be oriented either toward magic, aromatherapy, or muscle or mental relaxation. Anointing can be done with essential or infused oil, saltwater, spring water, or some other substance. Any or all of these substances may, optionally, be ritually consecrated prior to use and then kept for future working.

When adding ingredients to your bath water, basin water, or anointing blend, you can use the elemental nature of the ingredients to balance or augment elemental spells. For instance, when doing an Air spell, you can use herbs or essential oils associated with Air. Or you might balance the four elements by using, say, a saltwater (Earth/Water) sprinkle and a censing or smudging (Air/Fire).

Some people work in special magical garb, wearing a robe or other magical outfit and/or special jewelry. Some work skyclad (nude). Changing into magical clothes or disrobing can be part of the process of preparing your psyche for magic—changing the outside symbolizes changing the inside and cues the mind.

Grounding and Centering

It seems I need to include a section on grounding and centering in every book I write because it's so important.

The phrase "grounding and centering" is so commonplace that I'm using it to avoid confusion. However, in a group ritual, there is a third part to the process, so it should more correctly be called "grounding, centering, and merging."

Here are the steps:

1. GROUNDING—Getting in touch with the earth
2. CENTERING—Getting in touch with ourselves
3. MERGING—Getting in touch with each other

How to Ground

Most people find that a few simple visualization techniques connect them effectively and quickly to the earth. Here is one that works nicely:

Stand or sit, breathing calmly and slowly. Become aware of your physical self, sparing a brief thought for each part of your body. Start at your head and continue down to your neck, shoulders, arms, hands, chest, belly, groin, legs, and feet. Feel your feet touching the ground. If you are indoors, feel the floor beneath you, and imagine the floor's connection to the earth. Even if you are on an upper floor, continue imagining until you have established a connection from your feet all the way down to natural soil. Imagine that your toes are digging into the soil. Imagine that the soil is responding by caressing your toes and feet and supporting your entire body. The earth is your companion, holding you up, supporting you, encouraging you.

This technique is very simple and can be done for several minutes or started and finished in thirty seconds. You can quickly flash your awareness from the top of your head, through your body, to your feet, the soil, and back up again in the time it takes to tell.

Another technique involves the spinal cord instead of the feet. This is helpful for people for whom a standing meditation is challenging or impossible. This time, begin your visualization at the base of your skull. Imagine that your spine is alive with a steady glow of life-giving energy. In your mind's eye, follow your spine from your neck down through your upper back, your lower back, and reaching your tailbone.

As you picture this, allow each part of your body to relax—your shoulders as you pass them, then your chest, arms, and so on. When you reach your tailbone, imagine that your spinal cord continues, that you have a tail that is running straight down into the earth. Again, continue through any flooring until you've reached soil. Feel this vibrant, glowing tail dig into the earth. Now, feel that it has become a siphon, drawing life-energy from the earth, being nourished by the earth's ever-replenishing supply of solid, stable power. Draw that energy back into yourself.

There are many other ways to ground. Both of these examples are direct and physical and use the body itself. You can use more metaphorical imagery; for example, you can imagine yourself to be a tree with roots that reach into the earth. Trees are connected to all four elements—their roots are in the soil (Earth), their lifeblood is sap (Water), their branches are in the sky (Air), and they are nourished by the rays of the sun (Fire). Some people don't like the fact that trees are rooted to one spot; they say it breaks the visualization when they move, but most people find this tree meditation very effective.

How to Center

Find your center, the place in your body where you feel that "you" are located. This might take some experimentation. It varies from person to person, often being the solar plexus, but sometimes the heart or the head.

Centering is simply a matter of locating the center and bringing all of your energy into it. Once you've located your center, picture the rest of your energy flowing into and out of that spot. You should immediately notice a feeling of increased calm and clarity. Now "hook up" to your center the energy being drawn from the earth.

Once you've connected energy from the earth to your center, you can extend the energy up through the rest of your body, out the top of your head, and into the sky. If you're using a tree meditation, this would be the part where you visualize your top branches and leaves and feel the sun on them.

Alternately, you can center before grounding. This can be helpful because bringing your energy to your center helps with distractions. Imagine all your distractions, all your stray thoughts, as bits of you that are uncentered. I like to visualize my hopes, worries, and concerns as birds, and my center as the nest to which they return. Once everything is back home, nested, I can begin the grounding of my centered energy.

How to Merge

The last part of the process is done when you are in a group; you will form a connection with the others in that group. Do this by extending the visualization you have used so far. In other words, if you've drawn energy up from the earth and then connected it to your center, you should then extend that same energy out toward the others in the circle and feel the connections.

If you are all trees, at this point, you should add to the visualization that the trees are in a grove or forest, that the trees are forming a circle, and that the tips of their branches touch.

In a group, the grounding, centering, and merging instructions are usually said aloud so that everyone is visualizing together. Remember that merging works by awakening our knowledge of that which connects us. The verbal instructions should include at least one thing that connects this particular group. For ritual, this varies considerably. You might be united by your worship of the gods, by your membership in a community, coven, or tradition, by your age, gender, orientation, or profession, by parenthood or grandparenthood, by your political convictions, or by anything else that has brought this group together. For spellwork, the purpose of the spell unites you.

Preparing a Group

If you are working in a group, be sure that everyone knows what is coming. Even if you all know why you have gathered, before beginning a working it is best to review the target and goal, pass around any sympathetic objects that will be used (like photos), and discuss the visualizations you are planning to do.

PREPARING YOUR TOOLS AND INGREDIENTS

One of the questions that beginners often ask is, what tools are absolutely necessary to have before magic can be performed? The answer is none. You can do magic with nothing more than a focused mind, a firm will, and a quiet space in which to concentrate.

That said, tools are useful. They are a source of both symbolic and stored power, and they help as psychic reminders of the magical state your mind should enter. Holding, seeing, and sensing your tools is a tangible way of knowing that magic is happening.

The Altar

The altar is a central piece of Wiccan ritual gear and figures prominently in the rites of many other magical and religious systems. You don't need one to do a spell, but an altar is also a table, a place to keep stuff, and as such, it is incredibly convenient.

If you have an altar dedicated to one or more deities, you shouldn't use that altar for your spellwork unless you are invoking those deities in the spell. It's not polite. If you use the same altar for a lot of different purposes, one nice way to vary your presentation is with different altar cloths. You can use the color of the cloth as part of the spell, just as candle magic uses candles of different colors—pink for love, white for purification, blue for peace, etc. Symbols, such as runes, can also be incorporated into the cloth using embroidery, fabric painting, appliqué, and so on.

Basic Tools

For our purposes, the most important magical tools will be those used to bring the elements into a spell.

Candles, which can be used to represent Fire, also have a great many other magical and ritual uses. A good stock of candles in a variety of colors is very handy, but if your budget is tight, start with white candles and add the symbolic meaning in another way (that is, instead of using a pink candle for love, use a white candle combined with some other love symbol). With candles, you'll need candle holders.

Incense can be used to represent either Air or the combination of Air and Fire. You'll need some sort of incense holder as well. Many beginners are happy with stick or cone incense. After a while, though, most people prefer to burn loose incense on a charcoal briquette. This method gives you more flexibility: you can use your own homemade blends, and you can make your ritual very smoky at some points while letting the smoke dwindle at others.

For Water and Earth, have two dishes, one with water and one with salt. A cup is important for the many times that wine or some other sacred or symbolic drink is used.

Always have an unobtrusive ashtray around. No one would confuse it for a magical tool, but it is really annoying to be in the middle of something that requires a lot of focus and suddenly realize you have no place to put your burnt match!

Special Tools

There are magicians who like pared-down simplicity, magicians who like an elaborate assortment of tools and accoutrements, and those who fall somewhere in between. The "basic" list just described is only for beginners and those who really love a simple approach. Most of us prefer more window-dressing.

The fundamental Witch's tool is the athame, and few Witches wish to be without one. The traditional athame is a black-handled, double-edged blade, although many choose a nontraditional tool, perhaps one with a single edge or a deer-foot hilt. The purpose of the athame is to direct the will of the magician; it is never used to cut in Wicca, although Kitchen Witches, among others, will use the same knife in magical and mundane contexts.

The wand is another tool of energy direction. Both the wand and the athame are used in situations where the magician could simply point their hands, but both have magical properties of their own—symbolism and stored power—and are useful focal objects. Many people consider the wand more "natural" than the athame, and also gentler.

A magical tool not so commonly discussed, but quite useful, is the mirror. It is used to scry, to capture moonlight (water is also used for this), to represent the Goddess, to represent the sun, and to deflect and trap energy. You can pick up small, cheap mirrors in the handcrafts department of craft stores. Then, if a spell calls for a mirror or you think one might be useful in a working, you'll have it around.

Sound has been known as a source of power since ancient times. A bell, because of the purity and singularity of its tone, creates vibrations heard by both natural and supernatural beings. Bells are used to summon, and they mark beginnings and endings. They also induce trance, as the mind "travels" on the sound waves.

Riding the broom is also associated with deep trance, as the "Witches' flight" of medieval legend was apparently a hallucinatory trip. Old recipes for "flying ointment" contain hallucinogenic ingredients, leading many scholars to believe that tales of witches flying were tales of drug-induced trance. The broom could therefore be used in conjunction with trance or astral travel. (I don't know anyone who does this, but it *could* be.)

The most common use of the broom as a magical tool, though, is for sweeping. Sweeping is a powerful metaphor for removing the unwanted, for cleansing, and for starting fresh. Sweeping sacred space can be done to remove unwanted influences, be they psychic, astral, or psychological. Sweeping as part of a spell can remove something unwanted from your life; a symbol of the unwanted can be placed in the ritual area and swept out.

A white-hilt knife is used by some Wiccans who use their athames only for energy work. It is useful, from time to time, to have a knife with which to cut in a ritual, and some of the rituals in this book will suggest that. In traditional Wicca, the athame is never used in this way. If you don't cut with your athame, this second knife is quite handy.

In the Air section of this book (Chapter 6), you'll find a spell that calls for pen and parchment (or other fancy paper). Pen and paper as magical objects, although not core necessities when building a magical toolkit, are things you'll never regret having. Over the years, I've done a lot of writing spells—they concentrate the mind, they empower words, and they marry the effort of our hands to the language in our minds.

Finally, your magical toolkit will benefit from the presence of a decent collection of herbs and/or essential or infused oils. Normally, people acquire these one or a few at a time on an as-needed basis. This is how I've built my collection—by purchasing or harvesting what I need when I need it and keeping the leftovers. Growing herbs is a great way to augment your supply and can be done in a window box.

Herbs and oils keep best in tightly sealed dark containers (to avoid breakdown from light exposure).

Directing Power with Tools

In the various spells offered in Chapters 4 through 9, you'll find many spells that call for an athame and/or a wand. Sometimes this is to bring the elemental power of a tool to the spell. Often though, the tool is suggested as a way of directing power.

As stated above, tools like this have stored power in them, and are incredibly useful, in my experience. On the other hand, the athame in particular can be a problem when traveling: In the U.S., a knife in carry-on luggage is definitely a no-no. You may have any number of reasons for wanting to use your hands only, and that is fine. You may also have a magical practice that uses a different tool, such as a rattle, crystal, broom, or sickle.

If a spell is using a tool specifically for its elemental associations, the instructions will say so. Otherwise, feel free to direct power with whatever tool is most comfortable for you.

The Magic Box

One of the smartest things I ever thought of was my magic box. It's nothing more complicated than a small, highly portable wooden box in which I keep a set of emergency ritual supplies.

It contains:

- Wooden matches
- A candle shaver (the kind used to shave down the bottom of a candle to fit it in a holder)
- A compass (for marking out directions in unfamiliar locations)
- Spare charcoal briquettes
- Frankincense (an all-purpose resinous incense; it can be used in many rituals and can be added to powdery incense that isn't burning properly)
- A utility taper (a spare candle used to light other candles or melt the wax at the base of a candle that won't stand up)
- A corkscrew
- You might add other such items to your magic box. It is ever so comforting, when starting a ritual, to know the magic box is by the altar—just in case

Preparation Checklist

- Is the door locked?
- Is the landline unplugged and the cellphone off or silenced?
- Are necessary chores done (pets fed, children in bed, dishes done)?
- Am I in comfortable clothing (or comfortably skyclad)?
- Have I a comfortable place to sit?
- Is the temperature of the room comfortable?
- Have I the tools and supplies I will need?
- Have I spares of things that may run out (candles, matches, charcoals)?
- Is my magic box handy?

Consecrating Elements and Tools

There are, in essence, two parts to preparing for magic—the practical part and the magical part. Let's move away from the practical aspect of preparing tools for a moment and talk about the magical.

Consecrating the Elements

Some people don't consecrate the elements before using them, some people consecrate them only when fresh (i.e., consecrate a batch of newly made incense), and some people consecrate only one, two, or three of the elements. For our purposes, I am assuming that you will consecrate all four elements at least once.

The words of consecration can be simple or elaborate, descriptive or straightforward. However you consecrate one element, do all four to match. That is, don't use a simple, six-word Air consecration and a fancy, thirty-word Fire consecration. The basic action of a consecration is to focus your mind, heart, and will on the process while using your hand, athame, or wand to send the energy into the element. The first example here will give full "stage directions," and subsequent examples will provide just the words. The example is written for one person. In a group rite, you might split up the consecrations; if you have four or more people, a different person can do each element.

Example One: Consecrating the Elements

My preference for consecrating elements is to mix them into two pairs. The unlit incense represents Air, the lit charcoal briquette in the censer represents Fire, a dish of water represents Water, and a dish of salt represents Earth. I consecrate Air, then place the incense in the censer while consecrating Fire; then after consecrating the next two I place salt in the water dish and stir. This gives me an Air and Fire blend (the smoking censer) and a Water and Earth blend. Using this method, when consecrating an object by elemental powers, you'll do two consecrations for each object—once to consecrate by Air and Fire and once by Water and Earth.

The alternative is to keep each element separate. In that case, the incense smoke represents Air alone, a candle is used to represent Fire, and the water and salt are not mixed. If this is your preference, the following sample can easily be modified.

Begin by lifting the dish of incense.[18] Place your fingers or athame in the dish, visualizing pure energy pouring into the incense. Say:

Lord and Lady, bless this Air!

Put the incense dish down, and from it, take a large pinch of incense between your fingers. Hold it over the censer and while sprinkling the incense onto the charcoal, say:

Lord and Lady, bless this Fire!

Visualize pure energy pouring into the fire and rising in the smoke. Run your hand through the smoke.

Lift the water dish. Place your fingers or athame in the dish, visualizing pure energy pouring into the water. Say:

Lord and Lady, bless this Water!

Put the water dish down and lift the salt dish. Place your fingers or athame in the dish, visualizing pure energy pouring into the salt. Say:

Lord and Lady, bless this Earth!

Take a large pinch of salt and drop it into the water, stirring with your athame or fingers.

---

18 I'm assuming loose incense burned on a charcoal briquette. You can do the same thing with stick incense. When the instructions say to sprinkle the incense onto the censer, simply light it with a candle flame and place it in its holder.

Example Two: Descriptive Elemental Consecrations

There are numerous ways to vary consecrations. Are you using the power of gods (as in the previous example), or your own power? Look at the following variations:

> *Lord and Lady, bless this Water!*
> *I bless this Water.*
> *I bless thee, O Water.*
> *This Water is blessed.*

As a writer, I am sensitive to things like an active or passive voice, to third person versus second person. I think anyone can see how these slight differences change the tone and implication of each of these statements.

In this example, only the will of the magician (no deities) is used in the consecration. There is also a fully fleshed description for each element. This brings the qualities of the elements into conscious awareness and creates a sense of their presence.

> *I, Deborah,[19] do consecrate this Air, that it bring breath, inspiration, and intelligence to my spell. So be it!*

> *I, Deborah, do consecrate this Fire, that it bring heat, passion, and willpower to my spell. So be it!*

> *I, Deborah, do consecrate this Water, that it bring flow, feeling, and depth to my spell. So be it!*

> *I, Deborah, do consecrate this Earth, that it bring reality, strength, and commitment to my spell. So be it!*

I am always attracted to reciting things in sets of three, as in this consecration. It is very magical, has a nice rhythm to it, and is easy to remember. If you're in the middle of a working and can't remember

---
19 Using your name, especially a magical name, is an ancient act of power.

the words you meant to say, it is easy enough to come up with three things that are descriptive of each element.

Consecrating Tools

To consecrate is *to declare* or *set apart as sacred*, and also *to dedicate solemnly to a service or goal*.[20] That "service or goal" might be general or specific. Now that you have consecrated the elements, you can use them to consecrate tools and objects that will be used in the course of your spell-working.

With tools that you use often (such as your athame, which might very well be a part of every spell you do), you would probably consecrate them generally—to magic, to the gods, or to the purpose of working your will. Each tool would be consecrated once, and thereafter would always be considered consecrated, without ever "reviving" the consecration. You would either consecrate it the first time you use it or, more likely, set up a special ritual just for consecrating stuff and do it then.

With an item used only once or rarely, such as an oil blended specifically for one spell, or a photo used specifically to create sympathy with the pictured individual, you would probably consecrate it to its particular purpose. In that case, you'd do the consecration as a preliminary part of working the spell in the same ritual as the rest of the spell.

As a person and for spiritual growth, your ultimate goal is to be balanced in the elements, and this book does contain a spell for balancing the elements in Chapter 4. Most of the spells in this book, though, use a single element, bringing its power to bear for a purpose connected to it.

For most tools, I would consecrate them using all four elements, creating a balanced "self" for the tool, blessing and empowering it for all uses. In some cases, a tool might have only a single elemental purpose. For example, the parchment and pen would always have a connection to Air. Even if you used writing for a Water, Fire, or balanced purpose, the act of writing still remains in the realm of Air. You might choose to keep such a tool dedicated to, and consecrated in, a single element only.

---

20 *The American Heritage Dictionary*

Finally, you might do *both* the one-time, general, balanced consecration *and* the single-purpose, single-element consecration. The latter would be used to charge up something for the occasion. So, your wand might be consecrated in the four elements and in the names of the particular gods you worship. Tonight, though, you'll be using your wand in a spell to gain knowledge. So, you'll charge the wand by Air for tonight's working. This isn't common—most people charge their regular working tools once in a lifetime and do the per-occasion consecrations only for items that are being used *solely* in that occasion.

Balanced Consecrations

Consecrations that are balanced tend to focus on balance. This may seem circular, but it isn't. It means that when choosing to consecrate by all four elements, you're choosing to perceive the balance of the universe, the totality of all qualities brought together into a whole, and you're bringing that wholeness to bear.

The consecrations offered in examples 3 and 4 use the combined-pairs method described in example 1—incense is Air and Fire; saltwater is Water and Earth. Any of these can be unbundled, and any of the consecrations in examples 3 and 4 can be done in four single steps rather than two paired steps.

Example Three: Consecrating a Magical Tool

This consecration can be used for any tool that will be used generally in many spells and rituals, such as an athame, wand, censer, or broom.

After consecrating the four elements as in example 1 or 2, you are ready to begin. Hold the magical tool in one hand. With the other hand, dip your fingers into the saltwater, and run them all over the athame[21] or wand, top to bottom and on all sides. Say:

> *By the power of Water and Earth, I consecrate this (name of tool). By the power of Water and Earth, I bless and charge it to serve my purpose and my will. So mote it be!*

---

21 Saltwater is corrosive. After consecrating any metal object, clean and oil it.

Now pass the item back and forth through the incense smoke. (Before doing so, add extra incense to the censer, and stir it up, if necessary, to get it smoky.) Again, turn it up and down, side to side, so that every part of the item is touched by the smoke. Say:

> *By the power of Fire and Air, I consecrate this (name of tool). By the power of Fire and Air, I bless and charge it to serve my purpose and my will. So mote it be!*

Now hold up the magical tool in front of you, and say:

> *By the power of Water and Earth, by the power of Fire and Air, it is done!*

Now use the tool at once. Using something seals and finishes a consecration. For an athame or wand, draw an invoking pentagram in the air (see appendix D on page 205). For a broom, sweep a spot in front of you. For an item that cannot be used at once, or that doesn't have a physical "use" (such as a goddess statue), it is traditional to show the item to the four quarters—east, south, west, north, and east again. This constitutes "use" if nothing else is possible.

Example Four: Making a Consecration Particular to the Item

Sometimes a consecration needs to be particular to the item. Even if it doesn't *need* to be, it can add a nice quality to your working.

In this example, we'll consecrate a bell. As before, you should consecrate the four elements before you begin (example 1).

Hold the bell in one hand. With the other hand, dip your fingers into the saltwater, and run them all over the bell, top to bottom and all around. Say:

> *By the power of Water and Earth, I consecrate this bell. By Water and Earth shall its sound be sweet, by Water and Earth shall it summon with purity and clarity. When this bell is rung, O Water, O Earth, let its sound be heard throughout all pleasant realms. So mote it be!*

Now pass the bell back and forth through the incense smoke, making sure the smoke touches all parts of it. Say:

By the power of Fire and Air, I consecrate this bell. By Fire and Air shall its sound be sweet, by Fire and Air shall it summon with purity and clarity. When this bell is rung, O Fire, O Air, let its sound be heard throughout all pleasant realms. So mote it be!

Now hold up the magical tool in front of you, and say:

By the power of Water and Earth, by the power of Fire and Air, this bell is consecrated. May it ring ever sweetly! So mote it be!

Ring the bell.

Consecrating to an Element

Sometimes you will consecrate a tool to one element only. The following are four examples that consecrate one item, associated with a particular element, to that element alone. Just as the bell consecration in the last example customized the words to the particular tool, so too should these examples use words chosen for the particular element. This gives specialized power to each object.

Specialization has advantages and disadvantages. In medicine, a general practitioner is often the best person to see when you don't know what's wrong since they care for the whole person. A podiatrist may not know very much about anything except feet, but they're the one to see if you have foot problems, particularly if you have unusual foot problems that the general practitioner doesn't see very often. The same concept applies to these consecrations—they pull the tool out of general use and, you might say, out of balance, but they increase the focused talents and powers of one element.

You *can* also use these sample consecrations to consecrate something in balance, to all four elements—by using all four! You can use more specific phrases when doing balanced consecrations, as long as you match them in "weight." That is, don't say ten lines about Earth and two lines about Air—that isn't balanced at all.

Example Five: An Air Consecration

This is for consecrating the pen and parchment used in Chapter 6. The magical writing spell in that chapter also uses sealing wax and an essential oil, and these too could be consecrated to Air at the same time.

Consecrate a package or stack of paper all at once. The spell calls for one sheet of paper, but you'll have the rest for future use.

Because sage is purifying and is associated with Air, we will use sage for this consecration. Have it burning before you begin.

Pass the pen back and forth through the sage smoke, saying:

By Air is this pen consecrated. O Air, bring to this pen your power over thought, words, and wisdom. May this pen's words fly on your wings, O Air. May all the words it writes be true. So mote it be!

Pass the paper back and forth through the sage smoke, saying:

By Air is this paper consecrated. O Air, bring to this paper your power over thought, words, and wisdom. May the words written on this paper fly on your wings, O Air. May all the words written upon it become manifest. So mote it be!

Note that this consecration is specific to the tools as well. Words and writing are Air things, but so are inspiration, breath, and new beginnings. Choose the words of a consecration in accordance with your purpose. If you're not sure what the purpose will be or how to phrase it, concentrate on empowering the object with the element itself, and say something like:

By Air is this (name of tool) consecrated. O Air, bring to this paper your special power. So mote it be!

Complete the consecrations by writing something (perhaps your name) with the pen on the paper. (This is an additional advantage of consecrating a stack at once—you can write on a sheet now, and still have a clean, consecrated sheet for the spell.)

Example Six: A Fire Consecration

In this example, we are consecrating a candle. Candles are used for many, many purposes; they are a real mainstay in magical practice. So, we'll assume for the sake of this example that these particular candles are intended for a Fire purpose.

In this case, you will already have consecrated candles *as Fire*, and you are now consecrating candles *as* candles *to* Fire. It is your intent that makes the difference, and the different words of the consecrations will reinforce and focus that intent.

Although one normally touches an object with the element consecrating it, in this case, it wouldn't be a great idea. Pass the candles far enough above the flame of the consecrated Fire that it won't melt the wax. As always, make sure the candles are "touched" in this way from end to end and all around.

When passing the candles above the Fire, say:

By Fire are these candles consecrated. O Fire, bring to these candles your power over passion, heat, and will. May your power burn hot whenever these candles are lit. Allow these candles to fulfill your purpose, O Fire. So mote it be!

Briefly light and then snuff the candles using the Fire candle.

Example Seven: A Water Consecration

Not everyone consecrates the dishes they use on their altars for things like holding water or loose incense. The idea is that a container is part of that which it contains; hence a water dish is consecrated the first time the water it holds is consecrated.

Still, you might wish to consecrate a water dish if you are using it for a specific spell or other purpose. Suppose you are using Water meditations in order to open your heart. You might anoint yourself with water during or before the meditation. For this special purpose, you might choose to consecrate everything you're using to Water, including the dish.

When consecrating something with water, you dip your fingers in the water and use them to wet the object all over. If an item is small enough, your dish of water large enough, and if neither will be damaged, brief immersion is also fine. Say:

> *By Water is this dish consecrated. O Water, bring to this dish your power over love, dreams, and intuition. May your power flow deeply when this dish is used. Allow this dish to fulfill your purpose, O Water. So mote it be!*

Pour some of the consecrated water into the new dish.

Example Eight: An Earth Consecration

For this example, we are consecrating an herb that will be used for an Earth purpose. For example, you might be using vervain, an Earth herb, to protect your home, an Earth goal.

Because you wish to use Earth alone and not Water and Earth together, you won't use saltwater. You could use only salt and rub the herb in it while speaking the words of consecration. You could consecrate a pair of stones and place the herb between the stones while speaking. You also could consecrate soil, and briefly bury the herb in it. Say:

> *By Earth is this (name of herb) consecrated. O Earth, bring to this (name of herb), grown in your soil, your power over home, safety, and foundations. Weigh down this (name of herb) with your power when it is used. Allow this (name of herb) to fulfill your purpose, O Earth. So mote it be!*

Chapter 4

Magic that Brings the Elements to You

To be balanced in the elements is a powerful and achievable goal. In my book *The Way of Four*, I present exercises and meditations to help you balance yourself in the elements. Here our emphasis is on spells and magic, so that's what we'll use.

Most of the time when we talk about spells, we talk about thaumaturgy—about creating manifest, real-world results using the occult. The focus in this chapter, though, is theurgic—the goal is self-actualization. Some people might think of theurgy as ritual, not spellcraft at all. But if you think about it, *all* ritual, even the most spiritually oriented, has a bit of the thaumaturgic about it. Transubstantiation [22] is, for example, an act of magic as well as an act of religious ritual. The dividing line between thaumaturgy and theurgy, between operative magic and spiritual ceremony, is simply not that firm. On the following pages are six magical acts that you might consider spells because they make your will manifest in your life or that you might consider rituals of self-empowerment. In either case, they are a good prelude to the elemental spells presented in our later chapters.

---

22 The act, in Catholicism, of converting the substance of the Eucharist wafer and wine into the body and blood of Christ.

BALANCING SPELLS

The purpose of our first two spells is to bring elemental balance into your life. You can use them when you feel out of balance or when everything's fine because you can never have too much balance. It's a good idea to balance when you feel that one element is overemphasized in your life, for example, when there is a lot of positive Earth in you, but it seems that Earth is *all* there is. You wouldn't want to decrease the Earth, both because it belongs there and because it's positive, so you'd do a spell of balance to lift up the other three elements. You can also have an adequate presence of each element but still be out of balance; a balancing spell can allow them to work more in congress as a reflection of wholeness within, rather than as four separate forces pulling you in different directions.

In *The Way of Four*, there's a great deal of discussion on how to know which elements are present in what proportions in your life, in all the parts of your life, and how to notice when there's an imbalance. Please see that book for more information on the topic.

Note: For these spells use four separate elements throughout rather than Air/Fire and Water/Earth. I will be using incense, a candle, a dish of water, and a dish of salt as symbols of the four elements. You may, of course, choose different symbols and adapt the spells accordingly.

Balancing the Elements: A Spell of Self-Empowerment

Goal:
To balance yourself in the four elements; to bring yourself into a state of magical and spiritual balance, with the elements as the primary symbols of balance.

Target:
Yourself.

NEEDED TOOLS:
- Symbols of the four elements.
- A mirror. Ideally, this should be of a size and shape that can be kept on your altar or carried with you after the spell is complete.

OTHER:
- This is a solitary ritual. You'll see a group version next.
- You can work seated and hold the mirror to your face. In that case, in Step 8, you'll anoint your face with the elements. Or you can work standing and anoint your entire body. I recommend working skyclad if you're going for the whole-body experience. To perform Step 8 on your whole body, have a place to hang or stand the mirror so you can see yourself. Test this spot beforehand so you are confident that the mirror will be stable before you begin.
- When anointing the face, concentrate on the third eye, the mouth, and the throat. When anointing the body, use the chakras, or use genitals-heart-throat-third eye.

APPROPRIATE DEITIES:
Because this is a spell for personal empowerment, use your matron and/or patron if you have one (or more). Otherwise, call upon a deity of wholeness, one with many powers, such as Isis, Lugh, Rhea, Vishnu, or Mahalakshmi.

THE SPELL:
1. Ground and center.
2. Consecrate the four elements (see Chapter 3).
3. If you choose to invoke one or more deities, do so here.
4. Say:

> *I am Air. I am Fire. I am Water. I am Earth.*
> *I am balanced. I am whole.*
> *I am Air. I am Fire. I am Water. I am Earth.*
> *I am balanced. I am whole.*

5. Pick up the mirror, and see yourself in it. Say:

> *I see my reflection.*

6. Consecrate the mirror.
   Pass the mirror through the incense smoke. Say:

> *By Air is this mirror consecrated.*
> *By Air will it reflect my wisdom.*

Pass the mirror over the candle flame. Say:

> *By Fire is this mirror consecrated.*
> *By Fire will it reflect my passion.*

With your fingers, wet the mirror, especially its reflecting surface. Say:

> *By Water is this mirror consecrated.*
> *By Water will it reflect my love.*

Touch your fingers to the salt. Because your fingers are still damp from the Water consecration, some salt will stick to them. Use this to touch the mirror, again focusing on its reflecting surface. Say:

> *By Earth is this mirror consecrated.*
> *By Earth will it reflect my commitment.*

It's okay to have a cloth handy to clean the mirror's surface after consecrating it. The Water and Earth energies are still there even after the water and salt are wiped off.

Note: This spell is for *you*. Use words for each element that reflect your ideals. For Air, you can replace *"wisdom"* with *"intellect"* or *"inspiration."* For Fire, you might choose *"will"* or *"charisma."* For Water, you could use *"intuition"* or *"dreams."* For Earth, you could say *"stability"* or *"reality."*

7. Identify yourself with the mirror. This step will make the mirror a sympathetic object, representing you. It is unusual to use a sympathetic object when the subject is actually present, but we are creating a feedback loop, reinforcing our goal.

    Look into the mirror, and say:

    > *I am the mirror, and the mirror is me.*
    > *My reflection shows me truly.*
    > *I am the mirror, and the mirror is me.*
    > *As I am reflected to myself, so I am and become and will be.*
    > *I am the mirror, and the mirror is me.*
    > *I am the mirror, and the mirror is me.*
    > *So mote it be!*

    Gazing into the mirror, anoint yourself with the four elements.

8. Cense your face or body, however you are working. (When censing a person, you hold the incense just below where you want the incense to reach and allow the smoke to rise to the proper spot. To cense a face, hold the incense below the chin. You can use a fan or your hand to gently move the smoke to the spot.) Say:

    > *I am Air. I see my wisdom. I am Air.*

    Hold the flame close enough to your face/body to feel its heat. Say:

    > *I am Fire. I see my passion. I am Fire.*

    With your fingers, wet your face/body at the focal points. Say:

    > *I am Water. I see my love. I am Water.*

Touch your fingers to the salt and anoint yourself with it on your focal points. Say:

I am Earth. I see my commitment. I am Earth.

9. Continue to gaze into the mirror. Focus on your own image in the mirror. Focus on what you have just said and visualize wholeness and perfection in the mirror—see it in your own face.

    Gather your inner power and focus it toward the mirror. Say:

    I am balanced. I am whole.

    Continue to repeat this, perhaps chanting or intoning it, as you gather power. As intensely as you can, see yourself in the mirror as balanced and whole (whatever that means to you). As you chant the phrase over and over, know the balance you have achieved; *know* it firmly. Continue to say:

    I am balanced. I am whole.
    I am balanced. I am whole.
    I am balanced. I am whole.
    I am balanced. I am whole.
    I am balanced. I am whole.

    Repeat as often as you feel is right. This is your power chant/mantra.

10. When you are ready, send the power you have raised into the mirror (which reflects it back to you). Say:

    So mote it be.

11. If you have invoked any deities, thank them now.
12. Keep the mirror where you can look into it—such as on your altar or your desk.

Balancing the Elements:
A Spell of Group Empowerment

Goal:
To balance a group in the four elements, bringing the members of the group into a state of magical and spiritual balance with the elements as the primary symbols.

Target:
The individuals in the group.

Needed Tools:
- Symbols of the four elements. For this spell, use a small stone, one that fits nicely in the palm of your hand, instead of salt. Use an Earth stone—ordinary granite is fine (see page 209).

Other:
- This group ritual works on the principle of mutual empowerment. It isn't just a solitary ritual expanded for several people; it specifically takes advantage of the presence of a group. It uses a technique I have found very effective in many situations—that of group members giving each other reinforcement of their sacred power.
- For this spell, I'll assume that you (the reader) are leading the group, inasmuch as the one person who reads to others can be called a "leader." As long as the group can comfortably choose one person to fulfill this role, you'll be fine.
- There are a lot of steps. When you read through the spell, though, you'll see that it's simpler than it looks!

Appropriate Deities:
As a group, you may have one or more patron deities, and this would be an appropriate time to call on him/her/them. Otherwise, call upon a deity of wholeness, one with many powers, such as Isis, Lugh, Rhea, Vishnu, or Mahalakshmi.

The Spell:
1. Ground, center, and merge.
2. In a group, a declaration of intent is very valuable so that everyone's purpose is aligned.
    Say:

*We are here to balance ourselves.
We will know ourselves as Air, as Fire, as Water, and as Earth.
We will know ourselves as a balanced whole
where all elements are joined.*

3. Consecrate the four elements (see Chapter 3).
4. If you choose to invoke one or more deities, do so here.
5. Join hands. One person leads and all follow:
    Leader: *We are balanced, we are whole.*
    All: *We are balanced, we are whole.*
    Leader: *We are balanced, we are whole.*
    All: *We are balanced, we are whole.*
    Leader: *We are balanced, we are whole.*
    All: *We are balanced, we are whole.*
    Drop hands.
6. Pick up the incense.
    Turn to the person on your left. Face each other fully, with direct eye contact. Say:

You are Air. I see your wisdom. You are Air.

Cense the person to your left: take the incense to their feet, and lift it, bringing it to the crown of their head and then back down to their feet, so that you have circled them in incense smoke. Finish by handing them the incense. (In a Wiccan group, you would typically hand this to them with a kiss, but your group may not be big on kissing.)

While you are doing this, the rest of the group can repeat *"You are Air. You are Air. You are Air."* You can gesture to remind them to join in on this. They can drum or clap instead of or in addition to repeating this phrase, but drumming should be light and slow for the elemental consecrations and should not begin to build and peak until Step 11.

The person just censed will repeat the entire process for the person to their left, who will pass it to the person on their left, and so on, until everyone has been censed. If you are using loose incense, you'll probably have to pause once or twice between people to add more incense to the charcoal. It should produce plenty of smoke during this process. The last person returns the incense to its place.

7. Pick up the candle.

    Turn to the person on your left. Again, face each other fully, with direct eye contact. Say:

    You are Fire. I see your passion. You are Fire.

    "Fire" them by bringing the candle flame close to them, foot to head to foot, as with the incense. The rest of the group can repeat *You are Fire* and/or drum or clap, just as before. Finish by handing them the candle, with or without a kiss.

    Pass the Fire anointing around the circle, just as you did with Air. The last person returns the candle to its place.

8. Pick up the bowl of water.

    Turn to the person on your left, as before. Say:

    You are Water. I see your love. You are Water.

    There are different ways to anoint with Water. One method is to dip all your fingers into the water and then flick toward the person or place being sprinkled; you can use this method, going from foot to head to foot. Another method is to dip and touch, in this case using symbolic points of the body. You would touch the feet, knees, groin (touching above the groin, below the navel), heart, throat, lips, third eye, and palms of the hands.

    As you anoint the person, the rest of the group is chanting/speaking/drumming/clapping or silent as before. It is important that each elemental anointing be equal in weight and meaning and should stay at the same energy level. Don't let drumming be more excited for Water than for Air. Give them the bowl of water when finished.

Pass the Water anointing around the circle, as before. The last person returns the bowl to its place.

9. Pick up the stone representing Earth.

   Turn to the person on your left, as before. Say:

   You are Earth. I see your commitment. You are Earth.

   Touch the person with the stone, beginning at the feet and gently traveling up the body. Include the face and head, then return to the feet. Again, the group might be chanting, speaking, drumming, and/or clapping. When finished, hand them the stone, with or without a kiss.

   Pass the Earth anointing around the circle, as before. The last person returns the stone to its place.

10. Join hands. Say:

    We are Air. We are Fire. We are Water. We are Earth.
    We are balanced. We are whole.

    All repeat:

    We are balanced. We are whole.
    We are balanced. We are whole.
    We are balanced. We are whole.

11. Now is the time to start raising power as a group. Continue saying *"We are balanced. We are whole."* Build your energy through voice, rhythm, and movement. You may eventually reduce your chant to *"Balanced! Whole! Balanced! Whole!"* as power and energy build.

    Don't turn this into a drum party. Remember that it's a spell. Let the energy build and build and allow it to flow through, empower, and be enjoyed by everyone, but stay focused. This is a wave-energy spell as opposed to a shoot-it-off spell, but it's still a spell.

12. When you are ready, raise your arms in the air to catch everyone's attention, and slowly bring them down. People recognize this as a universal symbol for calming down and becoming quiet. Say:

We are balanced. We are whole. So mote it be!

All repeat:

So mote it be!

If you have invoked any deities, thank them now. Say:

Our work is done.

MAGIC TO BRING INDIVIDUAL ELEMENTS

The purpose of the previous spells is to bring balance. Use them when you have a sense that things are out of whack, when one or two elements have come to dominate your life, or just because they're *A Good Idea*. In contrast, use the next four spells when you notice a specific weakness in your life; when one element seems distinctly absent. For each spell, I'll give examples of how an absence of that element might manifest in your life. For a detailed examination, I refer you again to *The Way of Four*.

TO BRING AIR INTO YOURSELF: A FEATHER SPELL

GOAL:
To bring the element of Air into yourself. Use this spell when you feel or show symptoms of an absence of this element in your life. Look at the following list of symptoms. If you notice several of them in yourself (not just one or two), you will probably benefit from this spell.
- Inability to concentrate
- Difficulty studying
- Being at a loss for words; being unable to make words work for you

- Lack of inspiration
- Inability to start new projects
- Difficulty getting up in the morning
- Fear of change
- Respiratory problems

TARGET:
Yourself, especially your mind.

NEEDED TOOLS:
- Incense, preferably sage or lavender.
- A bag of feathers. These can be feathers you acquire from nature, or you can get them in a craft store. You'll need approximately enough to fill a paper lunch bag.
- A bowl to put the feathers in during the spell. (You don't want to work directly from a paper bag.)
- A bell (optional). The sound of bells has long been associated with Air, and striking a bell invokes the element's power.
- A sheet to cover the floor.
- A cloth bag. Use a store-bought one that zippers shut or make one yourself that you will sew shut.

OTHER:
- You will write an Air chant yourself.[23] This can be as simple as *Air! Air! Air!*, or you can dress it up. Writing it is an important part of the process since Air rules language.
- For the same reason, it's important to do this spell *out loud*. Many people silently think the words of a spell instead of speaking them, but words have power, both metaphysical power and the vibratory power of sound. Speaking words uses a different part of your brain than just thinking the same words and activates more neural synapses. Especially when using or invoking the power of Air, actual speech is needed. If privacy is an issue, *whisper*.

---

23 My daughter likes "Fly, my pretties, fly," but use your own judgment.

- This spell is messy—feathers will probably end up on the floor. Prepare the room (or the outdoors) by laying a sheet under the working area.
- Making your own pillow bag is an optional part of the spell. Since the pillow is used after the spell is completed, that's where I'll put the instructions; but the bag needs to be ready, and in your working area, before you begin.
- If you're going to sew the pillow bag closed, have your sewing supplies with you as well.
- The spell is designed to be performed solitary, but can easily be adapted for a group. Handcrafts are always an excellent group activity, and your group might really enjoy making the pillow bags together, not to mention pouring feathers over one another.
- Work this spell barefoot and have your shoes nearby.
- This spell is ideal for the last week of a waxing moon but can be performed at any time.

APPROPRIATE DEITIES:
You can invoke sylphs instead of deities, or you can call upon deities of intellect and/or flight, such as Thoth, Garuda, Hermes, or Sarasvati.

THE SPELL:
1. Ground and center (and merge, if working in a group).
2. Light the incense and inhale deeply, bringing the smoke toward you.
3. If you choose to invoke one or more deities, do so here.
4. Strike the bell (if you're using one).
5. Place the bowl of feathers in front of you and begin to recite your chant. Build power while chanting, increasing the intensity while visualizing Air *flying* into you. At peak, pour the power from yourself into the bowl of feathers.
6. Pick up the bowl and pour the feathers over your own head. (If working in a group, decide in advance if you will feather yourselves or each other.)
7. Strike the bell again (if you're using one). Say:

So mote it be!

8. Take two feathers, perhaps two that have stuck to you, and put one in each shoe. For the next week, you'll be "walking on Air."
9. If you have invoked any deities or sylphs, thank them now.
10. Gather up the feathers and put them in the pillow bag. While walking on Air by day, you'll be sleeping on Air at night. If the feathers are uncomfortable (sometimes they are awfully pointy), put them under or inside your regular pillow.

The Pillow Bag:
Making a pillow bag is a simple affair. It should be about the size of a paperback book. The fabric should be thick enough that the feathers don't poke through. You sew it up more or less like an envelope, leaving a flap rather than a slit so the feathers don't slip out.

Make the pillow, leaving the flap open (Figure 6). Use a fabric in an Air color, such as white or light blue. Decorate the pillow with the alchemical symbol for Air (see Figure 1, page 16). That symbol is traditionally yellow. You can use a gold marker, fabric paint, embroidery, or trim to create the effect—the symbol is simple enough to be reproduced through any number of means. You could use sequins, for that matter, but sequins are kind of Fiery.

Figure 6: Pillow Bag

Making the pillow bag can be a ritual act. Even if you don't sew it up in a ritual context, you can meditate on Air, wind, flight, birds, etc. while sewing. The semi-finished pillow bag should be with you when you do the spell itself so that you can quickly and efficiently pick up the feathers and put them into the bag. Next, sew the flap closed. Place the bag under or inside your regular pillow.

To Bring Fire into Yourself: A Body-Painting Spell

Goal:
To bring the element of Fire into yourself. Use this spell when you feel or show symptoms of an absence of this element in your life. Look at the following list of symptoms. If you notice several of them in yourself (not just one or two), you will probably benefit from this spell.
- Life seems flat and colorless
- Tired all the time, no energy
- No one notices or pays attention to you
- Lack of libido
- General apathy
- Disillusionment
- Fearfulness

Target:
Yourself, especially your will; your life force.

Needed Tools:
- Red body paint. This can be acquired at a costume store, as a "romantic enhancement," or as a cosmetic.
- A brush to apply the paint.
- A dish to keep the paint in during the spell. You'll be consecrating the paint in Fire, so it should be a dish that can be safely passed over a flame.
- A red pillar candle. Because the goal is increasing inner Fire, a larger candle is better.
- Incense (optional). I prefer to burn incense during spells, but it is not strictly necessary. Cinnamon, clove, and frankincense are all good choices.

Other:
- This spell is written to be performed by two people, though it can easily be adapted for one person or a group. I like this spell to be done by partners because I find Fire energy in two people facing each other, making eye contact, and in

being seen. Showing off is a Fire characteristic, and if you do this spell alone, you lose some of that.
- You will be touching each other. You don't have to be romantic partners to do this spell, but you do have to be comfortable with that. If you have specific boundaries about touch that need to be respected, discuss them thoroughly before doing the spell.
- This spell is ideally performed skyclad. After painting the Fire symbol, you can continue exploring the body paints, and clothing would get in the way.
- Raise power in a Fiery way. Drum, use cymbals, or use your voice in a guttural way, emitting short *Ho!*s rather than words.
- For lighting the candle and consecrating the paint, decide in advance which of you will do it, or hold the match and dish together.
- When painting the Fire symbol on yourself, note three things: the color red is associated with Fire; the idea of body painting, which is associated with Fire, is sexy; and face paint resembles "war paint," which is associated with Fire.
- Perform the spell on a Sunday.

Appropriate Deities:
You can invoke salamanders instead of deities. Or you can call upon Fire/solar deities, such as Agni, Brigid, or Ameratsu, or martial deities, such as Ares or Ishtar.

The Spell:
1. Ground, center, and merge.
2. Light the candle, concentrating on the candle as Fire. Allow yourself to see it not as a fire, but as *Fire*.
3. If you're using incense, light the stick or charcoal from the candle flame, visualizing the incense as part of the Fire.
4. If you choose to invoke one or more deities, do so here.
5. Pass the dish of red paint over the candle, visualizing Fire entering the paint through the candle flame. Say:

> *Fire, enter this paint. Paint, become Fire.*
> *Fire, enter this paint. Paint, become Fire.*

Fire, enter this paint. Paint, become Fire.
So mote it be.

6. Raise power.
7. As you send the power, send it both into each other and into the paint.
8. Paint the alchemical symbol of Fire (see Figure 1, page 16) on each other's face. Make it large, covering the whole face (Figure 7).
9. Continue to chant, grunt, or drum. As you do so, *look* at each other. *See* Fire.
10. You can chant or shout *Fire! Fire! Fire!* (provided no one within earshot will call 911). You can also continue to paint one another to whatever degree is comfortable.
11. If the level of touch is agreed upon in advance, painting the solar plexus, navel, or above the pubic bone is particularly Fiery.
12. Say:

So mote it be!

13. If you have invoked any deities or salamanders, thank them now.
14. If you are very brave, you can complete the spell by going out with your face paint on. Public display is very Fiery and can have a profound effect on you.

Figure 7: Face Paint

To Bring Water into Yourself: A Bath Spell

Goal:
To bring the element of Water into yourself. Use this spell when you feel or show symptoms of an absence of this element in your life. Look at the following list of symptoms. If you notice several of them in yourself (not just one or two), you will probably benefit from this spell.
- Emotionless; unfeeling
- Dreamless sleep or insomnia
- Out of touch with your intuition
- Unable to sense what's going on around you; unable to interpret nonverbal cues
- Intense need to control situations
- Creative dry spell, writer's block, etc
- Illness
- Lack of loving relationships in your life
- Blood disorder

Target:
Yourself, especially your heart (your metaphorical heart, not your cardiac muscle).

Needed Tools:
- A bathtub (you can use the shower if you don't have a bath).
- A pitcher or ewer, perhaps dedicated to ritual use.
- Appropriate essential oil and/or incense, such as sandalwood, myrrh, or vanilla (optional).
- A rose.
- Pure olive oil in a dish (about a teaspoon).
- An athame.
- Seven pink or blue candles.

Other
- This is a solitary spell.
- Power in this spell will be raised in waves, following the wave model discussed under "Releasing" in Chapter 2.

- You'll be immersing yourself in a tub and using a pitcher or ewer to pour additional water over yourself. If you don't have a tub, you can stand in the shower and use the pitcher. With a tub, you consecrate the water in it and put that water into the pitcher. With a shower, you consecrate the water in the pitcher and allow the magic of contagion to consecrate the whole shower via that pitcher.
- For a Water spell, preparing and beautifying the room is very important because beauty is Watery. Create "mood" in the bathroom with candles and incense and turn off any fluorescent lights. You can add seashells and other Watery decor as well. Make sure the robe or towels you put on when getting out of the bath are sensual to the touch and enjoyable to wear.
- Pink is the color of love, blue is the color of Water, and seven is the number of Venus. To work with the number seven in a Water way, prepare a list of seven Watery things you are bringing into yourself. This list is individual to you, but might look like this:

Deep feeling
Love
Intuition
Happy dreams
Understanding
Compassion
Peace

APPROPRIATE DEITIES:
You can invoke undines instead of deities. Or you can call upon love goddesses, such as Aphrodite, Lakshmi, or Oshun, or ocean deities, such as Yemaya, Mannanan, or Poseidon.

THE SPELL
1. Prepare the bathroom by lighting incense, dimming lights, drawing curtains, etc.
2. Set up the seven candles (unlit) in a way that is aesthetically pleasing. I think it's a good idea to fuss a bit over the layout so that you are in touch with beauty as a goal.

3. Ground and center. Decide in advance if you will ground and center in the bathroom (in which case you need a comfortable spot for that), or if you will go to your typical meditation/ritual spot, ground and center, and return to the bathroom. Either will work.
4. Fill the tub to a pleasing temperature. It should be as hot as you are comfortable with so as to take advantage of the relaxing and mood-altering qualities of heat and steam, but you should be able to *enjoy* the bath, so don't make it too hot.
5. If you are adding essential oils to the tub, do so while the water is running, adding no more than 3–5 drops.
6. If you choose to invoke one or more deities, do so now.
7. While the tub is filling, light your seven candles. Focus your mind, take a deep, cleansing breath, and with each candle say *Water*, followed by one of the words/phrases from your list. Here is an example.

> *Water. Deep feeling.*
> *Water. Love.*
> *Water. Intuition.*
> *Water. Happy dreams.*
> *Water. Understanding.*
> *Water. Compassion.*
> *Water. Peace.*

8. When the bath is full and the faucets have been turned off, it is time to consecrate the tub water. (If you're using a shower, light the candles, then fill the pitcher and consecrate the pitcher.) Plunge your athame into the bath (or pitcher), saying:

O bath, I charge and consecrate thee to be filled with the essence of Water. To soak in thee is to be one with Water. To be touched by thee is to be full of love and compassion. So mote it be.

Touch the athame to the rose, saying:

> *O rose, I charge and consecrate thee*
> *to be filled with the essence of Water.*

To inhale thy lovely scent is to be one with Water.
To hold thee is to be full of love and compassion.
So mote it be.

Dip the athame into the oil, say*ing:*

O oil, I charge and consecrate thee
to be filled with the essence of Water.
To be anointed by thee is to be one with Water.
To be touched by thee is to be full of love and compassion.
So mote it be.

NOTE: You will notice two things about these consecrations. First, they use the word "thee." I like "thee," but you might not. Feel free to change that. Second, they specify qualities of Water (love and compassion). Your goal may inspire you to use different qualities. Go right ahead.

9. Place the pitcher, rose, and dish of oil where you can reach them from within the tub and get in. Begin to meditate on immersion, on being in and surrounded by Water. As you do so, begin to gradually raise power. You might "Om" or hum, allowing a slow, steady, Watery flow to come out of you and surround you. Perhaps you will find words or a tune; perhaps not. Simply allow the power to flow in and out, building at a quiet, even pace.
10. Fill the pitcher from the tub and pour the water over you so that all parts of your body are touched by the consecrated water. Continue to raise power while doing so. Power flows in and out of you, like ripples in a pool.
11. Pick up the rose, and inhale deeply, so that you fully experience its perfume. Now dip it into the oil. Using the rose as a paintbrush, paint the alchemical symbol of Water (See Chapter 1, Figure 1) over your heart. Say:

I am a part of Water, and Water is a part of me.

Set the oil aside. Hold the rose, or set it aside, as you prefer.

12. Continue to "pulse" power in and out. It is all right, after a while, to allow yourself to drowse, letting the power move with you into a near-sleep state.
13. When you feel you have finished, say "*So mote it be*" and get out of the tub.
14. If you have invoked any deities or undines, thank them now.
15. Wrap yourself in a luxurious towel or robe. Snuff the candles and drain the tub. You may keep the rose on your altar as long as it is beautiful. When the rose begins to wither, leave it on the open earth somewhere as a gift to nature.

To Bring Earth into Yourself: A Cookie Spell

GOAL:
To bring the element of Earth into yourself. Use this spell when you feel or show symptoms of an absence of this element in your life. Look at the following list of symptoms. If you notice several of them in yourself (not just one or two), you will probably benefit from this spell.

- Feeling ungrounded
- Feeling disconnected from your body
- No sex drive
- No appetite
- Unhealthy weight loss
- No money; inability to hold on to money (seems to slip through your fingers)
- Life is unstable
- Trouble with your home; unstable living situation
- People tell you you're impractical
- People tell you you're unreliable[24]
- Repeated trouble with theft; if you've been robbed more than once recently, you need to reconnect to Earth
- Dislike of being touched or hugged

---

[24] Impractical and unreliable people are notoriously unaware of their deficits. It is a good idea, then, to pay attention to the input of your friends and family.

Target:
Yourself, especially your physical body; concentrate on your groin, stomach, and feet.

Needed Tools:
- A cookie recipe, preferably oatmeal, peanut butter, or maple, and the ingredients and equipment called for.
- Your athame.
- An apron (see the "Kitchen Blessing" in Chapter 9).

Other:
- This spell can be done either solitary or in a group. It is written with a single person in mind but can easily be adapted.
- This spell combines a number of things with strong Earth associations. Cooking and baking are very Earthy, and I have added to that by suggesting ingredients (oatmeal, peanut butter, and maple syrup) with Earth associations. Getting your hands dirty and messy is Earthy. Feeding others is also Earthy, so I have finished the spell by having you share the majority of the cookies you bake.
- As befitting an Earth spell, this spell is long on practical behavior and short on the spooky stuff normally associated with spellcraft.

Appropriate Deities:
You can invoke gnomes instead of deities. Or you can call upon deities of the earth itself, such as Gaia, Geb, or Danu, or hearth and home deities, such as Lakshmi or Hestia.

The Spell:
1. Ground and center. You might want to do the "Kitchen Blessing" from Chapter 9 before proceeding.
2. Prepare your kitchen so that it feels "Witchy" to you, whether that means candlelight, incense, cool music, or just "as is."
3. Have all the ingredients and the cookie sheet laid out. Make sure your hands are very clean.
4. If you plan to invoke any deities, do so now.

5. Lift your athame over the ingredients, pointing it toward them and concentrating. Say:

   I consecrate these ingredients by Earth.
   With these ingredients, I create Earth.

6. Mix the dough with your hands. If anything needs to be whisked or otherwise treated with a special tool, do that first, but choose a recipe that can be finished by mixing with your hands.
7. When the dough is mushed together nicely, flatten it out in the bowl so that the surface is smooth. Using your finger, dig a trough in the dough in the shape of the alchemical symbol of Earth (See Chapter 1, Figure 1).
8. Say:

   This is the stuff of Earth.

9. Shape the dough removed from the symbol-trough into one or more cookies, saying:

   I am forming food of Earth.

10. Put the Earth cookies on the cookie sheet and distinguish them in some obvious way: add an M&M, a chocolate chip, or a pecan to the top. Or use your imagination.
11. Form the rest of the cookies normally and bake the batch.
12. When the cookies have cooled, take your "Earth" cookies and eat them, saying:

    I take Earth into me. I am filled with Earth.
    Earth is within me. So mote it be!

13. If you have invoked any deities or gnomes, thank them now.
14. Feed the rest of the cookies to other people. Give them to your family, bring them to work, or give them to a neighbor.

Chapter 5

Using the Elements in Spells

Every spell can benefit from being balanced in the elements. Some spells have an obvious elemental focus, as the second half of this chapter will illustrate. Sometimes, you'll use all four elements in a spell.

USING ALL FOUR ELEMENTS IN A SPELL

Some spells have a mixed elemental purpose; or you can't tell what the elemental nature is; or you simply can't connect, on an emotional or psychic level, to the elements as the primary symbol system.

Mixed Elemental Purpose

What would a spell with a mixed elemental purpose be? You might be working to get someone a job. An Earth spell would normally be suitable for this purpose, as money, jobs, and stability are all Earth issues. However, the person you're working for might be a nurse, and nursing is a profession with strong Water associations.

Or perhaps you need a new car. Money issues are related to Earth, transportation is ruled by Air, and freedom (which may be what the car represents to you) is associated with Fire.

Unclear Elemental Nature

Healing has strong folkloric associations with both Water and Fire. The best way to choose an element for a healing is to have lots of information about the illness. Information is always important to a spell, as we discussed in Chapter 2. But you don't always know what's wrong, you don't always have time to find out, and heck, the *doctors* don't even know sometimes.

Lots of times nowadays, people "send energy" to people they know only from the Internet. Personally, I find it impossible to form the vital connection in most such cases, and I don't do spells when I can't connect. If you're working in this way, you may not have a clear visual image of what's going on, and that may impede your ability to choose the dominant element. Also, you have Air mixed in whenever you're dealing with the Internet, and that can muddy the waters.[25]

Not Connecting to the Elements

For me, there are times when I'm seeing a situation holistically: a whole person, an entire family, or a flow of events. I can see it in my mind as a single image, but I can't break it down into components. At these times, I don't try to find a single element to work with because I'm connected in a more holistic way.

Whenever any of these situations apply, you wouldn't choose to do an Air spell, a Fire spell, a Water spell, or an Earth spell. Nonetheless, you'd want to bring the power of the elements into your spell; you'd want balance. I accomplish this by consecration or by invocation.

Consecrating by the Elements

When an object is central to a spell, consecrating that object by the elements balances the spell. It also serves to purify the object. A central object might be a photograph, poppet, talisman, parchment, etc.

---

25 And I *just* realized that "muddy the waters" is a metaphor about mixed elements. Go figure.

Sample Consecration One: A Photograph

Suppose you are doing a distant healing for a sick friend. You are using a photograph of your friend to form a magical connection to her. Before you begin the healing, consecrate the photograph by the elements. The purpose of the consecration is twofold: to turn the photograph into a magical object (it will *become* your friend) and to make the spell whole by balancing it in the elements.

Note: This consecration uses two pairs of combined elements: water and salt for Water/Earth, and smoky incense for Fire/Air.

You will need:
- The photograph, saltwater, and burning incense.

1. Hold the photograph in one hand. Dip the fingers of your other hand into the saltwater, and run them all over the picture, front and back. Pay special attention to the parts of the body that are being healed (if they appear in the picture). Say:

By the power of Water and Earth, I consecrate this picture. By the power of Water and Earth, I make this picture (name of person being healed). This picture is (name). So be it!

2. Now, pass the picture back and forth through the incense smoke. Before doing so, add extra incense to the censer and stir it up, if necessary, to get it smoky. Say:

By the power of Fire and Air, I consecrate this picture. By the power of Fire and Air, I make this picture (name of person being healed). This picture is (name). So be it!

3. Now hold the picture in front of you, and say:

By the power of Water and Earth, By the power of Fire and Air, it is done!

Sample Consecration Two: A Car Mojo

One magical thing I've used for years is a mojo bag for my car. I load it up with a host of magical influences that are important in the car—antitheft, safety and protection, and alertness, to name a few.

When I first started studying Wicca, I was driving a car that stayed on the road by willpower alone, it seemed. Upon getting a new(er) car, I decided to put my studies into practice and make a protection bag. I started by making a list of goals for the car and then researched appropriate ingredients. I went with traditional things like herbs, stones, and embroidered symbols, but also innovated, such as by adding a bit of coffee to stay awake and alert in the car.

Looking over my ingredient list, I realized I could also balance it in the elements. By tweaking an herb here and a crystal there, I was able to come up with twelve ingredients so that there were exactly three associated with each element. The following example assumes you have put together some sort of bag, and most of the ingredients are already inside. You'll be charging the bag next, invoking forces of protection and whatever else you've decided on, but first you're going to consecrate it by the elements.

I've left a lot of room here for you to devise the bulk of the spell on your own. I'm focusing only on the elemental consecrations. Because the turquoise is being sealed into the bag, it will be more convenient to change the order of Air-Fire-Water-Earth. We will start with Earth.

Note: This time there are four separate consecrations—incense for Air, a candle for Fire, a sprinkling of water for Water, and a piece of turquoise for Earth. Turquoise serves a double purpose in the spell: it is also protective.

1. Hold up the piece of turquoise, envisioning safety and security. Say:

I consecrate this bag by Earth.
By Earth will the ground beneath my car[26] be secure.

---

26 You can obviously use a bag for other things besides cars. Just switch the wording as needed.

2. Place the turquoise in the bag, and close it.
3. Pass the bag through the incense smoke, imagining intelligence and clarity. Say:

   I consecrate this bag by Air.
   By Air will the winds upon my car be favorable.

4. Pass the bag over the candle flame, envisioning heat and power. Say:

   I consecrate this bag by Fire.
   By Fire will the engine of my car run true.

5. Sprinkle the bag with water, picturing flowing streams. Say:

   I consecrate this bag by Water.
   By Water will my car be safe from the unknown.

6. End with:

   So mote it be![27]

Invoking the Elements

With invocation, you're calling the powers of the elements to observe, watch over, or involve themselves in a spell or working. In the previous section, we directly *used* the elements in consecrations; here, they're more like witnesses, bringing balance by their mere presence.

The simplest form of invocation goes something like this:

I call upon (name of element) to be present for this spell!
Welcome, (name of element)!

Repeat this four times, once for each element.

---

[27] "So mote it be" is a traditional phrase in Wicca, and it's somewhat formal. If you prefer "So be it" or something like that, go for it.

I like to dress up an invocation. The basic rules of an invocation are to be specific (name and describe the element), enticing (be nice), and persuasive (with a strong voice, the sounding of a bell, the playing of music, or asking *really* nicely).

Dressed-up invocations might go like this:

> *I call upon Air, element of thought and of the wind.*
> *Come to me, Air, and balance my spell.*
> *Please, Air, bring your wisdom to my aid.*
> *Thank you. Blessed be.*
>
> *I call upon Fire, element of will and of passion.*
> *Come to me, Fire, and balance my spell.*
> *Please, Fire, bring your power to my aid.*
> *Thank you. Blessed be.*
>
> *I call upon Water, element of feeling and of the sea.*
> *Come to me, Water, and balance my spell.*
> *Please, Water, bring your love to my aid.*
> *Thank you. Blessed be.*
>
> *I call upon Earth, element of home and of fertile soil.*
> *Come to me, Earth, and balance my spell.*
> *Please, Earth, bring your strength to my aid.*
> *Thank you. Blessed be.*

Of course, you can also dress *down* the invocations, by being entirely nonverbal, or by using mime, music, drumbeats, or simple monosyllabic shouts (*Earth! Earth! Earth!* can really work).

USING A PARTICULAR ELEMENT IN A SPELL

When a spell has an obvious elemental focus, it follows that to use that element in the spell, or to orient the spell around that element, will contribute to the spell's flavor, focus, and success. For example, to layer Water into a love spell makes perfect magical and symbolic sense. You would at least put *some* Water in every love spell, and at most perform a Water spell—a spell entirely structured in Water.

So, an elemental spell is one in which an element is used to aid in achieving the spell's goal, or for a spell that is inherently of one element. Water spells include love spells and others that use Water because of Water's affinity to the purpose of the work. Water spells are also rooted in Water, such as those that use the ritual cup as the primary magical tool.

Some spells touch upon more than one element. For example, to be more creative you need Air for inspiration, Fire to put the "fire in the head" (to enliven the creative spirit), and Water to allow intuition to flow through your creativity.

Sometimes, finding the elemental flavor of a spell is a key to unlocking the true meaning of the spell. In the example of creativity, which has three strong elemental components (and also requires Earth to *finish* the project), you will need to ask serious questions about what is blocking your (or the subject's) creativity. What happens when you attempt to do something creative? What isn't working, and what still works just fine? What would an ideal outcome be? As you ask these questions, you'll find that your spell becomes more and more specific in its goal, and specificity is a vital (and often overlooked) part of any spell. Plus, the specifics will tell you a lot more about the elements.

Conversely, the elements may tell you more about the specifics. As a magical person, you can use divination, meditation, or other psychic arts to discover the elemental needs of a spell, and this can tell you what's going on with the subject. For example, you might find yourself saying: "My card reading tells me that this spell needs Water, and the situation already has lots and lots of Fire. I guess that (the person) is applying too much will and is forcing the creative process too much and needs to learn to flow, maybe to take inspiration from dreams. Let's do a Water spell that will help (the person) flow creatively."

In this example, you knew nothing about the situation except that it was to release a creative block. The reading gave you nothing but a lack of Water and a preponderance of Fire. You then applied your knowledge of the elements to put two and two together and create a narrative of meaning, allowing you to target the spell in the most effective way.

Psychic knowledge can often take the form of imagery. You allow yourself, in a meditative state, to picture the problem. What does it look like? Such images can be metaphorical; for example, an illness may look like a knot, a cloud, or rotted vegetables. You might not receive pictures but instead get vivid feelings, colors, or sounds. Just let it come. These pictures and feelings can be a great help in understanding the purpose and direction of your spell. As a clear picture takes shape, you'll often see an elemental relationship. For instance, if an illness looks like a dark cloud, then Air can blow the cloud away. If it looks like rot, then Fire can burn it.

Both psychic skills and mundane fact-finding can help you determine the elemental needs of a spell. The more you know, the better your spell. As we discussed in Chapter 2, the knowledge you bring to a spell empowers the spell, and the effort you expend in finding out more background data translates into energy sent into the magical work.

The process of discovery can lead you in unexpected directions. Let's say your friend Steve is unemployed. Steve needs a job and money, which are Earth things, so the obvious remedy is to do an Earth spell. But before you leap into doing the spell, you ask *why* Steve lost his job. You find out he was fired for poor performance; Steve has been depressed, he has little energy, and he can't seem to get things done. Instead of an Earth spell, you decide to do a Fire spell, which will give Steve energy, help break his depression, and allow him to take his life into his own hands.

In the next chapters, we'll explore ways that a spell can be an Air spell, Fire spell, Water spell, or Earth spell, and there will be numerous spells as examples. For now, let's focus on creating lists of goals that have a natural affinity for each element.

USE AIR IN A SPELL:
- To increase understanding
- To gain knowledge or wisdom
- To do well in school or on a test
- To be eloquent; to say the right thing
- To start or complete a writing project
- To gain inspiration

- To bring about a new beginning
- To travel
- For a positive legal outcome; for justice or fairness
- To heal respiratory ailments (asthma, emphysema, etc.)[28]

USE FIRE IN A SPELL:
- To increase sexual desire (libido)
- To increase sexual energy (performance, sexual stamina)
- To gain physical or psychic energy
- To increase personal power or autonomy
- To increase physical or psychic stamina
- To gain influence over others (charisma)
- For attraction (using charisma to attract)
- To make a decision (strengthen will)
- To increase life force, and therefore to heal
- To heal neurological and immunological disorders
- For courage
- To aid political action or to right a wrong

USE WATER IN A SPELL:
- To bring dreams
- To soothe and calm
- To ease pain
- To bring romance (both to bring new love and to bring romance into an existing relationship)
- To increase psychic powers
- To improve intuition
- To make a decision using intuition (inner Water rather than inner Fire)
- To increase "flow"
- To improve lactation
- To make childbirth easier
- To heal blood and lymphatic disorders
- To address past-life issues
- For privacy or secrecy

---

28 I assume, for all healing spells, that appropriate medical attention has also been sought. Use magic to augment and improve medical care, not as a substitute for it.

USE EARTH IN A SPELL:
- For fertility
- For wealth
- To get a job
- To improve appetite
- To grow (can combat wasting illnesses)
- To improve crops or help your garden
- For longer hair and nails
- For marriage (any marriage-related goal)
- To get a home
- To bless a new home
- To finish things; to bring things to fruition
- To aid the ecology of a specific ecosystem
- To heal broken bones or other structural damage

In the following chapters, we will address many of these issues with spells of the appropriate element. For example, you will find an Air spell for improving your performance in school, and an Earth spell for increasing wealth. My focus is on presenting different kinds of elemental spells so you can use them as a template for future spells and so that you have an understanding of the principles behind various kinds of elemental magic. I'm not in any way trying to present a spell for every possible need you might have. Once you've read this book and tried the spells that are meaningful to you and reviewed the others, you should be well equipped to devise your own spells, follow the spellworking guidelines in Chapters 2 and 3, and balance your spells as we've discussed.

Chapter 6

Using Air in Spells

In the previous chapter, we identified the following purposes for Air spells:

- To increase understanding
- To gain knowledge or wisdom
- To do well in school or on a test
- To be eloquent; to say the right thing
- To start or complete a writing project
- To gain inspiration
- To bring about a new beginning
- To travel
- For a positive legal outcome; for justice or fairness
- To heal respiratory ailments

USING AIR

How would we bring Air into a spell? As with the other elements, there are three basic methods: (1) directly, (2) through magical tools associated with the elements, or (3) symbolically through qualities of the elements.

Using Air in Spells

To use Air directly, we could:

- Use inhalation (and therefore scent)
- Perform a spell in the open air and/or while looking at the sky
- Wave a fan over objects associated with the spell, over the area in which the spell is being performed, or over ourselves while focusing on the spell's goal

To use Air tools, we could:

- Use the wand or athame (depending upon whether we associate Air with the wand or the athame)
- Use a ritual feather
- Use a ritual fan
- Use incense, especially an incense with air associations, like sage
- Use a bell or chimes
- Use a rattle

To use symbolic qualities of Air, we could:

- Use speech
- Use writing
- Use memory

AROMATHERAPY AND SCENT

Aromatherapy may be defined as "the use of true essential oils for healing purposes."[29] For this book, we can define it as "the use of scent to achieve a healing or magical goal."

I should point out that aromatherapy often goes beyond the use of scent and involves the use of essential oils for healing in general. I am acquainted with an amazing woman who was paralyzed in a car accident. After five different doctors pronounced her paralysis incurable, she met an aromatherapist who was able to heal her over a

---

29 Definition from *Magical Aromatherapy*, page xi.

period of months by applying essential oils directly to her body. Now, the woman not only walks, but she runs! This is an astonishing tale, one I never would have imagined or even believed if I didn't know the lady myself. My point is simply that, although this healer calls her work aromatherapy, she is using essential oils placed directly on the body, not simply inhaled. So, our magical definition of aromatherapy is not the only one available.

When using aromatherapy in magic, you visualize your goal and then inhale. Some traditional things to inhale include:

- Essential oils directly from the bottle
- A few drops of essential oil on a cotton ball
- A drop of a nontoxic essential oil on your finger, the back of your hand, or a magical tool
- Fresh or dried herbs
- Fresh or dried flowers

Aromatherapy doesn't have to be traditional! Any scent can stimulate memory, emotions, and psychic connections. Literature and science agree that scent has the strongest connection of any sense to memory. Proust was certainly not alone in having profound memories flood forth when triggered by a scent from the past. The sense of smell has a direct connection to the central nervous system, whereas sight, sound, touch, and taste travel first to the thalamus before reaching the nervous system.[30] It is aroma, then, that reaches us most directly, and at a primitive, often subliminal level. This visceral, image-laden experience is ideal for magical work. The things we work hard to achieve—visualization, direct connection to a moment in time, vivid memory—are often brought forth naturally by the right scent.

Some inspiring ideas for inhalation include:

- An article of clothing owned by someone to whom you wish to connect for magic. Instead of using a photograph for a visual connection, use an aromatic connection by inhaling the person's scent from their clothing.

---

30 *Essence and Alchemy: A Book of Perfume*, pp. 13–14.

- Similarly, use a toy, blanket, or food belonging to your pet when performing magic on them. You could inhale this scent while calling a lost animal home.
- Food is laden with scent-memory. Aren't we performing aromatherapy magic when we bake bread in order to inhale the aroma of comfort and hominess?
- Nasty-smelling herbs such as asafoetida are traditionally burned in exorcisms and banishings because the unpleasant smell drives away negative entities. You might try using unpleasant smells to rid yourself of negative thoughts or frightening mental imagery.
- That "new car" smell might be just what the magician ordered to bring the prosperity you desire.

The following two Air spells are a traditional aromatherapy spell and a nontraditional scent/memory spell. Use these spell recipes as you would use food recipes, making substitutions and adjustments to fit your kitchen and your personal dinner plans.

To Bring About Travel: A Simple Aromatherapy Spell

GOAL:
To travel; variously, to take a desired business or vacation trip, or to get a job that entails a great deal of travel.

TARGET:
Yourself; you will visualize yourself traveling.

NEEDED TOOLS:
- Fresh mint, with a dish to put it in
- A lid for the dish (optional)
- A hand-held fan
- Your wand
- A glass of cold water and a spoon

OTHER:
- This spell is done solitary.

The Magic of the Elements

- This is a simple aromatherapy spell in which the bulk of the work is done through inhalation and visualization.
- If you associate the wand with Fire rather than Air, use your athame.

APPROPRIATE DEITIES:
Mercury, Hermes, Garuda, Ra, Epona.

THE SPELL:
1. Ground and center.
2. If you're invoking a deity, do so here.
3. Hold your wand and point it at the fan, visualizing clear, bright, inspiring Air rushing from it. Say:

I consecrate this fan as a tool of Air. As it moves air, it brings Air. Each breeze it creates is a blessed and consecrated breeze. Let this fan be blessed! So mote it be!

4. Continuing to visualize Air rushing from the wand, point the wand at the dish of mint, and say:

I consecrate this mint by Air. By Air may it bring travel to me. By Air may it speed me on my chosen road. So mote it be!

NOTE: Both of these consecrations can include the deity invoked by saying, for example: *I consecrate this fan as a tool of Air and by the God Hermes.* Mint is a Mercury plant as well as an Air plant, so Mercury or Hermes would be especially good.

5. Using the fan, fan yourself and the mint thoroughly, feeling Air breeze over you (this is where a lid for the mint might come in handy so that the mint leaves won't be blown all over). As you do so, visualize yourself traveling. Visualize this however you see fit: see yourself on a plane, in an airport, at your destination with luggage, checking into a hotel, etc. Send power into this visualization in waves.
6. Continue to visualize yourself traveling as you pick up the dish of mint, lifting the lid (if needed), and inhale deeply. See

travel entering you through the scent. See the scent being an agent of travel (no pun intended) that moves you to where you wish to go. Inhale and visualize for several minutes, continuing to send power into the image and scent.

7. Crush the mint in your hand. Place it in the water and stir it with the spoon, sending a final wave of power into the water. Then drink. Say:

So mote it be!

8. If you have invoked any deities, thank them now and let them know the work is done.

To Increase Understanding: A Scent/Memory Spell

Goal:
To improve understanding and communication in a relationship. Use this spell when a relationship is basically good, but communication has broken down and you don't seem to understand each other anymore.

Target:
The couple (you and your partner).

Needed Tools:
- An article of worn clothing (a T-shirt is ideal) belonging to each partner. The clothing should not be laundered because you will be using the scent of your partner's body as a tool of Air
- Your wand
- A hand-held fan

Other:
- This spell uses Air for a relationship, although we usually think of relationships in terms of Water. To understand this, you need to see the *totality* of your relationship and that all *whole* things, including relationships, have all four elements. This is a healing spell for the Air part of a relationship that has healthy Fire, Water, and Earth.

- The two of you should do this spell together. If only one of you wishes to do the spell, you can basically cut it in half, using only your partner's T-shirt.
- If you associate the wand with Fire rather than Air, use your athame.
- The fan consecration is basically the same as in the previous travel spell. If you've consecrated it once, you need not consecrate it again.

Appropriate Deities:
Odin, Mercury, Lakshmi, Papa Legba, Ogma.

The Spell:
1. Sit or stand facing each other. Maintain as much eye contact as possible throughout the working.
2. Ground, center, and merge. When working as a couple, the merging is extra important.
3. If you're invoking a deity, do so here.
4. Hold the wand together, with each of your hands on it. Point it at the fan, visualizing clear, bright, inspiring Air rushing from the wand. Say:

We consecrate this fan as a tool of Air. As it moves air, it brings Air. Each breeze it creates is a blessed and consecrated breeze. Let this fan be blessed! So mote it be!

5. Continuing to visualize Air rushing from the wand, point it at the articles of clothing, saying:

These clothes are tools of Air. These clothes are carriers of scent, memory, and understanding. We consecrate these clothes to Air. So mote it be!

6. Use the fan to fan the clothes and each other. Hand the fan back and forth to each other, while maintaining eye contact. Visualize your minds being opened by the air that is being fanned onto you. Allow the fanned air to build and carry power.

7. Still maintaining eye contact, pick up your partner's article of clothing, and inhale deeply. As your partner's scent enters into you through inhalation, imagine inhaling an understanding of your partner at the same time. Allow images of positive, wonderful times with your partner to fill your mind as the scent triggers intimate memories. Breathe deeply for several minutes.
8. Say to each other:

    I understand. I breathe and understand.

9. End the spell with a loving embrace. If you are performing the spell solitary, simply say:

    So mote it be.

10. If you have invoked any deities, thank them now and let them know the work is done.

MAGICAL WRITING AND SPEAKING

Language, whether spoken or written, is the province of Air. Spoken words are formed of breath, and written words are formed of thought and intelligence. The pen is as much a tool of Air as the fan. Magic is replete with spoken words from *So mote it be!* to sacred and secret names. In fact, originally, the word *spell* was used for magic involving the spoken word; you "spelled it out."

Throughout the mythologies of the world, creation has been understood as an act of language. *In the beginning was the Word.* And what is creation but the first act of magic, performed by the first god?

To perform magic is to create—to work the miracle of transformation; to bring into being that which wasn't there before, whether it be a home, a healing, or an opportunity.

The spoken word in a spell can state its result; *Be healed!* can be part of a spell or can empower the result. Names of God, mantras, and incantations often lend power without being specifically related to the working—*Abracadabra* is such a power word, and grimoires such as *The Key of Solomon* are chock-full of such words.

Writing Magic

Writing for magical purposes can take many forms. A word or phrase might be written in the earth, inscribed in the air, added to an object, etched onto a talisman, embroidered on fabric, or tattooed onto the skin. Writing might augment a spell or be the main focus. For example, in the previous chapter, I talked about creating a mojo bag. Most of the "work" of that bag was in the ingredients and the consecration, but I also decorated it with written symbols.

In other cases, the spell itself is executed in writing. One way of achieving a goal is to write it down. Or you can do the opposite: write down something unwanted and, by disposing of the written words, dispose of the problem.

One technique is to write a desired goal repeatedly, filling a paper or parchment. You might write *My book has a publisher. My book has a publisher. My book has a publisher.* dozens of times, over and over, until the writing of the spell has induced a kind of trance. Continue to write until the page is full and finish with *So mote it be!*

Typically, you would use a special paper or parchment and a special quill or pen. These instruments are usually consecrated and are reserved strictly for magical use—you do not perform spells with the same pen and paper used for your grocery list! A magical alphabet, such as Runic or Theban, is often employed.

Such a writing spell may be done in a cast circle, in a meditation space, or at your writing desk. The paper and writing instruments are prepared either by consecrating them as a preliminary step during your spell or by consecrating them once as magical tools and then keeping them sacred. It is traditional to write by candlelight and you may also burn some incense, preferably incense attuned to your goal. You may choose to speak a simple invocation before you begin. You then write your statement over and over until the paper is filled. Declare the spell complete and fold the paper into a tiny packet or place it in a consecrated envelope and seal it with sealing wax. The paper may then be kept upon your altar, ritually burned, ritually buried, or made a part of another magical object (you could stuff it inside a poppet). The disposition will depend upon your intention and preference.

The Language of Magic (Affirmations)

The substance of magical writing, ancient though it is, survives in a very modern technique—affirmations. Affirmations are used by people who follow all sorts of different paths—Christians, Pagans, agnostics, New Agers—and many people don't realize that in structure, form, and history, affirmations are essentially an act of magic.

Affirmations are a spell of Air, using repetitive spoken or written language to imprint a magical goal onto the self, and/or to send energy in the form of a message out to a target. They work by creating a resonance. The language itself is an act of creation, and you are sending the energy of creation into the universe in a way that is effective and real.

Magical statements (affirmations) can be structured in a way that will empower them to succeed or in a way that will set you up for failure. When writing affirmations, you need to follow certain rules that will allow creation to happen. These rules are common sense and logical (which follows, since both affirmations and logic are Air), but many people don't realize how important they are. Let's go over them in detail.

Be Positive

When you make a statement, it begins to create a new reality within your own mind. You see, feel, hear, and imagine (in various combinations) that the statement is true. When storing the resonance in the memory, your mind throws away extra words. "The boat is red" resonates as "boat red." This also means that the mind remembers and retains the core positive words of the statement and eliminates the negative. "Not" is an extra word that gets thrown away. "The boat is red" and "the boat is not red" are both remembered as "boat red."

Politicians use this type of magic all the time. They force their opponents to deny some ludicrous charge, but the mind doesn't remember the denial, only the charge. If Senator Smith is forced to issue a statement saying, "I did not have sex with green aliens," his constituents will almost certainly associate him with alien sex, despite the denial and lack of evidence. He has made a statement that *magically* affirmed sex with aliens, even while *literally* denying it.

Your magical statements must avoid this pitfall. The statement "I am healthy" is infinitely more effective than "I am not sick," because you have not given any energy to the word "sick." Senator Smith gave energy to, and created resonance with, the phrase "sex with green aliens." Just so, "I am not sick" gives energy to "sick." The affirmative version, "I am healthy," gives energy only to that which you wish to create.

Always find the positive (affirmative—hence the name) version of your statement: "healthy" instead of "not sick," "employed" instead of "no longer unemployed," and so on.

Use Time Appropriately

Many people begin their affirmations with "I will," as in "I will be healed." But when? The future is a vague, amorphous place in which anything might happen, or not happen, sooner or later. "I'll call you" is a notoriously unreliable statement.

Will you be healed tomorrow? Next week? In your next incarnation? Your statement doesn't indicate this, so the visualization that naturally accompanies your statement isn't placed anywhere in time. While "I will be healed" is better than "I am not sick" (because it affirms the core idea of "healed"), it lacks some of the impetus to be made manifest.

Not only does the "I will" statement leave doubt as to when the result will be achieved—allowing the echo of that doubt to reverberate in your mind and in your magical work—but it also leaves you sick in the present tense. "I will be in the future" contains a germ of "I am not at present."

Finally, don't forget the old saying "Stick with the devil you know." People get attached to the reality they have, to the status quo, even when that reality is unhappy. That a patient is attached to their illness is not to blame the patient; it is simply to acknowledge that attachment is part of human nature. Nothing is wholly and completely negative. Sickness may suck, but it allows for bed rest.

Loneliness may stink, but it affords a great deal of privacy. We naturally attach ourselves to the positive side of our situation, even though we long for the situation to change.

When we seek to effect change, we must overcome this attachment. If I am attached to being sick (even while wanting very much to be well), my attachment may subconsciously push the "I will" of my statement much farther into the future than my conscious mind desires.

Use time appropriately by creating statements in the present tense: "I am healthy" is a wholly positive, present-tense affirmation. In fact, "healthy" is even better than "healed," because "healed" contains an echo of the past—you must have been sick or injured in the past to be *healed* in the present, but you can be *healthy* in the present just because.

Of course, there are times when disease and other negative conditions are firmly present in your mind. You don't have to pretend to be disconnected from reality in order to work magic. Use specificity (see "Be Specific and Exact" below) to make sure that your affirmation moves past the negative condition to create a positive reality.

You can also use a specific, clear deadline. The deadline can be used with either a present or future-tense statement: "Deborah is wealthy by the next full moon," or "Deborah will be wealthy by the next full moon."

Using a deadline or the present tense, or a combination of both, allows your affirmations to manifest unhindered.

Be Clear about Your Intention

What do you intend to happen? Your statement should contain only your intention. People often confuse desire or hope with intention. But desire and hope live in our minds and hearts all the time without being made manifest. Intention is something entirely different, as discussed in Chapter 2.

It is a common mistake to phrase affirmations in the form of hope or desire. "I want Deborah to be wealthy" and "Deborah should be wealthy" are forms of hope, not intention. If you give magical energy to "I want Deborah to be wealthy," you'll manifest your stated intention, and the end result will be…that you'll want Deborah to be wealthy. Thanks, but I prefer the wealth.

Always remember to phrase your affirmations so that they speak of your intention as a reality, and not a hope, wish, or ideal.

Be Specific and Exact

People sometimes don't know what they want, but as discussed in Chapter 2, uncovering that knowledge is part of your magical process. To have an optimal and recognizable result, send your intention exactly where it needs to be.

"I will have a good job" is far too vague. Everyone wants a good job, but what does that mean? Is a job with excellent pay and grueling hours good by your definition? How about the opposite: a congenial working environment and low pay?

With healing, "Rhonda is healthy" is sometimes the best affirmation possible, but when you are struggling with a difficult illness, "Rhonda's tumor is benign" can sometimes be a better choice. Because the tumor has weight and substance, creating a reality that addresses it specifically can be far more effective than "wishing it away."

Using exactness and specificity means including details of time, place, and/or result. Here are some examples:

- "The cancer is in full remission."
- "Healthy and strong."
- "Well-paying job in San Diego."
- "Passing grade in calculus."

The following three spells use magical speaking and two different forms of magical writing to achieve different Air goals.[31]

---

[31] The spell to improve school performance originally appeared in *The Way of Four*. In that book, I included four spells as examples of elemental magic, and they remain good examples to illustrate the principles of meeting an elemental goal with an elemental spell.

To Improve Memory: An Affirmation Spell

Goal:
To improve your memory. This spell could be used to combat an ailment causing memory loss, to improve your skill at memorization for school or for a theatrical performance, or to sharpen the mind and memory for any other reason.

Target:
Yourself; specifically, your mind.

Needed Tools:
- A sage bundle (one bundle per person), loose sage, or sage essential oil
- A mirror
- Your wand or athame—whichever you associate with air

Other:
- This is a solitary spell. I like the idea of doing it early in the morning before going out. Dawn is the time of Air.
- If you want to work this spell as a group, consecrate enough sage for everyone and do the first affirmation (steps 1–7) as a group, with or without the mirror. Then send the sage home with everyone to continue doing solitary morning affirmations, as described in Step 8.
- This spell involves inhaling the aroma of burning sage every day. If you have smoke allergies or asthma, use a cotton ball with a few drops of sage essential oil to achieve the same result.
- Begin the spell at the new moon and do the affirmations daily until the full moon.
- Since you'll be performing your affirmations while standing in front of a mirror, you have three options:
  - Put a mirror at your altar;
  - Move your sage and wand to wherever your mirror is;
  - Consecrate the sage and then bring it to your mirror.

APPROPRIATE DEITIES:
Mneme, Ogma, Odin (or Huginn and Muninn), Enki.

THE SPELL:
1. Ground and center.
2. If you're performing an invocation, do so here.
3. Pointing your wand/athame at the sage bundle/sage essential oil, say:

I consecrate this sage by Air, by intellect, by the powers of the mind. May it be charged with the power to aid thought and memory. So mote it be!

NOTE: Consecrating the sage is an optional step. Some people would consider it unnecessary.

4. Standing or sitting before your mirror, light the sage (or dampen the cotton ball) and inhale the aroma, visualizing clarity rushing into your mind.
5. Repeat the following affirmation five times (or a multiple of five times):

My memory is clear and accurate.

NOTE: Don't count aloud. Use your fingers, a rosary, or a pile of pre-counted crystals moved from one spot to another.

6. Say:

So mote it be!

Then put out the sage.
7. If you have invoked any deities, thank them now and let them know the work is done.
8. Repeat steps 4–6 daily throughout the waxing moon. It's not necessary to repeat the consecration.

To Improve School Performance: A Writing Spell

GOAL:
To do better in school. This spell is designed for someone who is really struggling with their studies—who is having a hard time understanding concepts, retaining material, or just keeping up. It still requires that you study, attend class, and do your homework (darn it).

TARGET:
This is a self-improvement spell; you are aiming at yourself.

NEEDED TOOLS:
- Ritual pen. This can be a fountain pen, a quill, or any pen you have set aside for ritual work
- Parchment or other ritual paper
- Envelope
- Sealing wax
- Candle and lighter
- Cotton ball or cotton swab
- Appropriate essential oil or blend (see below)

A Note on Air Oils: Mercury governs language, communication, intelligence, gathering information, and speed of thought. Air and Mercury: Caraway, Clary Sage, Lavender, Spearmint.

Jupiter governs good luck, the higher mind, success, growth, philosophy, and education. Air and Jupiter: Anise/Star Anise, Sage.

OTHER:
- This spell is meant to be done alone over a period of time.
- Before you begin, you should compose the spell proper (the part you're going to write and say) if you're not going to use the text provided.
- The sealed envelope will be used daily for a while. Decide where you're going to keep it and how you're going to dispose of it when the spell succeeds.

- Many spells have a time period based on nature. The cycle of one full moon, or one moon phase, is often used. Other spells are done for a week, or on the same weekday for a set period of weeks. This spell has a period of time based on your school calendar. If you've been worried about failing, there will be a point in time when you'll know you've passed—when report cards are issued, test results are posted, or what have you. The duration of the spell will be from its beginning—preferably during a waxing moon, but again, based on your school schedule and need—to the point in time that you've determined to be its end. Determine the beginning and end in advance, before doing the spell.

Appropriate Deities:
Sarasvati, Thoth, Apollo, Ogma.

The Spell:
1. Ground and center.
2. If you're invoking a deity, do so here.
3. Consecrate your tools to Air as follows:
   Bring the pen, paper, sealing wax, and essential oil to your altar. Have sage burning. Pass the pen back and forth through the sage smoke, saying:

   By Air is this pen consecrated.
   May all the words it writes be true. So mote it be!

   Pass the paper back and forth through the smoke, saying:

   By Air is this paper consecrated.
   May all written upon it be manifest. So mote it be!

   Pass the sealing wax back and forth through the sage smoke, saying:

   By Air is this sealing wax consecrated.
   May it hold, contain, and seal words of truth.
   May it do its work rightly! So mote it be!

Pass the bottle of essential oil back and forth through the sage smoke, saying:

*By Air is this oil consecrated.
May it open my mind and speed up my thoughts. So mote it be!*

4. Light the candle. Make sure you have sufficient light by which to write; add candles as needed.
5. Pick up your pen and have your paper before you. Say:

May this work be true, and for the good of all! So mote it be!

6. Visualize your goal clearly in your mind. Picture passing grades, excellent test results, or whatever it is you need.
    With this image firmly in mind, begin writing the spell. Write it over and over, slowly, until you fill the page. Write:

*My mind is open and alert.
I understand my course of study.
I am a success at school.*

Leave enough room at the very end to write *So mote it be!* Sign your name (your magical name if you have one). Say out loud:

So mote it be!

NOTE: For "course of study" you can substitute the specific course that is troubling you, e.g., "Calculus," "Physics," "Russian Poetry." This spell doesn't rhyme, so you don't have to worry about the name of the course changing the meter. On the other hand, you can rewrite it so it *does* rhyme.

7. Take the oil and, using a cotton ball or swab, scent the paper with the oil. Surround the outside of the writing in oil, as illustrated in Figure 8. If you'd like, you can add a rune or astrological symbol by painting it in oil (using the

swab) over the body of text. See Figure 9 and Figure 10 for two runes you might choose.

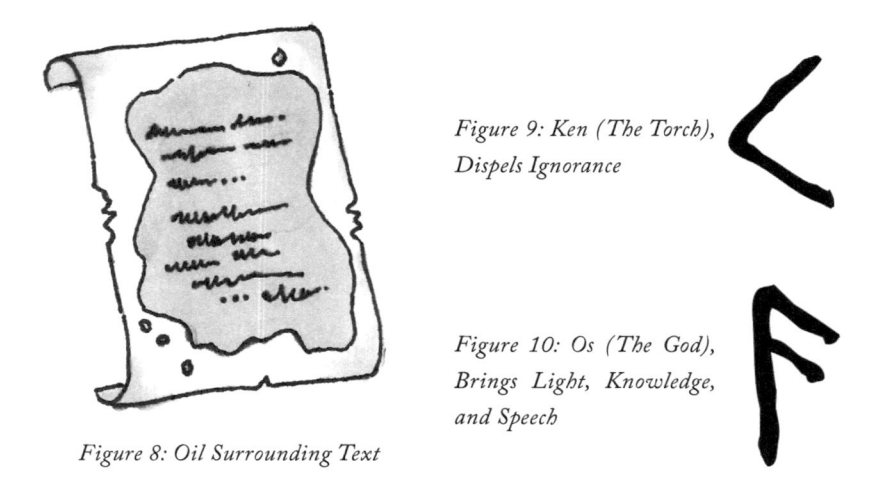

Figure 9: Ken (The Torch), Dispels Ignorance

Figure 10: Os (The God), Brings Light, Knowledge, and Speech

Figure 8: Oil Surrounding Text

8. Fold the paper and place it in the envelope. Seal with sealing wax. (If you've never used sealing wax before, practice beforehand. It can be tricky, and it is easy to burn yourself.)
9. Say:

So mote it be!

10. The spellcasting is complete. Place the envelope on your altar or wherever you decided to keep it.
11. If you have invoked any deities, thank them now and let them know the work is done.
12. For the period of the spell, every day, pick up the envelope. Inhale the aroma of the essential oil and visualize again your goal. Say:

My mind is open and alert. I understand my course of study. I am a success at school. So mote it be!

13. At the end of the period of the spell, give the envelope to Fire or bury it in the earth.

To Bring Justice: A Writing Spell

Goal:
A positive and favorable legal outcome. Do this spell when preparing to appear in a court, before a judge, at a deposition, etc.

Target:
The person or persons making the decision; for example, the judge or jury.

Needed Tools:
- A jar of "invisible ink" made of an herbal infusion, or of a mixture of water and a drop or two of essential oil. Create the infusion by steeping cinquefoil or marigold in water overnight or use a tincture or oil of either or both of these herbs, both of which are said to help win favorable legal outcomes.
- A writing instrument. Since you will not be using regular ink, your consecrated pen (if you have one) may or may not be appropriate.
- An article of clothing that you will wear to court. This could be anything: a tie, a skirt, a handkerchief, etc.
- A "cheat sheet" of what you will write, in Theban, Runic, Angelic, Malachim, or whatever magical alphabet you have selected (see Figure 11 on the next page for the Theban and Runic alphabets).
- Symbols of the four elements. Because a court appearance throws just about everyone out of kilter, the use of the four elements for balance is especially important.
- Also, with legal matters, there can be a wide range of issues being addressed, touching upon any or all parts of life; hence all four elements should definitely be present.
- Your athame. Even if you consider the wand the tool of Air, in court you will often need to be at your strongest and most powerful, and the athame is the strongest of magical tools.

The Magic of the Elements

A			K			U			
B			L			V			
C			M			W			
D			N			X			
E			O			Y			
F			P			Z			
G			Q			.			
H			R			,			
I			S			?			
J			T			!			

Figure 11: Magical Alphabets
From left to right, English correspondence, Runic, and Theban.
Adapted from an illustration courtesy of Isaac Bonewits.

OTHER:
- Decide which magical alphabet you will use, and more importantly, decide what you will write. This won't be an affirmation, but a keyword or phrase. The example illustrated in Figure 12 is the word "Justice," always a safe bet in these situations. You might choose a more pertinent phrase, such as *Not Guilty, Custody to the Mother,* or *Punitive Damages,* depending upon the outcome you seek.
- The nature of this work, and of the issue being addressed, is solitary. If you work in a group, that group might surround and support you, drumming, chanting, sending power, or simply holding hands in a circle while you do the writing. Or, the garment might be passed around, and each person in the group might do some of the writing.

- You could do this spell on behalf of someone else, presenting the person with the garment and instructing them to wear it to court after the spell has been performed.
- The moon phase, day of the week, and other magical timing will depend upon the outcome sought.

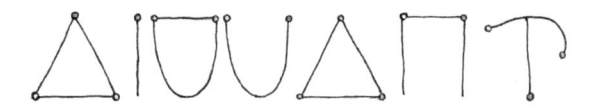

Figure 12: "Justice" in Angelic script

APPROPRIATE DEITIES:
Athena, Ma'at, Kwan Yin, Obatala.

THE SPELL:
1. Ground and center.
2. If you're invoking a deity, do so here.
3. Consecrate the four elements.
4. If you have not already consecrated your pen by the four elements as described in Chapter 3, do so now.
5. Consecrate the "invisible ink" as follows:

   Pass the container with the herbal infusion or the oil-water mixture over and through the incense, saying:

   I consecrate this ink by Air and Fire.

   Using your fingers, touch the entire exterior of the container with the saltwater. Add a few drops of saltwater to the ink, saying:

   I consecrate this ink by Water and Earth.

   Place your athame just over the container, and focus your will and strength through your athame into the mixture, saying:

   By the powers of justice and right do I consecrate this ink.
   As it writes words of justice, so justice shall be done.

By Air and Fire, by Water and Earth, by my true will, and in the name of the gods, so it is and so it shall be!

Plunge the athame into the liquid as you say *so it shall be!*

Note: For "in the name of the gods," you can replace "the gods" with the name of the deity or deities invoked, or use something else meaningful to you, such as "the Lord and Lady," or "my ancestors," or leave out the entire "in the name of" section.

6. If the garment is a shirt, skirt, slacks, or jacket, turn it inside out before consecrating it. This is obviously not necessary for a tie or handkerchief. Consecrate the garment as follows:
Pass the garment over and through the incense, saying:

I consecrate this (name of garment) by Air and Fire.

Using your fingers, touch the entire exterior (or the interior, if it's now inside out) of the garment with the saltwater, saying:

I consecrate this (Name of garment) by Water and Earth.

Touch the garment with your athame, again focusing your will and strength. Visualize clearly the goal of your work: see yourself in the courtroom or before the judge, wearing the garment, and succeeding in exactly the way you intend. Say:

The powers of justice and right flow into this (name of garment). To wear this (name of garment) is to be adorned in irresistible justice. I bring justice and right with me as I wear it, and only justice and right can come to me. By Air and Fire, by Water and Earth, by my true will, and in the name of the gods, so it is and so it shall be!

Note: If you're doing the spell for someone else, just substitute that person's name wherever it says "I wear the garment," "I go to court," etc. For "in the name of the gods," use whatever language you decided on in Step 5.

7. Now lay the garment on your altar. Pick up your magical pen, dip it into the invisible ink, and begin writing your word or phrase in the magical language you have selected. Write slowly and deliberately with focus, visualizing your goal constantly as you write. If the garment is a skirt, you might fill the hem with writing, starting at a seam or zipper so you know where you began. For a tie, you simply use the full length. For pants, you can write on the waistband or go up one leg and down the other. If a group is writing, each person writes the word or phrase once and then passes the garment to the next person. (Alternately, the garment is left at the altar, and each person gets up and lets the next person sit at the altar to write.) With a group, people might get multiple turns, which is fine.
8. When you're finished, say:

So mote it be!

Next, briefly put on the garment to seal the spell. (Do this even if someone else will be wearing it to court.) Then take it off and neatly put it away until it is time for the court appearance. If the court appearance isn't for some days, the garment should not be worn in the meantime.
9. If you have invoked any deities, thank them now and let them know the work is done.

CHAPTER 7

USING FIRE IN SPELLS

In Chapter 5, we identified the following purposes for Fire spells:

- To increase sexual desire (libido)
- To increase sexual energy (performance, sexual stamina)
- To gain physical or psychic energy
- To increase personal power or autonomy
- To increase physical or psychic stamina
- To gain influence over others (charisma)
- For attraction (using charisma to attract)
- To make a decision (strengthen will)
- To increase life force and therefore to heal
- To heal neurological and immunological disorders
- For courage
- To aid political action or to right a wrong

USING FIRE

How would we bring Fire into a spell? As with the other elements, there are three basic methods: (1) directly, (2) through magical tools associated with the elements, or (3) symbolically through qualities of the elements.

To use Fire directly, we could:

- Light a fire; perform ritual around a fire
- Burn things, either to destroy them or to send them to Spirit
- Use candles in ritual; perform candle magic
- Do smithwork

To use Fire tools, we could:

- Use the athame or wand (depending upon whether we associate Fire with the athame or the wand)
- Use a cauldron over a fire
- Use a scourge

To use symbolic qualities of Fire, we could:

- Perform sex magic
- Perform ritual combat
- Perform spells of destruction (i.e., break things)

As with the Air spells in Chapter 6, the spells in this chapter use a combination of the above purposes and methods but are not meant to be comprehensive. Mix and match and use your own ideas.

CANDLE MAGIC

Candle magic is the most convenient sort of magic there is, second only to magic done purely with the mind and using no tools at all. Candles are readily available; the last time I did a spell that required a candle of a particular color, I ran out to the drug store, and sure enough, I found what I needed. Candles provide a convenient and easily understood focal point, they are self-timing, they lend themselves to the use of all sorts of additional symbology (as we'll discuss shortly), and they dispose of themselves.

When you do a writing spell, you have to decide what to do with the paper afterward. Save it? Bury it? Burn it? Similar decisions exist for all sorts of spells, but not candles, which burn the evidence. This is not only convenient, but it creates a satisfying sense of completion. Candles use Fire's devouring quality to finish off the spell neatly.

A candle spell can be as simple as lighting a candle while visualizing your intention. The flame serves as a visual focal point; you gaze into it and allow it to induce a mild trance. You can see your target and/or goal in the flame—just as flame can be used for scrying in which visions are allowed to come as they will for divination, flame can be used for imposing a desired vision (water can also be used for both of these purposes).

The candle continues to "work" even after you have finished casting your spell. By this I mean simply that you light your candle, raise power, focus, send the energy, and finish, saying *So mote it be!* or whatever you like to say. You will leave the candle burning, and while it is burning, the energy continues to be sent toward its target. (Needless to say, fire safety is essential. Flames left unattended carry a risk; use safe candle holders, place the candle on a fireproof surface, and make sure your smoke alarms are in working order.)

One way I like to leave a candle working is to do a spell before bed using a standard twelve-inch dinner taper. This type of candle lasts for about eight hours, so it burns all night. Intermittently throughout the night, I will wake just enough to become conscious of the candle flickering in my room, and so my mind will continue to feed the spell until morning. It's not the deepest sleep, and I wouldn't do it every night, but it works.

Burning the candle down completely is something that is done only when a spell is accomplished in a single session, or when it is the last session of a multipart spell. The simplicity of candle spells can be attractive but need not be confining. You can add to candle spells in a number of ways, including color, decoration, "dressing," and movement. This gives them variety and makes each spell unique.

Candle Color

Color magic isn't particularly an elemental topic, although the elements themselves have colors associated with them—a great variety of colors, in fact, as different systems, groups, and individuals associate different colors with the elements.

The following chart shows some common color associations used for the elements.

Element	Colors
Air	White, light blue, yellow
Fire	Red, orange, yellow
Water	Blue, green
Earth	Black, brown, green

Colors are also associated with astrological signs. One simple way to color-code your magical work is to use a color corresponding to the sign of the person for whom you're doing magic. For example, when working to make me wealthy (I hope you haven't forgotten about that!), you would remember that I'm a Taurus, and thus might use pale-green candles.

Sign	Colors
Aries	Red
Taurus	Emerald green, pale green, pink, pastels
Gemini	Turquoise, silver
Cancer	Silver, pale blue
Leo	Gold, yellow, orange
Virgo	Brown, gray, white
Libra	Blue
Scorpio	Dark red
Sagittarius	Purple
Capricorn	Black
Aquarius	Aquamarine, rainbow
Pisces	Sea green, violet, indigo

Now, if you're working Fire magic for me, you already have to choose between a red or orange candle for Fire, and an emerald-green, pale-green, or another pastel-colored candle for Taurus, but that's not all! There are also color associations for various magical purposes. These vary from system to system and from practitioner to practitioner, but a typical set of associations would look like the following:

Color	Magical Associations
White	Purity, protection, spirituality
Red	Sex, blood, war, health, energy
Pink	Love, compassion
Green	Fertility, crops, money, healing
Blue	Feelings, psychism, the astral plane, intuition, peace
Purple	Anger, lust, violence, royalty
Yellow	Intelligence, beginnings
Orange	Pride, courage
Brown	Earth, soil, crops
Black	Death, old age

So, for a money spell for me, you'd have to decide between black/brown for Earth (money is associated with Earth), pale green for Taurus, or deep green for money. In general, I choose the color of the spell's purpose when working for myself, the color of the person's sign when working for someone else over a great distance (to establish the connection), and I use altar tools and other items to bring in the elemental influence. But that's me.

If you're out of candles of the color you need and you're in a hurry or flat broke, you can always use white. Because white is absorbent of energies, you can use decoration to add the influence that color would provide, and simply visualize the color you want surrounding the candle. This is a good backup plan. Just don't use it as an excuse to be lazy.

Candle Decoration

One of the cool things about candles is that they're made of wax, which is soft and malleable. It's quite easy to carve something into a candle in order to add energies to it. Writing words on a candle is a way to add Air to a Fire spell. Suppose, for example, that you were pressing a civil liberties case in the courts. This would fall under both justice (Air) and political action (Fire). You could use a red candle with a word carved into it; the color and candle would bring Fire to the spell, and the word would use the power of Air.

You can use symbols to add astrological or planetary influence to the spell. Suppose you decided to use brown (for Earth) for your *Deborah Is Wealthy* spell. You might then add a Taurus glyph to the candle to establish a connection to me. I sometimes simply add a person's initials to a candle or write their magical name.

Candles are easy to carve; you can use your fingernails. On the other hand, you might prefer a knife. It is traditional in Wicca to avoid cutting or carving with the athame, which is why some Witches have a tool called the white-hilt knife that is used for such things. Normally, this is a consecrated tool reserved for magical cutting only.

Candles can be decorated with paint, markers, or glitter, and objects can be embedded into them. For example, a consecrated crystal might be pushed into the wax and made part of a spell; the crystal would then be disposed of or saved after the candle burned down.

Some of the large seven-day candles that come in glass containers can be removed from the containers, but some are made by pouring the wax directly into the glass and cannot be removed for decorating. In that case, you can decorate the container. You'll have to decide how to dispose of the container when you're done. I think sending it to the recycling center is an effective way of returning it to Mother Earth.

Candle Dressing

The process of dressing a candle seems to have originated in Yoruban magical traditions (Voodoo, Santería, Candomblé, etc.). The procedure is simple: Using an oil, rub the candle upward and deosil (clockwise) for spells that create or improve, and downward and widdershins (counterclockwise) for spells that banish, shrink, or destroy. (You can think of it this way: waxing moon spells are upward, and waning moon spells are downward.) You prepare the oil, and then, concentrating on your goal, rub it into the candle. I do this at my altar just before beginning the actual spell.

The oil can be plain olive oil, but usually, it has a drop or two of an appropriate essential oil or a sprinkle of a powdered herb or herbal mixture. The oil may or may not be consecrated. It may have been prepared specifically for the spell at hand or a batch may have been made up, consecrated, and stored for when it was needed (in which case it is probably a general-purpose oil for success, healing, or some other common use).

If there is a spoken part of the spell, I often recite it while dressing the candle. If the spoken portion is long or complex, I might reduce it to repeating a word or two, like: *Success! Success! Success!*

Candle Movement

Candle movement is more or less what it sounds like—you move the candle. The candle functions as a symbolic representation of a person, thing, or condition. For example, a candle could symbolize you, your friend, your job, or your libido. When you set up the spell, you include a consecration that defines the candle—something that says: *This is now George!*

The candle's (George's) location is meaningful in this sort of spell. Your working area (altar, table, etc.) is laid out with some symbolism as to its geography. George may be in a specific physical relationship to another candle, to other altar items, or to a mental map you have of what certain spots on the altar mean. Such spells are typically used to bring the subject closer to a distant object, be it money, a lover, or inner peace. Both subject and object can be symbolized by candles, or the subject (George) can be moved toward some other symbolic thing (a photo, a ten-dollar bill, etc.). When doing this sort of spell, I like to use a dish-shaped candle holder; that way, the candle can end up actually touching its goal without creating a fire hazard.

I used this technique in *The Way of Four* as a balancing exercise. Each of four symbols of the elements starts out in a separate location. As the exercise progresses, each symbol is moved to touch the ones already used so that the exercise ends with all four symbols touching each other, representing wholeness.

Marking Candles

Candles can be marked with goal points as part of a spell. Perhaps you have seen "knob" candles; they look like a vertical stack of seven (usually) golf balls. The idea is to burn one knob each day, and at the end of a week, the spell is complete. Dividing up a spell like this is an effective approach, but it isn't necessary to buy special candles to do so.

Another method is to mark a candle for a spell by simply cutting horizontal lines as needed; for example, divide a candle into seven roughly even divisions for each day of the week. You can use a marker to draw the lines, or you can stick an ordinary straight pin into the candle at intervals. The intervals depend upon your plans for the spell. In general, you'll divide the candle evenly according to however many days or sessions you plan, let it burn down to the next mark, and then snuff the candle.

To Restore Libido: A Candle Spell

GOAL:
To bring the sexual excitement back into an established relationship. Just as the spell to increase understanding in Chapter 6 restored Air to an otherwise healthy relationship, so this spell restores Fire to an otherwise healthy relationship.

TARGET:
The couple; particularly the lustful part of each individual and their lustful focus on one another. Depending upon the situation, you could target physical energy and desire, emotional focus (of a libidinous nature), or plain old lust.

NEEDED TOOLS:
- Two red taper candles
- About three tablespoons of olive oil
- Fresh ginger (a few slices) or ginger essential oil (3–5 drops)
- A jar or dish for the dressing oil. If you plan to keep it for future use, it should have a lid, and you should label it "Passion Oil" or some such name
- A tool for carving the candles (a white-hilt knife or other tool)
- Saltwater
- Your athame or wand—whichever you associate with Fire
- Incense, preferably containing cinnamon and/or powdered ginger

OTHER:
- You will be moving the two candles closer to each other over a period of seven days. Decide in advance where you will start and about how far each candle needs to move each day (no need to measure, but have a rough idea of your start point, your end point, and your five points in between). Find a spot where the candles will be undisturbed for that length of time.
- The spell can be performed solitary, as a couple, or as a group, either for your own relationship or someone else's. You could do a combination of group/solitary work by consecrating the candles and doing the first lighting as a group and then bringing the candles home, setting them up, and moving them nightly in solitary practice.
- Love and lust spells are traditionally begun on a Friday night during a waxing moon. The moon should be waxing throughout the seven days of the spell.

APPROPRIATE DEITIES:
Kama, Eros, Aphrodite, Frigga, Erzuli.

THE SPELL:
1. Ground and center.
2. Prepare the dressing oil.

    If you are using ginger essential oil, prepare the dressing oil by adding 3–5 drops of the essential oil to the olive oil and stirring. You can stir using the tip of your carving tool.

    If you are using fresh ginger, leave a few slices soaking in the oil overnight or longer, remove the slices, and stir.

    Point your athame at the dressing oil. Feel and see Fire pouring from the athame into the oil, and say:

    I charge this oil to carry the power of lust and passion.
    I fill this oil with the Fire of life, sex, and energy. So mote it be!

3. Make sure the incense is lit and smoky.
4. Prepare the candles.

    Carve each candle with the symbol for the astrological sign of the partner it represents, and/or that partner's initials.

Then, consecrate each candle to the four elements, naming the candle as the person during the consecration as follows:

Dip your fingers in the saltwater, and wet the entire candle, top to bottom, skipping only the wick, while saying:

> *I charge this candle by Water and Earth.*
> *By Water and Earth it is (name of person).*
> *By Water and Earth does (name of person) have body*
> *and heart for my spell. So mote it be!*

Now pass the candle back and forth in the incense smoke, touching all parts of it, while saying:

> *I charge this candle by Fire and Air.*
> *By Fire and Air it is (name of person).*
> *By Fire and Air does (name of person) have mind*
> *and will for my spell. So mote it be!*

After consecrating both candles, you can dress them. Be sure to use upward, deosil strokes. Allow yourself to notice the sensuality of stroking the candle, and, if you wish, repeat *Lust! Lust! Lust!* to yourself while doing so.

NOTE: It is obviously important that the right candle, with the right symbol/initials, be consecrated to the right name. At your discretion, you can carve one candle, then consecrate it, then carve and consecrate the second candle, so as not to mix them up. You could, if you like, have a photo of each partner, and leave each candle near the photo during the consecration process.

5. Now you'll begin the actual spell. Set each candle in its holder in the start position—as far apart as possible.
6. If you're invoking a deity, do so here.
7. Gazing at the two candles, say:

> *By the powers of Air and Fire and Water and Earth (and in*
> *the name of deity) do I charge you, (name 1) and (name 2), to*
> *approach each other with passion.*

(Name 1) and (name 2), come near to each other.
(Name 1) and (name 2), have passion for each other.
(Name 1) and (name 2), come near to each other.
(Name 1) and (name 2), have passion for each other.

NOTE: It might be best, if you are one of the partners, to refer to yourself in the third person (by name) so that you can really project yourself into the candle. Try it out before you do the spell, both using your name and using "I" and "me," and decide which you prefer.

8. As you raise power and send it into the candles, continue to repeat:

   (Name 1) and (name 2), come near to each other.
   (Name 1) and (name 2), have passion for each other.

   Continue for several minutes and then snuff the candles.

NOTE: Some people believe it is an offense to Fire to blow out a candle. I've never ascribed to that view, but I do find a snuffer handy, because the wax makes less of a mess.

9. If you have invoked any deities, thank them now and let them know the work is done (for tonight).
10. Leave the candles where they are until the next night. Then move them to the second position (see Figure 13).

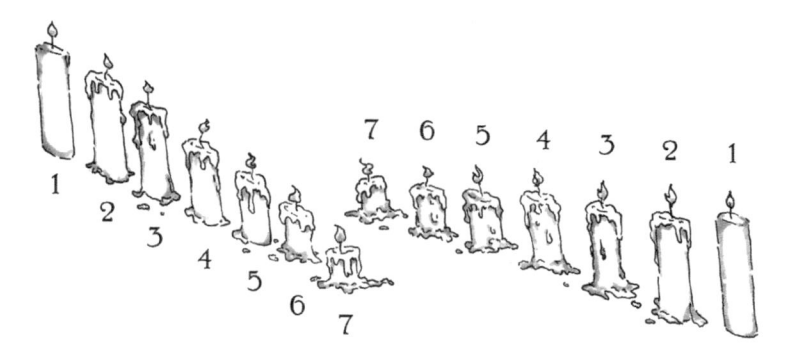

Figure 13: Candles Approaching Each Other Over Seven Nights

11. Every night, move the candles as illustrated in Figure 13, and then repeat steps 6–8.
12. On the last night, the candles will touch. Change the spell so that everywhere you have been saying *"Come near to each other,"* you now say *"Touch each other."*
13. On the last night, when you finish sending the power, say:

*It is done! (Name 1) and (name 2), have passion for each other.
(Name 1) and (name 2), touch each other with lust and joy.
So mote it be!*

14. On the last night, leave the candles to burn themselves out.

To Aid a Cause: A Candle Spell

GOAL:
This is a political action spell for whatever cause you choose. It is for someone who is working to get a candidate elected, to get a bill passed, or to otherwise effect change on a national or, especially, grassroots level.

TARGET:
The target depends on the goal. If you are working for a candidate, they are the target and will be surrounded by Fiery charisma and success. If it's a bill or law or other abstract subject, target that abstraction and visualize it as a thing surrounded by charisma and success.

NEEDED TOOLS:
- One red candle
- About three tablespoons of olive oil
- Essential oil of carnation and/or cinnamon (3–5 drops, if using one oil or about 2 drops each if using more than one oil)
- A jar or dish for the dressing oil. If you plan to keep it for future use, it should have a lid and you should label it "Success Oil" or some such name.
- Saltwater
- Incense containing woodruff, carnation, and/or cinnamon

- A tool for carving the candle (a white-hilt knife or other tool)
- Your athame or wand—whichever you associate with Fire

OTHER:
- This spell is designed to be worked by a group of people committed to the same political cause. If need be, you can work this spell solitary: the steps set up for a group working can be skipped, and each "notch" phase can be handled by the same person.
- A group working this spell need not be Wiccan, Pagan, or a magical group per se, but merely a group of people willing to include magic as part of their political action.
- Note that part of the power raised in this spell is in the commitment of each person to pass the candle to the next person in the chain on time. This is hard; it can push the individuals past their normal limits of time and energy. It can also uncover weak links in the group, and thus create interpersonal challenges that will have to be ironed out. This entire process will empower the group and the spell.
- The duration and timing of the spell work as follows: You are working toward a specific goal with a deadline, such as Election Day, the deadline for gathering signatures, or whatever it may be. Work during the waxing moon, either just prior to the goal date or as the campaign is starting up. Given those time constraints, set two dates when the group can meet. Then divide the time evenly between individuals. For example, with four people and one week, one person must commit to finishing and passing the candle in one day, and everyone else has two days:
  - Saturday: Group meeting
  - Monday: Person 1 works
  - Tuesday: Person 2 works
  - Thursday: Person 3 works
  - Saturday: Person 4 works
  - Sunday: Group meeting
- Obviously, this is just one example, and my real point is that you, as a group, need to plan this out at the first group meeting, or it won't happen.

APPROPRIATE DEITIES:
Oya, Durga, Nuada, Lugh.

THE SPELL:
1. Ground, center, and merge.
2. If you're performing an invocation, do so here.
3. Prepare the dressing oil.

    Add a total of 3–5 drops of essential oil to the olive oil, and stir. If you are using more than one essential oil, use about 2 drops of each. Pass the oil around from person to person and have each one stir.

    Place the bowl/jar of dressing oil in the center. Everyone points athames/fingers at the oil; feel and see Fire pouring into the oil. One person says:

    We charge this oil to carry justice and success.
    Our cause is just, and we have the Fire to fight for it.
    May this oil carry our Fire. So mote it be!

NOTE: If you're not being Witchy, you could substitute *So be it!* for *So mote it be!*

4. Make sure the incense is lit and smoky.
5. Prepare the candle.

    Notch the candle with horizontal lines that are roughly equidistant. Because the top of the candle tapers, allow the top section to be slightly longer. The number of notches should equal the number of people in the group (Figure 14 shows five notches).

    Consecrate the candle to the four elements, naming the candle as the candidate, bill, or cause, as follows:

    Dip your fingers in the saltwater, and wet the entire candle, top to bottom, skipping only the wick, while saying:

    We charge this candle by Water and Earth.
    By Water and Earth it is (name/purpose).
    By Water will we intuitively find the right ways to win.
    By Earth will our success become a reality. So mote it be!

Now pass the candle back and forth in the incense smoke, touching all parts of it, while saying:

We charge this candle by Fire and Air.
By Fire and Air, it is (name/purpose).
By Air will we find the right words to communicate our cause.
By Fire will we have the energy and drive to succeed. So mote it be!

6. Dress the candle with upward, deosil strokes.
7. Everyone in the group now raises power and sends it into the candle. Power raising can be freeform—drumming, chanting, whatever—as long as it's energetic.
8. If you have invoked any deities, thank them now and let them know the work for tonight is done; let them know the work will continue over the next (number of) nights.
9. Send the candle home with the first person, who will burn it to the first notch. Figure 14 shows a sample group with five members. Raven will burn the first part of the candle, raising power, using words of her own choosing, and sending Fiery, intense power to the target. If you have invoked deities during the group working, each individual should do an invocation prior to their private working.
10. When the candle has burned to the first notch, Raven snuffs it and says *So mote it be.*

    If she has invoked any deities, she thanks them now and lets them know the work for tonight is done.
11. Raven is now responsible for getting the candle to Amber within the agreed-upon timeframe.
12. Remember that a standard dinner taper burns for eight hours. If the candle is divided into five segments, each will last over an hour and a half. You don't need to raise and send for that length of time. Raise power, send it, and then let the candle burn on its own. Stay near the candle, reading, meditating, listening to music, or whatever you choose so that you know when to snuff it.
13. Each individual works as described in Step 9.

Using Fire in Spells

14. At last, each individual has worked and there is a final portion of candle remaining. The group now gathers and does the final working together. If you have been performing invocations all along, of course, you will do so again now.

    Power raising can be freeform and impassioned. Words can be improvised, shouted, and sobbed. Let your passionate belief in your cause energize your working and leave you with almost limitless Fiery energy.
15. When the power has been raised and sent, say a final *So mote it be*, and allow the candle to burn out completely.
16. If you have invoked any deities, thank them now and let them know the work is completely finished.

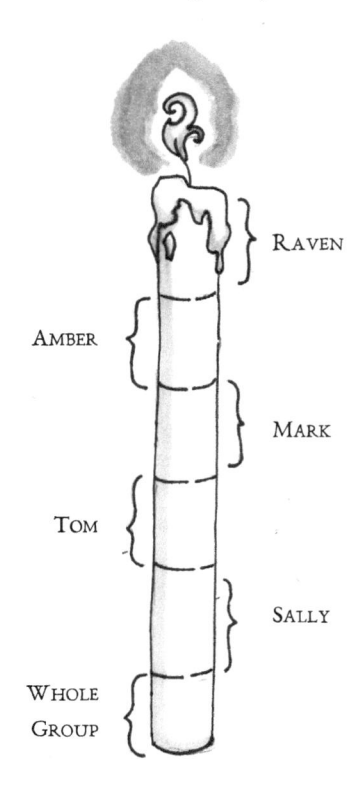

Figure 14: Candle Notches for Group Work

SPELLS THAT BURN THINGS

The simplest way to use *Fire* in a spell is to use *fire* in a spell—to burn stuff. Before I begin discussing the various ways that you can use burning as part of a spell, I must emphasize that fire safety is paramount. As discussed in Chapter 1, salamanders can be tricky things and working magic with an open flame will certainly attract them. When I light small fires in my home, I use a larger fireproof container (e.g., dish, cauldron) than I think I'll need, I keep tongs handy, and of course I know where the fire extinguisher is. Despite all that, I have a burn hole in my bedroom rug from a spell that got out of hand. When we go into an altered state of consciousness—visualizing, chanting, and staring into the flame—our self-control is not at its peak (nor should it be), and the compelling quality of Fire can move us to take risks we wouldn't normally consider and may not even realize we're taking. For that reason, set up your fire-safety tools well before the ritual begins and double-check everything.

Pure burning spells can fall into three categories:

- Sacrifice or offering
- Letting go or releasing
- Destruction or transformation

Burning as a Sacrifice or an Offering

Three of the four elements can be seen as deriving from "worlds": the world of the land (Earth), the world of the sea (Water), and the world of the sky (Air). Fire, however, doesn't come from a world. No creatures that we can perceive (except, perhaps, psychically) live in Fire, nor can we travel to, in, or on Fire. In this way, Fire is distinct from the other elements. The realm of Fire is not a natural realm where natural beings can live; hence it is a spirit realm.

Because of this, Fire has been assigned to "spirit" in some systems. (I prefer to assign Fire to "will," but it is clear that will and spirit have a connection, both being inward forces that move one forward in life.) Fire is unworldly; it seems like magic. It arises spontaneously or from the heavens (lightning). It isn't born, and when it dies, it's gone entirely. When a person or animal dies, the corpse retains the shape of the living creature. When a plant is cut, it looks just as it did when it was growing in the earth. But when fire is dead, it is gone completely. Ash and ember are nothing like fire. Unlike animals and plants, "dead" fire has disappeared utterly from this realm.

Hence, Fire has been connected to the gods since ancient times. It is thought to have come from them, and many mythologies have tales of fire-bringers, from the widely known Prometheus of the Greeks to Grandmother Spider of the Choctaw[32] to the lesser-known Yehl of the Tlingit.[33] The theft of fire and the bringing of it to human beings makes us more godlike. Fire is the first step toward civilization; its possession transforms us from animals into humans.

It is perhaps because the gods are seen as the source of fire that fire has, for millennia, been used as a means of communing with them. We send things to them in the fire, and we receive messages from them through the fire.

We can give something to the gods as an offering or a sacrifice by burning it in the fire with the knowledge that this sends it to them. By communing with the gods in this way, we might also send messages, prayers, requests, or bargains. A bargain spell, in which an offering to the gods is made in exchange for the granting of a request, can be performed using fire as the means by which the offer is made.

A Bit About Invocation

Spells of offering or sacrifice are performed by invoking (calling and bringing present) a deity and then making the offering/sacrifice. Such an invocation should be *specific*, *descriptive*, and *sincere*.

By specific, I mean that an invocation should go beyond "plug in deity name here." Your research will often turn up traditional phrases of invocation for this specific deity. It should be consistent with who and what this deity is. This is important both for the same reason a specific goal and target are important—so that the energy gets

---

[32] A Native American people originally from the Mississippi region.
[33] A Native American people of the Pacific Northwest.

where it's going. It's also important to recognize that, over centuries of worship, many ancient deities have been worshiped in a variety of ways. Do you want Mercury, god of communication, Mercury the psychopomp, or Mercury, protector of thieves?

For example, here is a translation of a traditional invocation of the Hindu god Ganesha:

> *We invoke you with offerings, Ganesha,*
> *making offerings to you as Love.*
> *Invoking you with offerings, He of Plentitudes.*
> *We invoke you with offerings, Ganesha,*
> *making offerings to the Sage great and wise.*
> *Invoking you with offerings, He of Rulers.*
> *Come to us quickly and join our gathering, be among us!*[34]

The Ganesha invocation names specific attributes of this god in particular: "He of Rulers" and "He of Plentitudes."

The Ganesha invocation above is also descriptive. Ganesha is a "Sage great and wise." Being descriptive can mean using visual imagery (*Brigid of flaming red hair*), naming personal characteristics (*Athena the just*), or detailing facts and stories about the deity (*Krishna who multiplied himself in the Vrindavana Forest* or *Odin one-eye*). Such description is evocative and effective and can even contribute to an altered state of consciousness.

Being sincere does not require faith or traditional religious belief. It *does* require a respectful attitude and a suspension of disbelief. This hearkens back to the section on magical language in Chapter 6. Even if you don't really believe in deities as "real" beings (whatever *that* means), your deep mind is hearing and responding to what you are saying, so say it sincerely. You cannot truly complete this call if you are convinced there's no one to call.

Finally, complete all invocations with a specific *invitation* (such as "be among us" in the Ganesha invocation), and the assumption of success—meaning, say "welcome" or some such once you are finished.

---

34 Sharanya: The Maa Batakali Cultural Mission, Inc. http://sharanya.org/mandala/th_gallery/invocation-of-ganesha/ accessed October 21, 2018.

Burning as Letting Go or Releasing

Sometimes the word *release* is used to mean giving up something negative, such as a bad habit, an undesirable behavior, or an old wish. This type of "release" is more along the lines of what I'm calling "destruction or transformation." Let's look at a different usage of the term.

To release or let go can be to set free. Like a bird released from its cage, something can be set free into the universe, to fly at will. Spells are often released in this way. In the writing spell in Chapter 6, you were instructed to decide how to dispose of the paper once the spell was finished. One method might have been to burn it. The principle behind this is that the fire distills the object into its spirit-form; its Fire-form. The object still exists, but not in the physical world; it is now a Fire object moving through a different reality toward its goal.

When we burn an object in a spell as a release, we first raise power into the object and then place the object in the fire. As it burns, we focus on the energy being released out into the universe. For example, you could charge up and then burn a copy of your résumé, visualizing its Fire-form flying toward the ideal employer. You also could contact a missing person or a long-lost friend by sending a letter through fire.

Burning as Destruction or Transformation

Destruction and transformation are one and the same—to transform a thing is to destroy its earlier form. When steel is made (in fire), the iron from which it was forged is gone. Death destroys life, and earthquakes destroy homes, so we often see destruction as entirely negative. But childbirth destroys (transforms) pregnancy, adolescence destroys childhood, and marriage destroys bachelorhood.

Sometimes we destroy something without knowing what will take its place. We leave an empty space for the universe to fill and we must trust that the vacuum will be filled with something positive and empowering—we might use magic to encourage this, and we might use magic, as well, to help ourselves trust the process.

Divorce is often like this. We destroy the marriage, which may be an occasion for grief, for celebration, or for both. We undertake this act of destruction because we know it is the right thing to do, but we don't know what will come next. When my marriage ended, I barely remembered what it was like to be single, and I had to relearn an awful lot about living my life. I just had to trust that destruction is also *always* transformation and give energy and nurturance to the person I was being transformed into.

Just as we sometimes choose destruction without being able to see the transformation ahead, so there are times when we choose transformation without knowing what it is that will be destroyed. Again, we must let go and trust, and we can use magic to help the process along.

In Fire, we can destroy grief or rage and transform it into peace and freedom. In Fire, we can destroy bad attitudes, addictions, poverty, and loneliness.[35] In Fire, we can seek transformation into a new kind of person or a new mode of being.

To use a burning fire as a means of sacrifice, offering, release, or transformation begins with intention. You must *intend* your fire to be a particular thing—a place of offering and communion, for example, or a place of transformation. You can consecrate the fire to that purpose and meaning and send power into it. Then, you send something, which might also be consecrated, into the fire. You might send energy and visualization; or shout words; or throw in a symbolic (flammable) object, or written words or phrases on slips of paper that will burn easily.

Even with setting a clear intention, you might find the different meanings and uses of Fire confusing. If this is true for you, then read through this section and determine for yourself what Fire means to *you* and stick with that meaning. That is, if you're clear that for you, Fire always destroys and transforms, then the spell of offering below is not for you.

---

[35] Real-world tasks must accompany each of these transformations, just as real-world job-seeking must accompany magic done to get a job and visiting a real-world medical practitioner must accompany magical healing.

For Courage:
A Spell of Offering

Goal:
To increase your own courage or the courage of someone else; use this spell to help someone faced with a frightening challenge.

Target:
The God, Goddess, or gods of your choice. You are sending an offering to a deity and asking for courage in return. You can perform this spell if you believe in deities as literal beings, as symbols of parts of the self (archetypes), or as metaphors. If you don't wish to work with deities at all, an offering would not be part of your magical repertoire.

Needed Tools:
- A setup for a small fire. You can create an indoor fire in a cauldron, or you can use a candle and then light something afire from the candle flame and transfer the burning item to a fireproof container. Whatever your setup, test it in advance with a "neutral" burn. Don't forget the fire extinguisher!
- An offering. An offering to a deity can be something specifically pleasing to that deity (as your own research will determine), something meaningful to you, or something symbolic of courage.
- If you don't know what to offer, tea is a plant associated with Fire and courage, and the leaves can be burnt as an offering.

Other:
- The spell is designed to be performed solitary but can be adapted for a group.
- Optionally, you can choose to offer something that is not flammable in addition to the offering you will burn. This is especially appropriate if you are invoking a patron deity who likes a particular sort of offering that isn't flammable. For example, lots of people give milk to Brigid and Isis. If you wish to do this, add a suitable offering just before the burnt offering and then dispose of the offering in your usual way (see steps 4 and 5).

- After you've finished the spell/offering, stay near the fire and keep your eye on it. Once the offering has been fully consumed, you can put the fire out or let it burn itself out.

Appropriate Deities

If you have a patron deity, make your offering to them. You might also choose a deity specific to the reason you need courage. For example, if you need courage for a court appearance, choose a deity of law and justice. If you need courage because you're facing a biopsy, choose a deity of healing.

Deities associated with courage include Mars, Inanna, Nana Buukun, and Thor.

The Spell

1. Ground and center.
2. Perform an invocation to the deity who will receive the offering.
3. Say:

O, (name of deity), I offer you this (offering). Find it pleasing, I pray, and see fit to fill me with the courage I need. I offer it from my heart and from my spirit. I offer it with hope but no demand. I give freely and pray for courage out of love and honor for you.

Note: You're doing this spell because you or someone you know is facing a frightening situation. So, it's important that the words in Step 3 are meaningful. Personalize them as you see fit.

4. If you're offering something in addition to the burnt offering, do so now.
5. Burn the offering. As you do so, visualize it flying in a stream of fire to the deity you invoked.
6. Meditate for a while on your offering and on courage.
7. Say:

So mote it be.

8. Thank the deity for their presence and let them know the work is done.

To Make a Decision: Releasing into the Fire

Goal:
To make a decision. Use this spell when you are really torn and cannot find the inner fire to choose.

Target:
Your own indecision: you are releasing indecision into the fire.

Needed Tools:
- A setup for a small fire. You can create an indoor fire in a cauldron, or you can use a candle and then light something afire from the candle flame and transfer the burning item to a fireproof container. Whatever your setup, test it in advance with a "neutral" burn. Don't forget the fire extinguisher!
- A small slip of paper on which you will write the choice you wish to make. It can be as simple as "yes or no," or it can be more detailed, such as "marry Joe or marry Charlie," or "keep job or quit." You can use consecrated paper, as described in Chapter 3.

Other:
- This is a solitary spell.

Appropriate Deities:
Again, if you have a patron deity, you can invoke them. You can invoke a deity specific to the choice (a marriage deity for deciding between Joe and Charlie), or a deity more generally associated with Fire, Will, or decision, such as Janus for choices, Odin for wisdom and mastery, Brigid for fire and knowledge, or Themis for wisdom and knowledge.

The Spell:
1. Ground and center.
2. If you're performing an invocation, do so here.
3. Light your candle or fire.
4. Hold your slip of paper over the flame, and say:

True or false, yes or no,
To the Fire, it shall go.
True or false, yes or no,
Let it go, let it go.
To inner Fire, set it free,
Fire knows how it should be.
Know the answer, right or wrong,
Fire knows it all along.

5. As you visualize indecision burning up and wisdom emerging from your inner fire, set your slip of paper on fire and watch it burn completely.
6. Say:

So mote it be.

7. If you have invoked any deities, thank them now and let them know the work is done.
8. If you like, you can bury the ash of your paper.

To Gain Freedom from Obsession: A Spell of Burning

GOAL:
To free yourself from an obsession or addiction. I designed the spell with a sexual or romantic obsession in mind—an unhealthy longing for the wrong person, either from the past or present. This combines three Fire qualities: lust, obsession, and freedom. However, any obsession or addiction can be released into the fire. The goal is freedom.

TARGET:
The target is the obsession itself, which will be burned up in the fire.

NEEDED TOOLS:
- Fire-safety materials (sand, fire extinguisher)
- Fire-building materials (wood, matches, kerosene, etc.)
- Drums and other instruments
- Blankets to sit on.

- Symbols of obsession, such as notes with significant words written on them or any token that represents the object of obsession.

OTHER:
- This spell is designed for an outdoor setting, such as in the woods or around a campfire. It can also be done indoors with the fire built inside a cauldron. However, keep in mind that the noise level is liable to be pretty high, so don't try this where neighbors are likely to complain.
- This spell is meant for a group. It is ideal for a group of people who share a common addiction or obsession and perhaps are meeting to support one another in recovery. It is less "Witchy" than most spells, and, if no circle is cast and no gods invoked, it is suitable for people who enjoy New Age–style ritual but would be uncomfortable with Paganism or Witchcraft.
- You'll probably want some chants related to fire and/or freedom and/or empowerment. *Chants: Ritual Music* by Reclaiming and Friends[36] has an appropriate song called "Rise with the Fire."

APPROPRIATE DEITIES:
Agni, Kali, Thor, Hathor, Dionysus, Zeus.

THE SPELL:
1. Gather in your location and build the fire. It should be going nicely before you begin. Make sure your fire extinguisher and sand are nearby before you start. Make sure everyone is comfortable, with blankets laid out and drums at hand. All participants need their symbol, token, or slip of paper with them by the fire.
2. Ground, center, and merge.
3. If you are going to cast a circle or do invocations, do so now.

---

36 Available as a CD, digital download, or free streaming from www.reclaimingquarterly.org/music/.

4. Chant softly and get your drums warmed up. Begin your freedom chant. Let the drumming build slowly. It is important at this point not to cut loose, not to let the drumming go into that wild, ecstatic thing that drumming often reaches toward. A slow, steady climb is what you're after.
5. Whoever is moved to do so goes first. The first person stands up and says something in the following pattern while throwing their token into the fire:

I, (name), release X. Go to the fire, X! I, (name), am free!

Here is an example:

I, Mary, release my obsession with John. Go to the fire, obsession! I am free of my longing for you. I, Mary, am free!

NOTE: Do not send people into the fire! Release the obsession, not John.

6. Everyone now begins to chant:

Mary is free! Mary is free! Mary is free!

The drumming builds to a higher pitch (but still not completely cut loose, as the work will continue). While everyone drums and chants for Mary, she can chant along, scream, drum, or do whatever moves her.

Gradually the intensity is allowed to subside, the drumming remains at a low tempo, and Mary returns to her place.

7. Each person, one by one, will release their obsession and throw their token into the fire. Each person will have their name chanted and drummed and be declared free.
8. When everyone has gone, the chant can change to:

We are free! We are free! We are free!

9. *Now* cut loose. Let the drumming build as much as you like. Shout, scream, dance, shake rattles, shake your groove thing, let go! You are free!
10. As the drumming dies down, resume your opening chant. Let it fade slowly, and say:

So be it!

(Everyone should echo the first person who says this so that all say it.)
11. If you have invoked any deities, thank them now and let them know the work is done.
12. Make sure you have safely doused the fire before you leave.

Spells of Destruction

The ability of fire to literally destroy and transform means that Fire is also symbolically connected to destruction and transformation. If a spell involves destroying something, even if it's not by burning, then Fire's power to destroy and reshape is invoked.

The spell of destruction that follows is somewhat controversial. It is a spell to release rage. In the spell, it is rage that is being brought forth, acted out, destroyed, and, it is hoped, transformed into peace and freedom. Because the rage *is* acted out, quite viscerally, some people have looked on the spell as negative. You should be very clear, though, that no harm is being done in this spell. If I work to act out my uncontrollable rage at, say, Pee-Wee Herman, and if I destroy a symbol of that rage, I have not harmed, or attempted to harm, Pee-Wee Herman in any way. Even if I write Pee-Wee Herman's name on something and then destroy it (which is what happens in the spell), I have not cursed or done magic against him, provided I am very clear that my work is about rage and not about any individual against whom I feel rage.

Because this spell is done in the context of a supportive group of people, you can help keep each other honest about your intentions. In addition, you will not invoke, consecrate, or charge the dishes being "named"; they will not be magically connected to people, but only to rage.

To Release Rage:
A Spell of Destruction

Goal:
To release rage and find peace. Use this spell if you are experiencing destructive or uncontrollable rage.

Target:
The inner Fire of rage. You will transfer the rage to your symbolic objects (the plates) and then destroy it. You can visualize your rage as a bright-red glow moving from within you into the plates, as you write on them.

Needed Tools:
- A set of breakable dishes. You can probably find dishes you're happy to destroy at a garage sale or a thrift shop.
- Grease pens or laundry markers for writing on the plates. Practice beforehand to make sure that the kind of pens you've got really do write on the kind of dishes you've got. Have enough pens to pass around to everyone.
- A heavy-duty broom (a janitor's push-broom is good), dustpan, and heavy-duty garbage bags for clean-up.
- A set of blankets or chairs to sit on before you begin while you're marking up the plates.

Other:
Here are some possible uses for this spell:
- This spell is excellent for people who are recovering from rape, incest, abuse, or other forms of victimization. Sometimes abuse survivors are full of rage right away; usually, though, they go through a period of guilt, depression, or numbness until the rage emerges. This emergence is healthy, but it can be agonizing and the rage can be a destructive force within.
- It can be used in situations where you are unable to express rage directly, such as when you have been the victim of an injustice or when the person against whom you are raging has died.

- In addition, this spell is for people who are experiencing a great deal of day-to-day anger and rage without a clear cause; rage that may be harming their relationships or their sense of self.
- The spell is designed to be performed by a group. Ideally, by a group of people who meet to deal with issues related to this work, for example, a rape survivor's group. Unlike other spells worked so far, this spell is ritual theater, in which feelings are literally acted out in order to exorcise them.
- You'll need someplace like an empty parking lot or vacant location of some kind. The ground or floor must be hard so the plates will shatter, and of course you'll need privacy so you can really let go.

APPROPRIATE DEITIES:
Kali, Sekhmet, Hera, Shango.

THE SPELL:
1. Gather in your location and set up your seating area with the blankets and grease pens.
2. Ground, center, and merge, focusing on joint purpose and commitment to recovery from rage.
3. If you're performing an invocation, do so here.
4. Sit on your blankets in a circle on one extreme end of the location, with the plates in a pile in the middle of your group. Begin writing on the plates; each plate will represent one object of rage. You can write a person's name, a situation, a symbolic phrase—anything of one or two words that is your rage trigger. If all your rage is focused on one person or instance, try to break it into component parts.

    For example, if you are releasing rage over rape, you might have one plate for the rapist's name (or just "RAPIST" if you don't know the name), one plate with the word "HELPLESS" to rage at your feelings of impotence, one plate with the word "SEX" that expresses rage at what has happened to your sexuality since the attack, and so on. While you're doing this, you can talk amongst yourselves, telling stories of rage, hurt, loss, and even humor (don't forget that it's okay to laugh). Show each other what you're writing, sometimes one person's plate can inspire someone else to think of something to write. Be encouraging; sometimes it's hard to get in touch with exactly where it hurts.

5. When you're ready, stand up and hold hands (provided everyone is comfortable with touch). Each of you should have your personal plates in your own pile, but all the piles should be more or less in the center of the circle. Say something simple and direct like:

> *Here is our rage. We hate it. We will crush it.*
> *We will destroy our rage. So be it!*

6. Now it's a virtual free-for-all. Start one at a time, but there's no set order. Each person picks up the first of their plates and throws it as far and as hard as they can, screaming the word written on it. Screaming can be improvised; don't censor yourself!

    Everyone will throw a plate, and everyone else will be yelling encouragement ("Yes!", "Do it!", etc.).

    Keep picking up plates, throwing them, and screaming. By the end, you may not want or need to take turns. In fact, you may not even need plates; the screaming and group energy may carry you along.

Note: You would ideally stand in the south, the direction of Fire, and throw the plates north. However, the most important considerations are the layout of the location you've chosen, and what is safest.

7. After a while, things will die down, and all the plates will have been smashed. Return to your circle and just stand for a moment, catching your breath. After a bit, say:

> *We have freed ourselves. The way to peace is open. So be it.*

8. If you have invoked any deities, thank them now and let them know the work is done.
9. Clean up the broken crockery thoroughly before leaving (that's why you need the broom, dustpan, and garbage bag).

SEX MAGIC

I have read a number of books on sex magic, but my bibliography here includes only two.[37] This is because most of the books I've read are:

- About sex but not about magic
- About magic but not about sex
- Confusing, or icky

(Of course, there may be plenty of wonderful books about sex magic out there, because, as I may have mentioned, I still have not read every book ever written!)

In addition, most of the writing about sex magic, including the excellent writing, is about using either Tantra (Eastern techniques) or Ceremonial Magic (Western techniques) to achieve a higher spiritual state or state of enlightenment. Clearly, this is a fairly demanding goal. It is also, I should point out, not a *Fire* goal. Sex magic is Fire magic because it uses the energies of lust and passion. In this book, we are focusing on using elemental techniques to achieve elemental goals. But enlightenment is not elemental; it is a thing of Spirit—that is, it combines and transcends the four elements and reaches toward the quintessence.

You've doubtless already noticed that the spells in this book are not of the Ceremonial/High Magic sort. My bias in Witchcraft has always been toward the simple, Low Magic sort of spell; I like folk magic, and I like a sort of arts-and-crafts approach. Although I use techniques, systems, and symbols borrowed from Ceremonial Magic (like the Theban and Angelic scripts illustrated in Chapter 6), I am not a Ceremonial Magician (capital *C*, capital *M*—I don't mean that I don't perform ceremonies

---

37 *Ecstasy Through Tantra* by John Mumford and *Modern Sex Magick* by Donald Michael Kraig.

or magic or the two in conjunction), and none of the techniques offered in these pages is beyond the ability of a moderately experienced practitioner or a smart beginner. Thus, my sort of sex magic is within your reach as well and doesn't even require you to go to India to practice it!

In contrast to Tantra or Ceremonial Magic, sex magic, for the more mundane purpose of spellcasting, is a relatively simple affair. Most of the verbiage and most of the complexities of sex-magic instructions arise in preparation and in rituals needed to work toward profound spiritual elevation. Also, complex are the techniques of energy work that enhance both sexual satisfaction and spiritual awareness. Energy work used to achieve sexual satisfaction, nirvana, or other such goals is at a pretty advanced level; it tends to require a deep understanding of how to perceive, move, and (usually) share energy. On the other hand, when raising energy for a spell, this greater level of understanding, while helpful, is not strictly necessary.

What are the basic requirements? Sex magic performed alone requires the ability to achieve orgasm, and some forms of sex magic require a couple to achieve simultaneous orgasm.

The understanding, sensing, and manipulation of energy can allow a nonorgasmic person to achieve orgasm (provided there is no physiological reason for the absence of orgasm). Given the ability to achieve orgasm, energy manipulation can allow a couple to achieve simultaneous orgasm. Lots of people have wonderful, intimate sex lives without simultaneous orgasm but others find that this particular sort of togetherness is exceptionally magical and worth experiencing. Simultaneous orgasm is certainly a convenient way of doing sex magic, as we'll soon see. Energy manipulation of this sort can improve sexual satisfaction in other ways as well. I find, for example, that if one partner is hyped up after sex while the other falls asleep, it is usually due to an imbalance of psychic energies. Energy manipulation can leave the couple more together after sex, rather than in totally disparate states.

Obviously, one can use energy-manipulation skills in many ways that are life-enhancing and enjoyable. However, this is a book on spells, and teaching this sort of energy work is beyond our current scope. The good news is you can work with the abilities you possess now.

The way I see it, there are basically four ways of moving sexual energy in a spell.

Method 1: Raising and Sending Power Alone

Method 1 is for one practitioner to raise the power, focus it, and send it to the target. This is done by masturbation or by one partner being magically passive—participating in the sex, but allowing the other partner to do all the magical work.

This is not substantially different from the basic power-raising techniques described in Chapter 2. This book has presented numerous solitary spells, so the concept of raising power alone and then sending it toward your target should already be quite familiar. In sex magic, you raise power by arousal and use orgasm as the "send" trigger. (Remember, you send just *before* the orgasm so that the energy is sent *through* the orgasm. If you don't start sending until you climax, you can miss your moment.)

When raising power alone you can masturbate, focusing mentally on dedicating your arousal and energy to your magical purpose. It is likely that your mind will move away from magic and toward the erotic in order to become aroused. When you are sufficiently aroused, you'll need to move your mind back to your magical work.

You can also make love with a partner, simply letting them know that you will be dedicating your sexual energy to a magical goal. Your partner should agree to this since it is likely that some of the energy you send will be "siphoned" from your partner (a couple's energies naturally mingle during lovemaking).

Method 2: Raising and Sending Power Together

A couple can raise the power together, focus it together, and send it together. This is usually done with simultaneous orgasm as a single "send" trigger. Again, remember to send just before orgasm. You should have the target in mind before you are fully immersed in orgasm so that you can retain the thought through orgasm.

What if simultaneous orgasm is not something you, as a couple, are able to achieve? You *can* send together without simultaneous orgasm. Each person can simply have an orgasm and then send the power at whatever timing works for them.

Method 3: Raising and Sending in Waves

Another alternative for a couple working together is to maintain magical focus from the first person's orgasm/send (Figure 15) through the second person's orgasm/send. In Chapter 2, we discussed two kinds of power raising: a build-and-peak likened (burst), and a build-and-undulate (wave). A couple can send together without simultaneous orgasm by switching from one to the other. That is, first build and peak toward the orgasm of the first partner. At the peak-and-send, pull some of the power (using visualization and energy management) toward an undulating wave, and send that wave toward the orgasm of the second partner.

As you can see, this method requires a somewhat sophisticated ability to manage energy, and that management has to happen at a moment when many people have a difficult time concentrating!

You can also *both* (or all, in a group-sex situation) send in waves, but for many people, this requires sophisticated training and practice in sex magic and energy control.

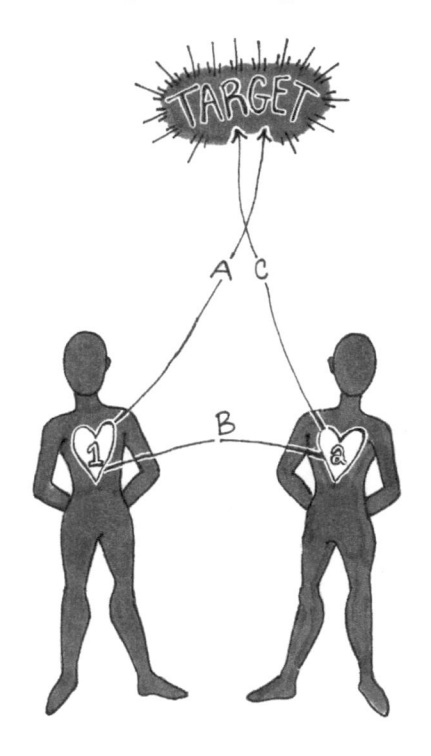

Figure 15: Waves

- *Orgasm 1 divides; it peaks and sends (A) and also undulates (B).*

- *Orgasm 2 then peaks and sends (C).*

- *Note that the energy from (B) helps partner 2 to reach orgasm.*

Method 4: Sex Magic Battery

So, we've seen that power can be raised and sent by one person; power can be raised and sent by two people together, either jointly (simultaneous orgasm) or sequentially (separate orgasms); and power can be raised and sent by one person and then by the other in connected waves.

The final method is to perform sex magic with only one partner needing to reach orgasm (Figure 16). The other partner can climax, but only one climax is sent to the target. In Chapter 2, we talked about the difficulty of visualizing both the target and the goal and of maintaining a sort of bifocal attention. We also illustrated how a group "battery" working can divide up the duties, with the group being in charge of visualizing the goal and sending to the battery, and the battery being in charge of visualizing and sending to the target.

Sex magic provides additional impetus for using a battery technique; you are paying attention not to two things, but to three—not just to the target and the goal, but also to arousal. So, it is quite helpful to divide up the duties.

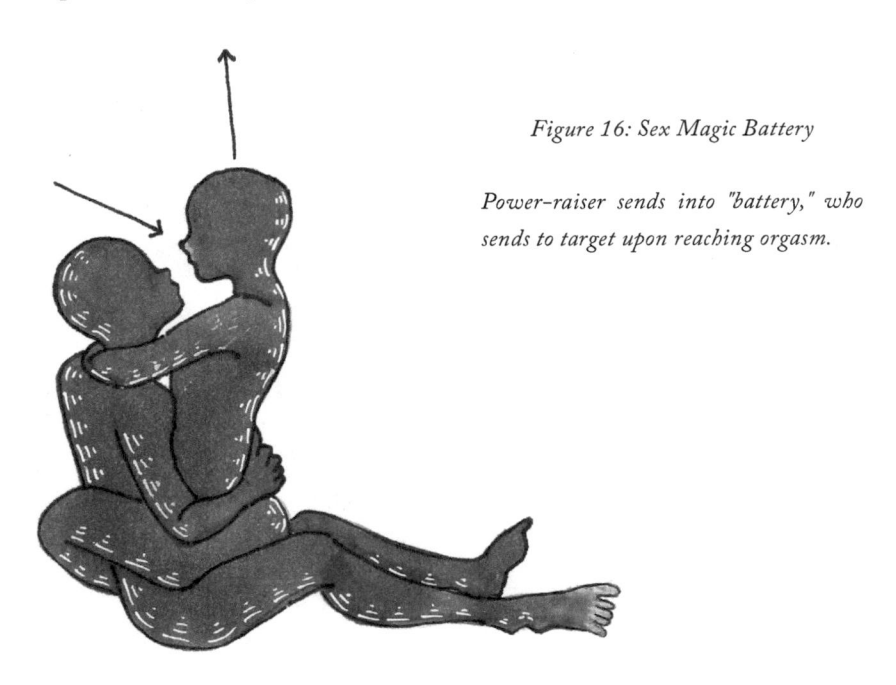

Figure 16: Sex Magic Battery

Power-raiser sends into "battery," who sends to target upon reaching orgasm.

As with the battery working described in Chapter 2 (Figure 5), this form of sex magic assigns raising power and sending power to different people. The person raising the power does so via orgasm. They concentrate strictly on power raising (arousal) and on the goal. When the participants are both ready, the power-raiser sends into the battery, who then sends the power on to the target.

Not only does this avoid some of the difficulties of diffused concentration that can occur in sex magic, but it also works for people who achieve orgasm best through manual or oral stimulation. This method can also work well in a group-sex situation, where multiple partners focus on one person's orgasm and send power jointly.

Suppose Jane and Amelia are a magical and sexual couple. They want to work sex magic. Jane is best able to reach orgasm by receiving cunnilingus. They agree that Amelia will be the power-raiser and Jane will be the battery. Amelia stimulates Jane while focusing on the goal. She visualizes the energy of both her arousal and Jane's moving toward the goal. While performing cunnilingus, she pays attention to Jane's arousal level and is very aware when Jane nears orgasm. (In addition, they can communicate verbally and/or with hand signals about their relative readiness.) Jane, meanwhile, pays attention primarily to her own arousal and to the target. As she becomes more and more excited, she begins to visualize sending her excitement to the target. As she approaches her peak, she signals Amelia. Amelia focuses all her energy into Jane, both physically (helping her reach orgasm) and magically (sending power). Jane focuses all her energy outward, taking her own orgasm and the power that Amelia is sending and sending them toward the target.

A Note about Safer Sex

I have been told that there are so-called sex magicians who will tell a potential partner that the act of sex magic protects them from the normal consequences of sex—that is, that it acts as both disease protection and birth control.[38] I was so angry when I heard this that I didn't know how to write a response or warning here. Shall I say

---

38 Donald Michael Kraig, personal communication.

simply that the gods help those who help themselves and aren't in the business of protecting fools from disease when those fools eschew the methods available to prevent it? Shall I say that many sex-magic practitioners believe that a birthing person is *more* likely to get pregnant when magical energy is present, drawing life force, and hence fertility, to the body?

Nope. I shall simply throw up my hands at the sleaze that some people call magic and at the depths to which some people will sink in order to enjoy the transgressive and repulsive pleasure of manipulating someone into unprotected sex. Even if this nonsense were true, in what way is it respectful or loving to ask someone to break their normal rules about sex? I implore you to always use your usual methods to prevent conception and disease; but more than that, I beg you to reject *anyone* who suggests that *any* form of sex *or* magic should be done in a way that violates your boundaries, standards, concerns, or sensibilities.

To Create a Beacon: A Sex Magic Spell

Goal:
To create a beacon of attraction. A beacon is visualized like a searchlight or a lighthouse. It is visible only to those whom you wish to attract, and to them it is bright and appealing. Beacons are used to attract buyers, tenants, or roommates for your home; members for your coven, grove, or rock and roll band; or any other time that a select group of people should be attracted to your space.

Target:
The beacon is placed on the home, apartment, covenstead, etc., and that is the target. You are creating a thoughtform and placing it in a specific location.

Needed Tools:
- A circle-casting tool (athame, sword, etc.)
- Seven red candles

- Symbols of your specific goal. For example, if you are creating a beacon to attract a coven, put tools of Witchcraft on your altar. If you need a drummer for your band, put drumsticks on your altar.
- Symbols of the four elements for consecration. The incense should be cinnamon and/or frankincense. If you don't use incense as part of your elemental consecrations, include the cinnamon/frankincense anyway.

A Note on Incense: I don't know of any incenses specifically associated with this beacon spell. I have selected Fire incenses with generally attractive, positive, and sexual energies. Feel free to improvise.

OTHER:
- You can perform this spell solitary or in a group, but the instructions are written assuming two participants.
- This beacon spell is one of the first spells I was taught. There are many ways of performing it. I think it is ideal for sex magic because the energies of attraction are already a part of sexual activity.
- Any kind of sex magic can be used. You can be alone, part of a couple, or in a group. You can work jointly or in a battery style. Decide in advance what you're doing. If you're a couple (or triad or more), you should agree to this jointly before you begin.
- You should also choose in advance how you will communicate with one another at crucial points in the ritual. You will need some sort of signal for "Now!" when you're sending, and probably some sort of build-up phrase to indicate that sending (orgasm) is about to happen. It could be as easy as *come to us…come to us…come to us…Now!* Some couples prefer to be entirely nonverbal and are so attuned to one another that they don't need a verbal signal to indicate approaching orgasm, but again, you should agree to this in advance.

- Casting a circle about the bed (or wherever the sex will happen) isn't strictly necessary, but it is a powerful way of focusing the mind and will on your purpose—of letting yourself (yourselves) know that this is sex *magic* rather than sex.
- Move your altar next to the bed (or wherever the sex will happen) or set up a special table to be this rite's altar.
- It is very important to have any external protection that you use (condoms, etc.) on the altar before you cast your circle. This is so that you don't have to leave your magical space, and also so that you don't introduce something disconnected from the energy you are creating. People often complain that protection breaks the mood in mundane sex. In sex magic, any subconscious thoughts you have along those lines can be exacerbated. Having the birth control/protection on the altar and included in the consecrations will transform it from an interruption into part of the magic. The same is true for any enhancement devices you use (such as a vibrator).

APPROPRIATE DEITIES:
You can invoke deities of lust, such as Kama, Eros, or Inanna; or you can invoke deities specific to your purpose, such as Hecate to form a coven or Orpheus to attract musicians; or you can invoke deities of general beneficence and good will, such as Isis or the Dagda. If you are working as a couple, you might choose to invoke a pair of deities who are themselves a couple, particularly if there is sexual mythology or folklore associated with them, such as Shiva and Parvati.

THE SPELL:
1. Ground, center, and merge.
2. If you are using quarter-candles, light them now.

NOTE: In Wicca, the circle is cast before the gods are invoked. If you are not Wiccan and wish to perform your invocation first, reorder the steps to suit the system you're most comfortable with.

3. Pick up your circle-casting tool. If possible, you can both place your hands upon the tool. Otherwise, one person holds the tool, and the couple will join hands. Prior to casting the circle, visualize exactly where the space will be. Some people mark the circle on the floor with chalk or cord or by putting candles at the quarters. If you are using your bedroom and your bed, this might not be practical. But even if you can't walk all the way around your bed or place a candle at each quarter, you can know where each quarter is, and visualize a round space surrounding the bed (Figure 16). If, for example, the head of your bed is against a north wall and there's no room to pull the bed out from the wall, you can imagine the circle going around that section of the bed. When I have to cast a circle in a tight space, I simply lift up my athame and cast vertically, as if the circle was drawn on paper, and part of the paper was folded up (Figure 17). That way I can continue to visualize a circular shape even when pressed flat against a confining wall.

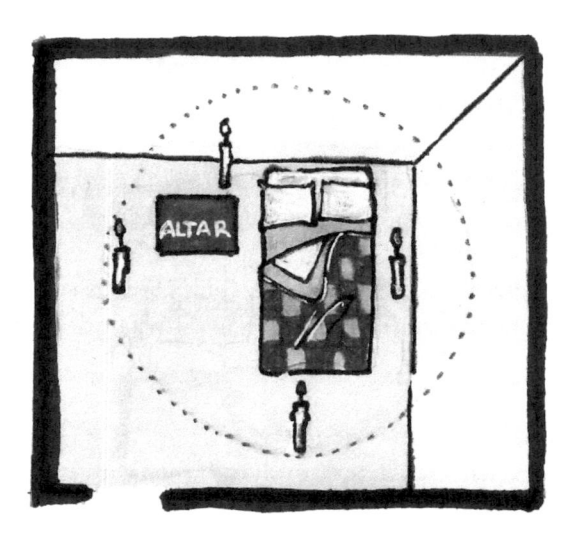

Figure 16: Casting a Circle around the Bed (above)

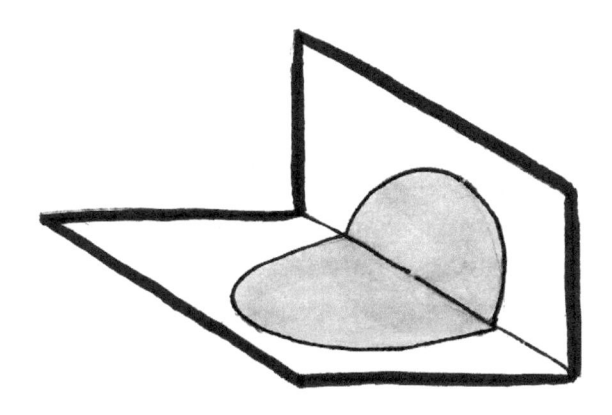

Figure 17: Including a wall in the circle

Visualizing the circle and standing inside it, begin casting clockwise from the east and ending in the east by walking or standing and turning around. See bright white or clear blue light emitting from your ritual tool and forming a sealed and sacred magical space about you.

One person says:

This is a place of love and magic.

By my (or our) Will, and in the names of (partner 1) and (partner 2), do we consecrate this circle and dedicate it to our work, the work of the Beacon Spell. Be consecrated, O circle, to contain and enhance the magic we shall make within you. Be a boundary and an amplifier and make our magic strong.

So mote it be!

4. Light the red candles on the altar. You can each light three and light the seventh together.
5. Using your chosen tool (athame, wand, etc.), draw an invoking Fire pentagram over the entire altar (see appendix D).

One person says:

This is a place of love and magic.

By my (or our) Will, and in the names of (partner 1) and (partner 2), do we consecrate this altar and everything it contains and dedicate it to our work, the work of the beacon spell.

So mote it be!

6. If you're performing an invocation, do so here.
7. Now you will begin sexual activity. This can be any sexual activity that is suitable and leads to orgasm for the one, two, or more people participating. You have decided in advance if you are using a solitary, joined, wave, or battery style for raising and sending power. You have decided in advance what signals you will use to indicate the phases of the power-raising. To begin with, don't worry about the spell at all. You've cast a circle and consecrated an altar; let that be the magical part for the moment and focus on the erotic. Do whatever works to stimulate and excite each other.
8. At a high point of excitement, shift your consciousness back to the purpose of the spell. (You may have a verbal or other signal for this shift.) Visualize the beacon, bright and shining atop the location you've chosen (home, rehearsal space, covenstead, etc.). Visualize wonderful, appropriate people being drawn to it. Visualize the beacon being built from the power of your excitement and sexual energy.

If you are using a battery method, the power-raiser can visualize long-term results: that is, the people being drawn to the beacon, the ultimate happy group, a rented apartment, etc. Meanwhile, the battery visualizes the beacon itself.

Remember to begin sending just before you reach orgasm so that the clear visualization and energetic sending will happen during and through orgasm.

After sex is completed, you will wish to rest for a while. Although I don't normally fall asleep after sex, it happens to

me often after sex magic, perhaps because I send so much energy. However, do not neglect the following steps.
9. Thank the deities you have invoked and let them know the work is over.
10. Allow the altar candles to burn out completely. Afterward (probably the next day, depending upon the type of candles used), you can, if you choose, deconsecrate the altar with a banishing Fire pentagram (see appendix D).
11. Open the circle by using the same tool, again going clockwise, east to east, and saying:

This place of love and magic is opened, and its energies can return to the earth. So mote it be.

NOTE: Some Wiccans open a circle widdershins, but I don't wish to unwind or dismantle the circle, simply to end it and allow it to dissipate.

Chapter 8

Using Water in Spells

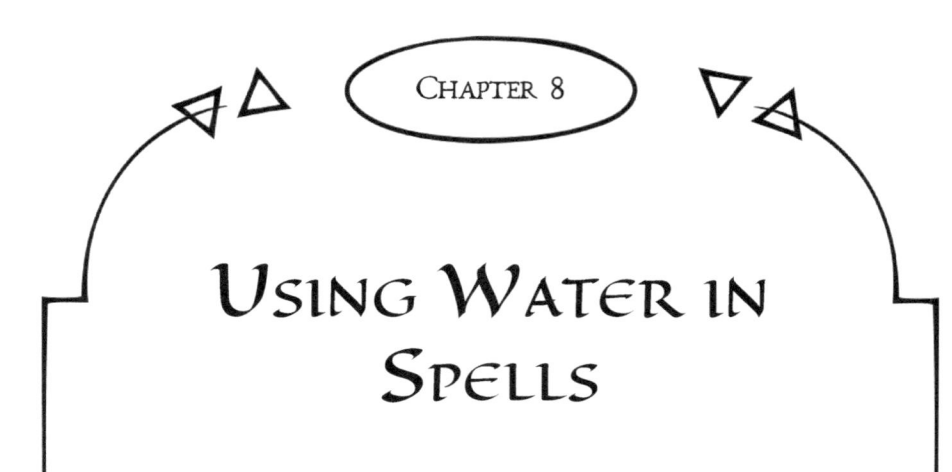

In Chapter 5, we identified the following purposes for Water spells:

- To bring dreams
- To soothe and calm
- To ease pain
- To bring romance (both to bring new love and to bring romance into an existing relationship)
- To increase psychic powers and improve intuition
- To make a decision using intuition (inner Water rather than inner Fire)
- To increase "flow"
- To make childbirth easier and improve lactation
- To heal blood and lymphatic disorders
- To address past-life issues
- For privacy or secrecy

USING WATER

How would we bring Water into a spell? As with the other elements, there are three basic methods: (1) directly, (2) through magical tools associated with the elements, or (3) symbolically through qualities of the elements.

To use Water directly, we could:

- Wash someone or something with water
- Soak someone or something in water
- Sprinkle someone or something with water
- Paint/write on someone or something with water
- Drink as part of a spell

To use Water tools, we could:

- Use the cup
- Use the cauldron (some people assign the cauldron to Fire, and some to Water)
- Use a mirror to represent the reflective quality of water

To use symbolic qualities of Water, we could:

- Do spells involving dreams
- Do spells involving divination or scrying
- Do spells that involve moonlight, such as capturing reflected moonlight

WASHING, SOAKING, SPRINKLING

The techniques of washing, soaking, and sprinkling are all used for some level of cleansing, purification, or exorcism. They differ mostly in technique, for practical as well as magical reasons.

Soaking is the most intense method, as an object can be left overnight or even longer in a container of water. Other influences are sometimes added—saltwater might be used for the added purification of salt and/or the influence of Earth. The container might be left in direct sunlight or moonlight; in general, the sunlight would be for purification and exorcism, and the moonlight for the blessings of the Goddess or the restoration of Water's purity (i.e., moonlight would make the water more Watery, less diluted by other elements).

An object is generally soaked to remove strong psychic influences from it. These may be negative influences, or they may be benign but not consistent with the object's purpose. For example, if you are to be married with an antique wedding ring, prior to blessing it, you may wish to leave it in a dish of purified water under the full moon to release it from the energies of past relationships. These may have been good relationships or bad, or the ring may have come to you without information about its history; the point is, you are starting your marriage fresh and wish to leave past influences behind.

Soaks are used to break a psychic connection that is part of an object. For example, if a person gives their lover a piece of jewelry and then the couple breaks up, it is often the case that the person with the piece of jewelry finds themselves unable to wear it. A spell involving soaking would help remove the psychic influences that linger on the item.[39]

Another sort of soak is that which uses water to soak up psychic influences or noncorporeal entities. In this case, you definitely *wouldn't* add salt to the water because salt would remove something you're trying to contain. What you're doing is using water to catch a negative psychic influence and then disposing of the water.

The technique is to charge dishes of water and then leave them overnight near the openings (doors, windows, vents, faucets) of a room that has the problem. If you had a problem with undines in the house (as evidenced by both physical and symbolic water—both floods and drips *and* depression and tears), this would be a benign way to remove them. They'd go into the blessed water and then you'd take the water and dispose of it in a stream, river, or other body of moving water. If you were disposing of negative psychic influences—an oppressive atmosphere you suspect has psychic causes—you'd do less of a blessing and more of a charging up, changing the words to be more forceful.

A magical washing is really a rinsing; it involves no soap—the object is dipped in water and turned over as needed to make sure that water touches all parts of it. Washing might be used when the psychic influence is less intense and therefore easier to remove, or it might be used on an object that would be damaged by soaking.

---

[39] A spell such as that sometimes fails because memories, thoughts, and dreams, not to mention actually seeing each other, can re-establish the psychic connection as fast as you can break it.

You would also wash an object if you needed to use it in a hurry and couldn't wait twenty-four hours for a soak. It might be used instead of a soak to take advantage of the psychological impact of washing; after all, we've all washed a few thousand times in life and have always known it to be cleansing, so it has powerful conditioning associated with it!

Washing uses less water than soaking, and sprinkling uses less than washing. Sprinkling is most appropriate when a small, symbolic amount of Water is needed as an addendum to a larger working. Water is often introduced into a spell by sprinkling when performing a spell that is balanced in all four elements. It is also used to introduce a magical infusion to a working, such as the infusion in Chapter 6 that was made to create invisible ink. The technique can be very simple or more elaborate. Most people will simply dip their fingertips into a dish of consecrated water and flick the drops over whatever is being sprinkled. Some people use a tool called an *aspergillum*, which is dipped into the water for this purpose. An aspergillum is often a handle designed to hold the fresh herbs or leaves that are dipped and used for sprinkling.

Instead of sprinkling, one sometimes anoints with water, wetting the fingers and then touching a person or object at specific spots. The third eye is frequently anointed in this way.

To Cleanse an Object of Negativity: A Soaking Spell

Goal:
To remove negative energy from an object. Perhaps you acquired something secondhand that you now wish to use as a magical tool. You sense an aura about the item. Your goal is to purify the object and remove the aura so that you can work with the item magically. In the case of a magical tool, this would normally precede an actual consecration. In the case of an ordinary object, such as a piece of mundane jewelry, the soaking spell is all that is needed.

Target:
The object to be cleansed.

Needed Tools:
- A dish or container of water large enough to submerge the object completely. You should use either clear glass or, preferably, an open-topped container (like a bowl) so that the sunlight will penetrate it.
- The object to be cleansed
- Your athame or another power-directing tool
- A location where you can leave the item undisturbed for a night and a day, meaning no neighborhood kids picking it up, no cats knocking it over, etc. Finding a good location may be your first order of business!

Other:
- The owner(s) of the object should do the spell. If it is an individual's magical tool, the spell should be done solitary. If it is a coven tool (such as a sword), the coven should do it jointly. If it is something like an engagement ring, the couple should do it together.
- You can do the spell with the dish already in the location you've selected or do it at your altar and carry the dish, with the object in it, to the desired spot.
- Perform this spell at twilight during a big moon. The moonlight should be bright enough to be visible, so the moon should be bigger than half, but it doesn't matter if it's full, waxing, or waning. A waxing moon will use the energy of increase to add to the purity and blessings for the object; a full moon will use the pure light of the Goddess to that end; and a waning moon will use the energy of decrease to remove impurities.

Appropriate Deities:
If you have a patron deity, invoke them. Or use a deity connected to the meaning of the object (for example, a deity who rules marriage for an engagement ring). Otherwise, use a deity of purity and goodness, such as Tara, Kwan Yin, Lakshmi, the Dagda, or Baldar.

The Spell:
1. Ground and center.
2. If you're performing an invocation, do so here.
3. Pointing your athame at the water, say:

> *Be purified, O Water, (in the name of deity)!*
> [Put the athame in the water.]
> *So mote it be!*

Note: Always be sure to wipe off your athame after getting it wet. After the ritual is over, you should oil it as well.

4. Hold the object above the water, and say:

> *Be purified, O (name of object), by the cleansing power of Water (and in the name of deity).*
> [Put the object in the water.]
> *So mote it be!*

5. If you have invoked any deities, thank them now.
6. Leave the object exposed to moonlight all night and exposed to sunlight all the following day.
7. The next twilight, after the object has soaked for twenty-four hours, take it out and dry it.
8. Present the cleansed object to the directions as follows: Face east, hold the object up, and say:

> *East, see this (name of object) that is now pure!*

Repeat for west, south, and north. Then return to the east and hold the object up in silence.

9. If you have invoked a deity for this spell, finish by presenting the object to the deity while standing in the center. Thank the deity and let them know the work is completed.

To Drive Away Bad Dreams: A Bathing Spell

Goal:
This spell is to drive away bad dreams if they have been bothering you. Slight modification can make this a spell to relieve waking anxiety instead.

Target:
Yourself; your dreams, your subconscious mind.

Needed Tools:
- A bath, drawn to a pleasantly hot temperature
- Fresh hyacinth flowers
- A pink or white candle
- Frankincense and myrrh incense

Note: If you have a stall shower and no bathtub, you can modify the spell by using a basin of water. Step into the shower but don't turn it on, rinsing yourself from the basin in steps 5–7. Then turn on the shower and pour the remaining basin water over yourself.

Other:
- Obviously, this is a solitary spell. Even if you have a partner with whom you like to share a bath, dreams and nightmares are fundamentally private matters.
- Since you'll be getting into the bath, you'll perform the spell skyclad (nude).
- Note that this spell takes advantage of the mundane effects of a hot bath. Even without magic, a hot bath relaxes the body and soothes the emotions and can therefore affect the subconscious. Never hold back from using mundane aids in a spell because they're not "magical." They certainly *were* considered magical before someone thought of a proper physiological explanation!
- In that vein, lighting a candle and having fresh flowers in the bathroom do more than impart magical qualities; they

beautify the atmosphere and soothe the mind, which helps to reach the part of you that is having nightmares.
- This spell is designed to ease nightmares caused by anxiety and general negativity, as well as to protect the sleep from psychic invasion. Sometimes, though, nightmares have something important to tell us. Like process servers, they don't go away until you receive the message. If this is the case, you will have to work *with* the dream, not to drive it away but to understand it.

Appropriate Deities:
Nuit, Morpheus, Rhiannon, Dream of the Endless.[40]

The Spell:
1. Prepare the bathroom. First, make sure it is clean and appealing. Then draw the bath. Set up the flowers, and inhale deeply of their scent. Light the candles and incense, again inhaling the scent. Notice how you feel soothed, protected, and at peace. Fill yourself with the pleasure of beauty and a sense of peace.
2. You will probably find that this sense of peace has already begun to lead you toward a grounded, centered state. Go ahead and finish that process now with a grounding and centering.
3. If you're performing an invocation, do so now.
4. Stand facing the bath. The candle, incense, and flowers should be in sight. Open your arms in a gesture that includes the whole scene, and say:

This is a place of purity and peace.
By the powers of Water (and in the name of deity),
I consecrate this place that its purpose be pure and true.
So mote it be.

---

[40] My use of a fictional "deity" is somewhat influenced by having met Taylor Ellwood, author of *Pop Culture Magick*.

5. Step into the tub. Lower yourself into the water and get comfortable.
6. Visualize the bath water sparkling with a pure and gentle light. Allow that light to touch you as the water touches your skin. Take water in your cupped hands and touch yourself all over with it, visualizing the lovely protective light clinging to your skin.

Say:

Pure Water brings peace of mind.
Water of dreams, bring peace to my dreams.
Water of hidden depths, soothe and protect my nightly journeys.
Water, protect me in the night.
Water, bring me dreams of sweetness.
Water, cleanse and purify my dreaming.
So mote it be.

7. Dunk under the water, submerging yourself completely. Visualize the light of protection and good dreams clinging tenaciously to your skin—it will not wash off.
8. Enjoy the rest of your bath. Before draining the water, thank it and release it on its journey.
9. If you have invoked any deities, thank them now and let them know the work is done.

PAINTING WITH WATER

In Chapter 6, we created invisible ink for a justice spell. We could almost say that we used water as a tool of Air since ink and writing are connected with Air. But, although writing is an Air activity, the use of "invisible ink" is worth revisiting in our chapter on Water spells. It is a powerful way of secretly adding Water's influence as well as almost any other influence you can think of. Both Air and Water are transparent; you can see through them. Invisibility is usually associated with Air, but secrecy is associated with Water because secrets hide in depths. (And just to complicate things, some people associate secrets and secrecy with Earth: buried treasure, for example, is a secret held in Earth.)

I like invisible writing because it strikes me as being connected to the roots of
Witchcraft, a discreet and sometimes covert art. Today, Witchcraft is stepping out from the shadows, but most of us who practice it feel a strong connection to our predecessors, and most of us understand that *To Remain Silent* is still a vital part of the Witches' Pyramid.

Invisible writing is also imaginative. Any word, phrase, symbol, picture, or idea can be painted with water. As long as we have an emotional reaction to the symbol used, the spell can work.

To Keep Something Hidden: An Invisibility Spell

Goal:
To keep prying eyes away from something hidden. This spell will not impart literal invisibility, but it will make the "invisible" item uninteresting to those who shouldn't look at it; it will be below the radar for eyes other than your own.

Target:
Whatever it is you are painting on. Sometimes Witches and Pagans who are still "in the broom closet" struggle with how to keep their magical gear discreetly hidden. This spell could be used as a "lock" on a box where such gear is kept, on a book cover, etc.

Needed Tools:
- A clear jar with a tight lid, labeled "Invisibility" or "Sealing" or some such name
- Water in a pitcher or ewer
- Keys and/or locks. You can use old keys from your key ring, or the cheap little keys or locks that come with diaries, skates, luggage locks, or anything like that. Don't use car keys, which *start* things rather than *close* things.
- A shattered mirror. I keep small mirrors around for use in spells; they often come in handy. You can buy small mirrors (one or two inches in diameter) in craft stores, you can remove them from makeup containers, or you can get cheap

The Magic of the Elements

hand mirrors for this purpose. The safe, easy way to break a mirror is to wrap it in a towel and use a hammer.
- A stick or twig of bamboo or birch. A chopstick can be used.

OTHER:
- This spell can be performed solitary or in a group. A working group doing the spell jointly would meet twice. The first time, each person would contribute something to the water jar (see the spell), and one person would be in charge of the jar until the next meeting. The second time, each person would bring their magical things to the meeting, the spell of invisibility would be performed jointly, and then you all would take your things back home.
- Perform this spell during a waning moon.
- In other spells in this book, we use runes, Theban, astrological symbols, and the like. This time, try something more creative and modern. Despite what I said earlier about connecting with our predecessors, there is nothing wrong with connecting with the twenty-first century as well. Figure 19 shows traffic signs that mean "No" "Stop," and "Do Not Enter." All of these symbols are easy to draw and will convey the meaning you need.

Figure 19: Traffic Signs

- A bind rune is a rune that combines two or more runes into a unique shape. Figure 20 shows an example.

Os   Beorc

Figure 20: Bind Rune

Using Water in Spells

- Bind runes are used often in Norse magic, but the concept can be applied to modern symbols. For example, you could combine the "No" symbol with the word "No" by simply writing one over the other, as follows:

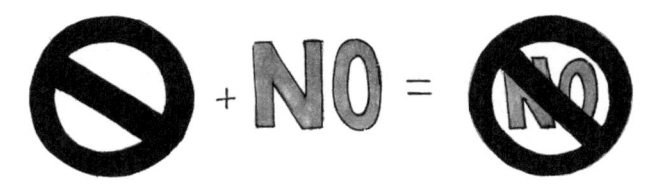

Figure 21: A "No" Rune

- But you could get more creative, designing your own unique symbol:

Figure 22: A Unique "No" Rune

The possibilities are endless.

Appropriate Deities:
You might choose a deity related to the object(s) being hidden; for example, if you're hiding a book, invoke Thoth. Otherwise, I'm inclined to use a deity of Witchcraft or magic, such as Hecate or Isis, or a blind god such as Hod. Treasure-keeper and secrecy deities tend to be those who are considered dangerous to invoke, such as Pluto, and I wouldn't advise it.

The Spell:
1. Ground, center, and merge (if working as a group).
2. If you're performing an invocation, do so here.
3. Pick up a shard of mirror, and say:

   Reflecting back. Reflecting back.

Put the shard in the jar.

4. If you are working in a group, pass the jar around widdershins. Each of you picks up a shard and repeats this phrase, putting the shard in the jar. If you are working alone, repeat the same phrase for each shard you put in.
5. After all the shards have been added, say:

   Reflecting back, it cannot be seen.
   The eye that looks sees only itself.
   So mote it be.

6. Now put a key or lock in the jar, and say:

   Lock and key. Sealed and safe.

7. As in Step 4, pass the jar and repeat the phrase in a group, or repeat the phrase for several items if working alone.
8. After all the keys and locks have been added, say:

   Lock and key. Sealed and safe.
   No one gains entry who is unwelcome.
   So mote it be.

9. Fill the jar with water from the pitcher and put the lid on tightly. Raise power and send it into the jar.
10. If you've performed an invocation, offer thanks now.
11. Place the jar in the moonlight. Leave it exposed to moonlight every night until the dark of the moon. You can leave it out in the sunlight or bring it in during the day. It doesn't matter; your focus is on moonlight.
12. The next ritual should take place at the dark of the moon. Have the jar of water, the bamboo stick, and the object(s) you will make "invisible."
13. For this ritual, ground and center (and merge, if in a group).
14. If you performed an invocation at the time you set up the jar, use the same invocation now.
15. You'll be using the stick as a writing implement (both birch and bamboo have protective qualities). You can keep it as

a magical tool with your ink pen. Consecrate it by the four elements as described in Chapter 3.
16. Open the jar and dip the stick in, using the water as ink and the stick as a pen. Having decided on the symbol you will use, paint the symbol on the front of the object (or the first object), saying:

> *Reflecting back. Sealed and safe.*

Repeat this phrase as often as necessary until you finish writing. If working in a group, pass the water and pen around widdershins. Each person makes the symbol on their own object (in a group, you each should do only one object, or at most two objects). The act of repeating the phrase over and over raises the power. If working in a group, everyone should say the phrase together, keeping the power going while each person writes.
17. Say:

> *Reflecting back. Sealed and safe.*
> *The eye that looks sees only itself.*
> *No one gains entry who is unwelcome.*
> *So mote it be.*

18. If you've invoked any deities, thank them now and let them know the work is done.

DRINKING AND THE CUP

The cup as a magical tool is a perfect example of how a concrete thing becomes an abstract idea and of how the two remain connected.

Water is water. Water also symbolizes Water. By that I mean, the physical *stuff* water is used magically to symbolize the pure and abstract *qualities* of Water. As we discussed in Chapter 1, the four elements are abstractions and ideals; in the real world, water has components of Air, Fire, and Earth as well as Water. You know this as you drink water from the tap and taste a mineral flavor—that's Earth.

Since water is Water, then the act of drinking water is also Water. This gets more nuanced when looking at different kinds of drinks—most alcohol is, in fact, associated with Fire, and beverages like milk are associated with Earth. But brews made with water—teas, infusions, and broths—are magically connected to Water, and the idea of putting liquid into your body is a Water idea. From here we can magically associate the physical act of drinking with the symbolic act of taking Water in.

Finally, this brings us to the tool of Water: the cup. If the act of drinking is Water, then the tool used in drinking must be Water. This is how magical thinking travels from the real (liquid) to the abstract (a tool). Along the same sort of path, we can move from drinking as a means of quenching thirst (taking in physical water) to drinking as a means of bringing Water qualities into a person and/or achieving magical goals related to Water.

Magical Brews

In a sense, there are two kinds of magical brews: those that take advantage of the mundane properties of the brew, and those that work strictly on nonphysical levels. The spell "To Drive Away Bad Dreams" earlier in this chapter uses the former sort of brew, taking advantage of qualities that hyacinth has, whether or not a spell is worked. (If you add essential oil to a bath, you could loosely call it a "brew," as it mixes water with other ingredients. If you use fresh flowers next to the bath, you are using aromatherapy, but not a brew.) The spell "To Keep Something Hidden" (also earlier in this chapter) uses the latter sort of brew. Without a spell, using keys and mirrors in the way prescribed would not work to keep anything hidden.

When making a tea or infusion to be ingested, you normally use ingredients that would be good for you anyway. It's a good idea magically to treat your body well. Setting physical health at odds with magical purposes creates a dissonant energy, a conflict that is good for neither health nor magic. Sometimes an ingredient is added that really isn't meant for swallowing. For example, a human hair is often added to a brew in spells you'll find in books of old folklore or medieval magic. Here you would ingest the magical energy of the person, but presumably, the hair itself would remain on the bottom of the mug with the tea leaves.

Don't think that using "real" treatments in a spell isn't magical! Many "real" treatments, such as the use of willow bark to relieve pain or foxglove for heart conditions, were first learned from magic.[41] Both of these folk remedies are now mainstream medicines: aspirin and digitalis, respectively. There is nothing even wrong with saying a spell over some aspirin before taking them. Aspirin usually works on its own but if you have any reason to think your body might not respond or if you want to add qualities, go for it. For example, a parent might recite a spell of comfort over baby aspirin before giving it to a sick child.

Raspberry leaf tea is a well-known treatment for a variety of uterine issues. It is used to improve uterine tone during pregnancy, to relieve menstrual cramps, and to ease the symptoms of menopause. Raspberry is also associated with Water, as are menstruation and childbirth. The following spell uses an ordinary brew of raspberry leaf tea and adds magical energy. Modify the words and visualization as needed for any issue related to the uterus or use the idea of this spell and create your own to accompany another healing tea.

TO IMPROVE HEALTH DURING PREGNANCY: A MAGICAL TEA

GOAL:
To improve uterine tone and generally ease pregnancy and childbirth. During pregnancy, you'll be doing many things to improve your health; this is just one of them.

TARGET:
Your uterus (womb).

NEEDED TOOLS:
- Fresh or dried raspberry leaves
- A power-directing tool of your choice

---

[41] Precisely because foxglove affects the heart, it is dangerous to ingest. Don't do it!

OTHER:
- A normal dosage would be 2–3 cups a day. This dosage is usual for all treatments (pregnancy, menstrual cramps, menopause). When I was pregnant, I made the tea in two-liter batches, kept it in the refrigerator, and heated a cup at a time.
- This spell is most convenient to do solitary, as you will repeat it often. A group of magically-inclined pregnant people could make a batch together, but you'll still have times when you'll be making a fresh batch alone.

APPROPRIATE DEITIES:
Artemis, Eileithyia, Juno, Hathor, Ermutu, Bhavani.

NOTE: In both the Greek and Egyptian pantheons, there is a well-known goddess associated with childbirth (Artemis, Hathor) and a specific midwife/childbirth goddess/aspect who is lesser known (Eileithyia, Ermutu).

THE SPELL:
1. Prepare the tea as follows:
   Boil water and pour it over the raspberry leaves, about a tablespoon of leaves per cup of water. Let steep for 15 minutes.
2. Ground and center.
3. If you're performing an invocation, do so here.
4. Gather power within yourself. Send power into the container of tea using your hands or a tool while saying:

Healthy womb, happy birth,
By Air and Fire and Water and Earth.

Repeat as often as you feel is appropriate, until you feel the power has been fully sent into the cup. Say:

So mote it be!

NOTE: Modify these words to create a spell for easing menstrual cramps or for other needs.

5. If you've invoked any deities, thank them now, and let them know the work is done.
6. Drink some tea right away to seal the spell.

Finding Love: A Cup Spell

Goal:
To find a loving relationship. This spell is not to attract a particular person, but to bring a person as yet unknown into your life.

Target:
The target is yourself; specifically, your heart—your emotional heart, not your cardiac muscle. This spell places an attractant around the heart. For most people, the best visualization is of a pink-white light surrounding your heart, drawing your beloved inexorably toward you. However, if you prefer, you may imagine a sweet sound or a delightful aroma, irresistible to your beloved but undetectable to others.

Needed Tools:
- A piece of rose quartz or a rose-quartz bead
- Your ritual cup
- May wine or other strawberry-flavored wine (wine is preferable, but if you don't drink alcohol, a strawberry-flavored beverage will do)
- Your athame or other power-directing tool of your choice
- Pink or red flowers
- Representatives of the four elements (a dish of water, a dish of salt, incense, and a candle). You will consecrate the stone by the four elements and use the wine and cup for the additional Water influence.
- A sweet incense. There is a vast array of herbs and flowers associated with love. The following are some that have Water as their element, Venus as their planet, *and* a folkloric association with love or love magic: apple blossom, freesia, geranium, thyme, and violet.

OTHER:
- This spell should be done alone, under a waxing moon.
- You should be skyclad (nude).
- Friday is the traditional day for love spells.
- If you are planning on using a bead rather than a stone, have a string or chain for it. If the string isn't waterproof, put the bead on it after the spell is completed.
- Candles, if you use them, should be pink.
- It is always best if the bottle of wine to be used is uncorked before the ritual begins so that you can pour without any awkward pause for the corkscrew.

APPROPRIATE DEITIES:
Aphrodite, Freya, Lakshmi, Oshun.

THE SPELL:
1. For love spells, it is important that the altar/spell area be beautiful and pleasant in every way. Arrange the flowers around the goblet, get the incense going nicely, and set up everything so that it is appealing to you.
2. If you're performing an invocation, do so now.
3. Visualizing your target, consecrate the rose quartz as follows. Pass the stone through the incense smoke, saying:

    By Air may my love begin.

    Pass the stone through the candle flame, saying:

    By Fire may my love be passionate.

    Dip the stone in the water dish, saying:

    By Water may my love be deep.

    Roll the stone in the salt dish, saying:

    By Earth may my love be firm.

You can moisten your finger in the water to wipe off any excess salt from the stone so that your wine won't taste salty.
4. Continue your visualization. Place the rose quartz in your ritual cup. Fill the cup with wine.

   Plunge your athame into the cup, saying:

   I consecrate this wine to love!

   Lay your athame aside (wipe the blade—wine left on the blade will damage it).
5. Still visualizing as strongly as possible, dip your finger in the wine and make a love rune (Figure 23) or the sign of Venus (Figure 24) over your heart, while saying:

   I make my heart a place where love will come.

   Figure 23: Beorc (The Birch), Brings Love or Fertility

   Figure 24: Venus Symbol

6. Say:

   I bring love into me, love is in me,
   Love will come to me, love belongs to me.

7. Drink down the entire cup. Say:

   So mote it be!

8. If you've invoked any deities, thank them now.
9. Carry the rose quartz with you at all times (this is why a strung bead comes in handy). Sleep with it as well.

DREAM MAGIC

Dream magic refers to one of three things: Either lucid dreaming or dream induction can be used to achieve magical goals, or both can be used in combination. The third form of dream magic is sending a dream to another person.

Lucid dreaming is an ability in which you become conscious and aware that you are dreaming while still asleep and remaining in the dream. Some folks have a spontaneous ability to lucid dream while others work to develop it. Lucid dreamers develop, with practice, the ability to control and change their dreams while in them. Dream induction is the act of predetermining what you will dream. You can induce either the content or the result of your dream, or both. If you decide that "tonight I will dream about the airport," this would be *content*. Or, if you decide that, "tonight I will discover the solution to my dilemma," that would be the *result;* the solution might be in the airport, or the schoolyard, or you might even wake up and not remember what you dreamt at all but have the solution in your head.

When I added this section to the initial outline of this book, it was with no small amount of concern. I had induced dreams successfully, but not recently, except in a nonliteral sense (see the section below, "The Psychological Power of Dreams"), and I had never experienced a fully lucid dream. So, I set out on a program of study.

I read books, I did prescribed exercises, and I sought the advice of skilled, experienced magicians. I experimented with a wide range of techniques recommended by these various people. I began this process when I began to write the book and got earnest about it when I finished the Air chapter (I tend to write in order). Still unsuccessful, I skipped my dream-magic section and continued to do dream exercises until the rest of the book was finished. The whole time period I'm talking about was approximately one year.

I still have not succeeded. I come away from this work knowing a lot more about dreams and dream magic than when I began, but I have not "field-tested" the dream spell I offer here. The writing in this section reflects my research much more than my experience.

I've given the fate of this section a lot of thought. It really belongs in this book; I didn't want to take the easy way out and just chop it from the outline. I believe my information is valid and that it's useful to gather it here. Many people, perhaps most, find that dream induction and lucid dreaming come quite easily to them. Certain factors work against me. First, I don't sleep well and haven't for many years. As a result, I've developed sleep habits specifically advised against by the experts. Second, my daughter gets up much earlier than I do, so my last hour of sleep each morning (considered the ripest and most productive time by dream experts) is always disrupted by various noises. Finally, there's the book. The flowing, Watery world of dreams doesn't respond well to the Fiery, demanding, will-imposing world of a book outline and the compulsion to finish it up, already![42]

At this point, I invite you, the reader, to say, "Hey, she doesn't know what she's talking about!" and skip to the next section, "Divination Magic" (an area in which I have had considerable success). If, however, you decide to continue reading, I intend to make it worth your while!

Increasing Your Dream Awareness

Before using dreams as part of your spellwork, you need to increase your awareness and control over your ordinary dreams. Every source (and there are many) will tell you to begin by writing down your dreams immediately upon awakening (this I'm good at). One of the best pieces of advice I read[43] was to change your morning alarm from noise, talk radio, or anything loud or jarring to classical music (actually, I use light jazz). When you wake up gently, you are more likely to remember your dreams.

The trick to remembering your dreams is to ask yourself what you dreamt the moment you awaken. What works against you is that you might start thinking about your day; deciding if your armpits need to be shaved, reminding yourself of an appointment, remembering a tiff with your partner. What works very well is to let go of such thoughts as soon as you realize you're thinking them and

---

[42] Note for the new edition: A dozen years after originally writing the above, I sleep well. My daughter no longer lives at home. I've had some minor success with lucid dreaming, and considerably more success with dream induction. Lucid dreaming remains an elusive art for me, and my dream expertise remains mostly in the area of book-learning.

[43] In *Lucid Dreams in 30 Days*.

ask yourself, "What did I dream?" Sometimes you think the answer is "nothing" or "I don't remember." In that case, ask yourself what images are in your head, what you are seeing, feeling, etc. Ask yourself: "What was I just doing? What did I just see?" Often by asking that question, I find that a whole dream floods back when the moment before I'd thought, "I don't remember any dreams."

In addition to writing down your dreams, increase your awareness of the different states of consciousness. Several times a day, ask yourself if you're awake or dreaming. Look around carefully; sometimes I notice that there are dreamlike things going on during my waking hours that *could* be a dream. Once, when doing a dream-state experiment, I discovered a stream behind a building I visit often. I had no idea the stream was there. Seeing it, I felt the sensation of "changing scenes" that is so common in dreams. This was as far as my success took me, but I found these experiments valuable; I greatly expanded my conscious awareness of the difference between dream states and waking states, and I got a better feel for the dream state than I'd ever had before. For many people, this is all it takes to become lucid dreamers. If you accustom yourself to asking the question "Am I awake or dreaming?" and if you don't answer perfunctorily, but rather stop and look around, you might start asking the same question in your dreams, just out of habit. For further advice on becoming a more aware dreamer, you're on your own.

There is a host of excellent books available on the topic. A few appear in the bibliography to get you started.

The Psychological Power of Dreams

Something that I have experienced directly, and which has meant a great deal to me, is the psychological power of dreams. Indeed, we are often told that dreams have psychological *meaning*, but we are not always told that dreams have psychological *effects*. We work on problems in dreams. We test scenarios, such as when we dream about different options for a decision or when we experience something in a dream that we are reluctant to experience in waking life. One kind of healing dream that can be induced explores the possibility of forgiving someone. You enact this possibility in a safe space; you have taken no irrevocable actions. It might feel wonderful. It might feel like a violation. How it feels, of course, is very informative. You can wake up with strong feelings in response to this experiment and explore those feelings while awake.

The interesting thing, the wonderful thing really, is that we undertake these explorations all the time, perhaps every night. We probably don't remember most of these dreams, yet they *work*. We are experiencing these explorations and growing, changing and healing as a result of these experiences, even when we don't remember a thing about them. That's a miraculous gift of our dream life. It's like going to bed with a high fever and waking with a temperature of 98.6; we heal in our sleep. Just as our bodies heal without our conscious awareness at night (if we care for them during the day), so do our psyches. If we do our healing work (therapy, meditation, self-help, ritual), our dream selves participate.

Once, in about 1987, I had an amazing dream. I was in therapy at the time, working intensely on a particular issue, a situation in which I felt paralyzed and helpless. In the dream, someone approached me and proceeded to do exactly the sort of thing that was troubling me in real life. As I told my therapist this part of the dream, I could see her wincing; she knew me so well and knew a bad thing was about to happen. But the dream took an unexpected turn: the person told me that *nothing bad would happen*, and then he resolved the situation in a gentle and loving way. I can't say I'd always wished the situation to resolve that way because I'd never *consciously* wished for that outcome; it was a desire and a longing of which I'd never been aware. The dream fulfilled for me a secret wish, and it modeled for me a kind of healing; it showed me what I needed and gave it to me all at once. And as I recalled the dream, I knew that I was healing, because I knew that a mind capable of giving me such a dream was a healthier mind than the one I'd once had. All these years later, I still recall it as a profound turning point and a testimony to the healing power of dreams.

So, on those occasions when I don't remember my dreams, or when I try to induce a dream but apparently fail, I don't sweat it. I know my dreams are doing their work whether I remember them or not and whether they make sense to me or not. If I ask for a dream about my relationship and instead dream about work, I take that work dream to be my answer and allow it to percolate in my mind to see what metaphors might arise from it that are applicable to my relationship.[44] In other words, I don't assume that dreams follow waking-life rules for success; the success of dream magic might be…dreamlike. My recent explorations of induced dreams have produced no results that make literal sense, but my nonliteral results, the ones that seem to make no sense at all, have their own wisdom which I may discover in time.

Uses of Dream Magic

When I began to explore dream magic for this book, I asked myself: What use is dream magic? What needs do I, or does anyone, have that can be addressed by dreaming? After a few minutes of brainstorming with my daughter though, we had amassed quite a list:

- Psychological healing, including:
  - Dreams of receiving love; feeling loved
  - Dreams of being forgiven
  - Dreams of giving forgiveness (as just described)
  - Healing suicidal thoughts by dreaming of wanting to live
  - Healing trauma by reliving it "right"
- Releasing creative blocks
- Accessing intuition, i.e., for decision-making
- Love magic: seeing the face of an unknown beloved in a dream
- Location spells, including:
  - Deciding where to move
  - Viewing a location from afar in a dream
  - Finding lost objects or missing persons
- Prophesy
- Getting advice from someone by bringing that person into a dream
- Performing sex magic in a dream

---

44 Just for entertainment value: I wrote that sentence late at night and went to bed shortly thereafter. I dreamt that night about having a relationship with a co-worker (who I have no such feelings for in real life). Apparently, writing about inducing a dream about relationships and work was all it took!

All of these are dreams that you, the magician, will have. I have also read numerous sources that offer spells for sending a dream to another, most typically sending a dream of you to someone you desire as a lover or someone who jilted you. These spells strike me as enormously unethical, a sort of psychic stalking.

I can only imagine one sort of dream sent to another that would be ethical, and that is to connect or reconnect to someone who cannot be reached through mundane means. A spouse, for example, might send a "love letter" to their military spouse whose location is secret and who cannot receive mail or phone calls. Or a pregnant person might communicate in this way with their unborn child. Years ago, I had a pen pal named Garry (yes, a real pen pal, using pens and paper in those bad old pre-Internet days), with whom I had a falling out. At that time, I was living with my mom, and she saw that I had thrown away a number of Garry's letters unopened.

Ultimately, Garry and I made peace and renewed a warm correspondence. However, my mother, when she got home before me and saw the mail first, was still throwing away his letters! She trashed about three of them before I noticed and asked her to stop. My friend must naturally have assumed that I was done with him. He had just moved, and my old letters didn't have his correct address. My attempts to reach him have since been futile. Garry has a very common last name and lived in a sizeable city, so phone searches back then and Google searches today have done no good. In such a case, a person might send a dream. If I sent someone a dream suggestion that he Google me, that person would certainly find me. Of course, such a dream is a message in a bottle. Sending it doesn't guarantee it will arrive. Recalling Chapter 2, you can see that a dream message like this might not have sufficient information or connection.

Before beginning dream work that seeks to alter reality, i.e., that fits a supernatural definition of magic, work toward dream goals that are considered conventionally accessible. Use dreams and dream magic for psychological goals. These include psychological healing, accessing intuition, and accessing information buried in the subconscious, such as the location of a lost object. This allows you to move into dream magic in steps, first getting your "sea legs" in the realm of dream manipulation before combining it with the realm of the supernatural.

Some dream experts see dream induction as a precursor to lucid dreaming; that is, they suggest learning to manipulate the subject matter of dreams while awake before trying to manipulate dreams from within while asleep. Others approach lucid dreaming directly, so I doubt it's a *necessary* step, but it appears from the literature and my own limited experience to be easier for many people to induce dreams than to dream lucidly. For this reason, it seems like a good idea to offer a dream induction spell.

One way to use lucid dreaming in magic is to use a dream induction spell, and once you are within the induced dream, use lucidity to help achieve desired changes or experiences. For example, if you are dreaming about forgiving someone, an induced dream might bring you face to face with the person; you would then use lucidity to say exactly what you wish to say, to ask the person questions, and so on.

Treat such a dream as purely psychological. Upon waking, understand that you spoke with an aspect of yourself—a *perception* about that person, not the person. A skilled lucid dreamer could also skip the waking induction of a dream and instead induce from within the dream state. That is, once lucid in the dream, bring forth the person with whom you wish to speak.

To Bring a Dream: A Sleep Spell

Goal:
To induce a dream. In this spell, the specific purpose of the dream is up to you. There are many possibilities. Look over the list of uses of dream magic in the previous section and decide what you are working toward.

Target:
Your mind; your dream state; as well as the specific target of the spell goal.

Needed Tools:
- A ritual cup, filled with water
- Your athame or other power-directing tool of your choice
- A bell, cymbal, or chime

- Visual reminders of your intended dream. If you wish to dream of a person, you could use a picture of that person. If you wish to dream of Paris, you could use a miniature of the Eiffel Tower. More than one such reminder will allow you to surround your bed so that all visual fields from your sleep position contain these reminders.
- Your dream journal and pen. Before beginning dream magic, you should have established a habit of writing your dreams in a journal immediately upon awakening before waking thoughts cause dream images to flee.
- Mugwort
- A candle and candle snuffer

OTHER:
- Obviously, this is a solitary dream. You might experiment with a partner in inducing the same dream on the same night and then comparing notes—but don't perform operative magic (a spell) at the same time.
- You'll be writing a rhyme to go with this spell. Writing rhymes is easy if they can be bad, and for spells, they *can* be. If the meter works and the words mean what you need them to mean, literary merit is beside the point.

  The structure of your rhyme should be:

  Line 1: Dream induction.
  Line 2: What kind of dream.

  So, something like the following could work with a location spell to find out where you should move:

  Tonight, a dream before my eyes,
  Show me where my new home lies.

  Or this, to free a creative block for a musician:

  Tonight, the dream that sets me free,
  Let the music flow from me.

One tip: It's harder to write line 2 because the meaning has to be more precise, so write it first. After that, you can attach a "Tonight I dream" line to the front with relative ease. Also, try to end your line with a sound frequently found in the English language. "Free/me" and "eyes/lies" are incredibly simple, and "free" also rhymes with "be," "see," "key," etc. If you like to write rhyming spells, you might purchase a rhyming dictionary as a magical tool.

Appropriate Deities:
Selene, Hypnos, Somnus, Evaki, Nyx, Morpheus.

The Spell:
1. Prepare your bedroom with your dream-inducing symbols. Have the cup, athame/power-directing tool, and bell near the bedside. The dream journal is wherever you normally keep it (mine is under my pillow).
2. Make sure you are ready for sleep and that you don't have any last-minute things to do. Do all your bedtime preparations in advance (i.e., don't brush your teeth after doing the spell!).
3. Move the blankets, sheets, and pillow to one side so that you can sprinkle the sleeping area.
4. Light the candle and turn out the electric lights.
5. Ground and center.
6. If you wish, you can cast a circle about the bed and use a bedside altar, as described in Chapter 7 in the spell "To Create a Beacon." You'll have to modify the words, of course.
7. If you're performing an invocation, do so here.
8. Holding your athame/other tool, direct power into the water in the cup, saying:

I charge this water with the power of dreams (in the name of deity). So mote it be!

9. Now direct power into the mugwort, saying:

I charge this herb with the power of dreams (in the name of deity). So mote it be!

10. Sprinkle the mugwort lightly over the area, including over the visual reminders, your dream journal, the bed, and under the pillow. Repeat your rhyme over and over, the whole time you're sprinkling.
11. Get in bed.
12. Now dip your finger into the water and anoint your third eye, again repeating the rhyme.
13. Hold the bell, and say:

This is the sound that will bring dreams.

Ring the bell.

NOTE: If the bell has a long tone that sustains for a while, you can ring the bell before anointing your third eye with water, listening to the sound while doing so. Experiment before you do the spell, so you know which works best for you. You definitely want to still hear the tone when you close your eyes.

14. Snuff the candle and go to sleep.
15. Immediately record any dreams you have during the night in your journal. Do this even if it's not yet morning.

    You may end up waking once or twice in the night to record dreams. Record them again in the morning.
16. Upon getting out of bed in the morning, thank any deity you invoked.

DIVINATION MAGIC

Most people associate divination with Water: divination addresses the mysterious and hidden; it arises from the subconscious, and it is generated by randomness, which is to say, like water, it follows a winding and unpredictable course.

Some forms of divination lend themselves more to magic than others. Specifically, it is more typical to use a structured system of divination such as Tarot, runes, astrology, or I Ching rather than something unstructured, like scrying or tea leaf reading, or something with a set and unchangeable "tablet," such as palmistry.

All divination works by the interaction of randomness with form. Randomness is the shuffle of the cards, the toss of the yarrow sticks, or the accident of the moment of birth. Form is the astrological chart, the pattern of tea leaves, or the bumps on the head in phrenology. In divination magic, we control the randomness: we stack the deck literally or figuratively, and we lay our controlled pattern onto the form. So, we choose a divination method in which the randomness *can* be controlled.

Ideally, I like to choose something that allows me to enact the reading so that what is essentially a theatrical performance becomes part of the spell. That is, after stacking the deck for a reading, I will then lay out the cards and read them aloud, preferably to another person, just as if the deck had not been stacked. This convinces my subconscious mind and the minds of any witnesses that the reading is "real." It imprints the idea that the outcome of the reading is true. This creates both a placebo effect (it works because I believe it will work) and a psychic resonance that reinforces the strength of the spell/reading.

Is it still Water, though, if it isn't random? Yes. A divination spell alters reality by reaching back into the pool of randomness. I impose my control onto a chart or a deck of cards, and then I mentally wipe the slate clean. Then as I reach for the cards, I reach into my internal divinatory state; I open myself to the cards just as when I'm doing a shuffled reading. I reach into the waters of my deep mind, and what do I find there? The stacked deck. It's a very powerful experience.

Use whatever divination method you're already good at. If you're not good at any divination method, study one—it's an invaluable tool for a magician. In the meantime, don't do this sort of spell. I believe that my intimacy with the Tarot is part of why Tarot spells work so well for me. I think if you don't know the Tarot and try a Tarot spell, it will be little more than a bunch of pretty pictures.

For its neat symmetry, I can't think of a better spell to use as an example of divination magic than one designed to increase psychic ability.

To Gain Psychic Ability: A Tarot Spell

GOAL:
To increase your own or another person's psychic abilities. You may have a general goal or a more specific one, such as increasing clairvoyance or adding a psychic skill (like scrying) not currently in your repertoire.

TARGET:
Yourself; specifically, your third eye. If doing the spell for someone else, target their third eye.

NEEDED TOOLS:
- A Tarot deck. Have the seven cards listed in the spell (see Figure 26 and Step 6 of the spell) pre-stacked, i.e., make sure that the Sun will be the first card you lay down, etc. If you want to use a significator, have that be first and then proceed from there.
- The four elements for consecration (see step 3)
- Whatever tools you normally use when doing a Tarot reading, i.e., a candle, cloth, etc.

NOTE: If you want to make Tarot spells a regular part of your magical practice, you might want a deck set aside just for magic.

OTHER:
- You can do this spell alone or with another person; you can read for yourself with another person present. Sometimes, even when doing an ordinary reading for myself, I find it helps to read to a second person. You might say it keeps me honest. If reading for another, substitute "you" wherever the spell has "I."

APPROPRIATE DEITIES:
Odin, Hecate, Apollo, Orunmila, Carmenta.

The Spell:
1. Ground, center, and merge.
2. If you're performing an invocation, do so here.
3. Consecrate your Tarot deck following the outline in Chapter 3.

Note: If you already have a deck set aside for your magical practice and it's consecrated, then skip Step 3. If, on the other hand, you want to set aside a deck but it's not yet consecrated, now's the opportunity to do so. Or, you may have a deck that you've been using for so long that it has already got a "charge," and you feel no need for a consecration.

4. Prepare your reading area, and have it set up in the way you like. You might wish to cast a circle about it or to consecrate the area where you will lay down cards.
5. Say:

> *What I say here is and will be true. So mote it be.*

6. Lay down the cards in the reading as follows. Lay each card, in order, in the position shown in the spread Figure 25. As you lay each card, say its name and description. You can improvise the description once you have memorized the general idea. (Figure 25 is a simple spread of my own, adapted from dozens of past/present/future spreads I've seen. It can be used for readings as well as for spells.)[45]

If you're using a significator, lay this down first in position 7. Say:

> *This is me.*

Lay the Sun card in position 1, and say:

> *In the past, the Sun. I leave my wondrous garden.*
> *It nurtures me but limits me.*

---

[45] For more spreads and more about Tarot, see my book Tarot Interactions.

Using Water in Spells

Lay the Hermit card in position 2 and say:

*Influencing the past, the Hermit.
I seek inner wisdom and begin my studies alone.*

NOTE ON THE HERMIT: If you have a teacher, replace the Hermit with the Hierophant, and say: I seek wisdom from one wiser than me.

Lay the Hanged Man card in position 3 and say:

*In the present, the Hanged Man.
I am willing to do what it takes to achieve my spiritual goal.
I am not afraid of hard work or discomfort.
I am able to commit myself to my goal.*

Lay the Fool card in position 4 and say:

*Influencing the present, the Fool.
I willingly step off into the unknown.
I trust the gods and my fate.*

Lay the High Priestess card in position 5, and say:

*In the future, the High Priestess.
I see beyond the veil and read from the book of mystery.
I am connected to the hidden source of truth.*

Lay the Moon card in position 6 and say:

*Influencing the future, the Moon. Secrets arise from the depths.
The dogs of night howl to the High Priestess,
and she understands their howls.
Truth is revealed to the eyes that can see it.*

Lay the Magician card in position 7 and say:

*Crowning the question, the Magician.
I have mastered the powers I seek. I can use them at will.*

I control my psychic arts; they do not control me.
My tools are laid out before me, ready for me to use.

NOTE ON THE MOON AND THE MAGICIAN: Here you see my habit of describing the picture as I read. I think it's a very powerful and reinforcing way to read the cards. I am using a Rider-Waite deck here. You'll have to change the descriptions to suit the deck you use.

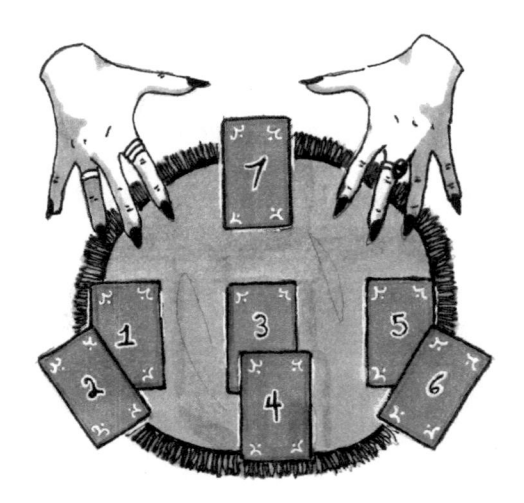

Figure 25: Tarot Spread

1. The past (the Sun)
2. An influence on or cause of card 1 (the Hermit)
3. The present (the Hanged Man)
4. An influence on or cause of card 3 (the Fool)
5. The future (the High Priestess)
6. An influence on or cause of card 5 (the Moon)
7. The crown (the Magician)

7. Put down the deck of cards. Move back from the reading, either by pushing your chair back or by allowing your posture to show that you encompass the reading as a whole. Say:

The reading indicates that my psychic powers will increase. I will access the mysteries and have mastery over this ability. My psychic skills are and will be a result of my study and hard work. What I say here is and will be true. So mote it be!

CHAPTER 9

Using Earth in Spells

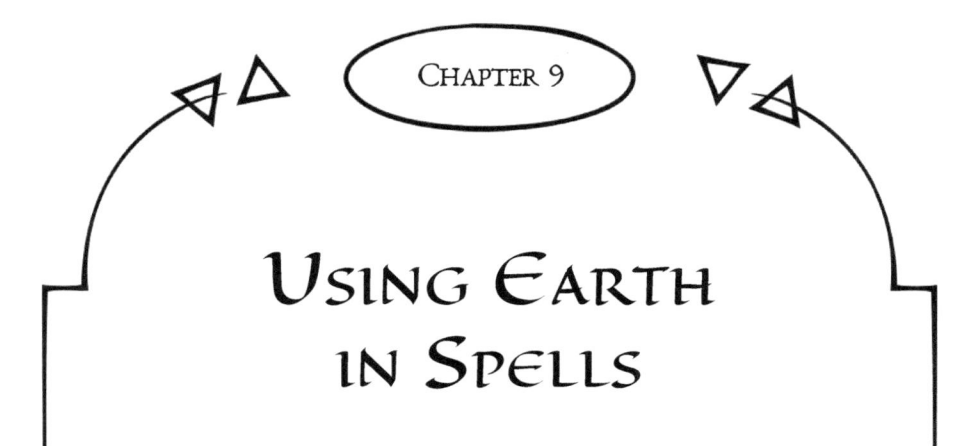

In Chapter 5, we identified the following purposes for Earth spells:

- For fertility
- For wealth
- To get a job
- To improve appetite
- To grow (can combat wasting illnesses)
- To improve crops or help your garden
- For longer hair and nails
- For marriage (any marriage-related goal)
- To get a home
- To bless a new home
- To finish things; to bring things to fruition
- To aid the ecology of a specific ecosystem
- To heal broken bones or other structural damage

USING EARTH

How would we bring Earth into a spell? As with the other elements, there are three basic methods: (1) directly, (2) through magical tools associated with the elements, or (3) symbolically through qualities of the elements.

To use Earth directly, we could:

- Bury something
- Plant something or use a plant in a spell
- Use a stone as part of a spell
- Use salt as part of a spell
- Use earth (soil, dirt, sand, mud, or clay) in the spell

To use Earth tools, we could:

- Use the pentacle
- Use the broom (the broom is variously attributed to Air for flight, Fire or Earth for the hearth, or Earth for domesticity—use your best judgment)

To use symbolic qualities of Earth, we could:

- Use food or cooking in our spell
- Do spells involving money or that use money as a tool
- Do spells slowly, over long periods of time that use patience and slow growth as a magical quality
- Use qualities of heaviness, i.e., lifting something, weighing something down
- Use foot-stomping or slow, bass drumbeats

FOOD MAGIC

Food magic is Earth magic because it is grounding, solid, and connected to the physical body and physical needs. Food comes from the Earth, either directly as plants or indirectly as herbivorous animals (most people don't eat carnivores if they can avoid it). Both agriculture and husbandry are Earth activities. Sustenance is an Earth quality, as is patience, and patience is needed to grow or raise and prepare food.

Food magic must be among the oldest of magics humans have worked. To eat is an essential need and a sensual pleasure. Meals are a time of communal gathering, a source of strength, and a means of sharing. Meals can take an elaborate effort in their preparation, yet one can also simply graze, picking an apple from a tree or a leaf from the ground. The acquisition, creation, and storing of food was the main work of our ancestors. Food's central importance in our lives to this day makes it a natural place to work magic.

There are a great many ways that cooking and food can be imbued with magical power. Any of the ingredients of a dish can be consecrated or charged to be symbolically meaningful or have inherent magical properties. For example, consecrate salt and add it to stew to bless the stew. Add cumin to a dish when working magic for an Aries, because hot, red, and orange spices, such as cumin, are symbolically associated with Aries. Sprinkle rosemary on chicken to bring peace because rosemary has that magical property. Nonedible ingredients can be added to magical food, in a way similar to the rose quartz added to a beverage in the "Finding Love" spell in Chapter 8. Just be careful not to add anything dangerous to ingest or upon which you could chip a tooth! Examples of nonedible ingredients are abound in folklore, such as love spells that require the hair of one person to be ingested by the other person.

The fire, water, oil, charcoal, or other cooking mediums can be magical, either permanently (like a sacred cauldron) or for a specific occasion (such as a Beltane fire) or purpose (a spell). Dishes for cooking and serving can be magical, perhaps set aside for ritual purposes. Just as observant Jews have special dishes used only for Passover, you can have special plates, bowls, and other dinnerware used only for your kitchen magic.

Stirring, sifting, kneading, churning, and other repetitive motions used in cooking are a great source of magical power and an opportune time to imbue food with magic. Rhythmic and repetitive activities were mentioned in Chapter 2 as a source of power; churning butter can be just as hypnotic as drumming.

Serving can be magical. Food can be arranged on a serving dish (perhaps a consecrated one) in a symbolic shape, presented with specific colors, or placed on the table while words of power are recited. The layout of the table setting can also be planned to be congruent with the work being performed. Numerology can be brought into play with the number of ingredients in a dish, the number of dishes served, or the place setting (number of utensils, bowls, etc.).

Eating itself can be very magical because what greater magic is there than preserving life? We remember the magic of eating when we say grace before a meal. We can say grace with magic in mind or substitute this simple reverent prayer with a more specific spoken, sung, or intoned spell.

Kitchen Blessing: A Home Spell

Goal:
To bless your kitchen so as to make it a good place to do kitchen magic. Do this blessing either once to inaugurate your kitchen magic or before each kitchen spell, as you prefer.

Target:
Your kitchen and its contents.

Needed Tools:
- An apron. If you wear an apron when you're cooking, put it on for this spell. In fact, if you haven't before, get one. This is the kitchen-magic equivalent of your magical robes.
- Your favorite kitchen things (see Step 1 of the spell)

Other:
- Make sure your kitchen is clean and cozy before you begin. There's no point in blessing a dirty kitchen.
- Do this solitary if you work kitchen magic as a solitary, or with a group if you work kitchen magic as a group.

Appropriate Deities:
Zao-jun, Anna Purna, Cerridwen, Kojin.

The Spell:
1. Put on your apron. If you are doing the blessing for a specific spell, put your ingredients, utensils, bowls, and other items that will be used for the spell on the counter. For a general kitchen blessing, put out the things that really represent the kitchen to you, such as your favorite bowls, knives, etc.
2. Ground and center.

Note: This spell is written to consecrate the kitchen in an east-to-east circle four times with the four elements. You might prefer to do this by moving east-to-east with Air, south-to-south with Fire, west-to-west with Water, north-to-north with Earth, and then return to the east.

3. Stand in the center of the kitchen facing east. Take a deep breath, visualizing your lungs filling with the bright energy you have gathered into your center. Exhale while pivoting in place, making a clockwise spin from east to east. Visualize your breath filling the kitchen with the same bright, sparkling energy.
4. Stand in the center of the kitchen facing east. Visualize your body full of Fire. Visualize the life force in your center. Do the same pivot, this time shouting, pushing Fire out of your throat and filling the kitchen with it. You don't need any words in your shout, but if words come, that's okay.
5. Stand in the center of the kitchen facing east. Place your hands over your heart and visualize yourself filling with a liquid love. Visualize a soft blue energy that feels like compassion. Pivot again, sending this loving kindness into the kitchen. You might choose to sing or speak while doing so.
6. Stand in the center of the kitchen facing east. Again, connect to your center, this time visualizing your strength and solidity. Allow this strength to flow from your center to your hands. Now walk around the kitchen, east to east, touching surfaces and objects, so that you make a physical touch–circle of the kitchen.
7. At this time, you can call your kitchen deity, silently or with words, to inhabit and bless the space.
8. Stand in the center, and say:

Blessed be.

Note: Why *Blessed be* instead of *So mote it be*? "So mote it be" declares that some-thing is to happen; it is the magical equivalent of Captain Picard's "Make it so." "Blessed be," on the other hand, simply imparts blessing. Here, there is nothing specific you are making so you are simply blessing your kitchen.

These are both Wiccan phrases; if you're not Wiccan, substitute an equivalent that feels comfortable to you.

9. Thank the deity you have called (if applicable).

To Gain Strength: A Magical Bread

Goal:
This is a healing spell to combat any illness that involves wasting, weakness, or weight loss, such as AIDS or cancer. The goal is to increase strength and appetite and to gain weight. The spell is used when simply eating is not enough, either because of appetite problems or because of the nature of the illness.

Target:
The body of the patient. The digestive system, the appetite, and the musculature are all target areas.

Needed Tools:
- A bread recipe, its ingredients, and the necessary kitchen equipment
- A picture or other representation of the patient to place before you in the kitchen. Be sure that the patient is represented in perfect health; do not use a picture where their illness is apparent
- If you want to burn incense, use something that has a food/kitchen aroma, something with spices you might cook with, such as cinnamon, clove, rosemary, or sage

Other:
- This is a solitary working performed by the cook. If you work as a group, use a battery operation; have drumming, chanting, etc., used by power-raisers who send the energy into the cook.

Using Earth in Spells

- Perform the spell during a waxing moon. Begin in the morning. Sunrise is ideal.
- Most grains, including wheat, rye, alfalfa, buckwheat, oats, and barley, are associated with Earth. This gives you considerable leeway in choosing a recipe.
- You might wish to add Fire to the bread, perhaps in the form of cloves, cinnamon, or curry in order to add enlivening and invigorating Fire to the body of the patient.
- In keeping with the earthiness of the spell, don't use a power-directing tool like an athame for the bread-making; use your hands.

Appropriate Deities:
Brigid, Dugnai, John Barleycorn, Fornax, Isis.

The Spell:
1. You can begin by performing the "Kitchen Blessing," or you can choose to bless your kitchen once and not repeat it for each spell.
2. Ground and center. If you performed the kitchen blessing as Step 1, you are already grounded and centered.
3. If you're performing an additional invocation (for a deity to aid the spell in addition to a general kitchen deity), do so here.
4. Have a short chant, word, or rhythm that you'll use as a part of this spell. Repeating a single word like *Strong! Strong!* is good. If you drum, you might create a rhythm instead of a chant, and if you sing, you might sing or hum a repeating melody line. You can grunt, tone, or tap your feet. Just make sure the sound you use is something that you will connect to your magical work. Visualize the patient and/or look at the picture or other representation to connect the sound with the goal. Begin using this sound as you combine the ingredients. After the ingredients of the dough have been put together, there's usually a part in breadmaking where you beat the ingredients for a few minutes. Allow this relatively long period of repeated rhythmic activity to become part of the sound/trance/energy.

5. Once your dough is blended, you can raise power more intently, sending it fully into the dough. You might have your drum in the kitchen and drum into the bowl of dough. You might place the bowl in the middle of the kitchen floor and dance around it. Raise the main force of power and send it into the dough while repeating your sound.
6. I usually suggest that people making magical bread avoid the use of a bread machine, because the hours of pounding and allowing to rise, pounding and allowing to rise, can be part of the work. Each time you pound the bread down, you'd use your sound. You would certainly repeat your sound as you form the loaf, as you put the bread in the oven and set the timer, and as you take the bread out of the oven.
7. When the bread comes out of the oven, thank any deity you invoked.
8. Serve the bread to the patient, perhaps as part of a magical ritual. If you are doing a distant healing, "serve" the bread to the picture/representation of the patient, and then pack up the bread and mail it.

House Blessing: A "Grace" Spell

Goal:
To bless a new home and make life in it safe, happy, and harmonious.

Target:
The home: think of the house (or apartment, or other dwelling) as having an aura, just as people do. You are charging the aura of the home with energy conducive to a happy life lived within.

Needed Tools:
- A hearty meal. Champagne, wine, or beer (champagne or wine for toasting, beer because it's Earthy) would be an appropriate beverage. Milk (also Earth) is excellent for teetotalers. Earthy dishes include pumpkin pie, breads, grains, and cheeses.
- Your best table setting, including a vase of flowers.

OTHER:
- This spell should be performed as soon as possible after moving into a new home (although, moving day being as chaotic as it is, it probably won't happen on the first night!). The spell can also be used to restore good will and harmony to a long-established home.
- Ideally, all the people who live in the home will participate. For this reason, the spell is not at all spooky or Witchy and will be acceptable to open-minded people of all paths.
- Since you don't have your usual ritual cues at a family meal, it is important that your mind be focused before you begin. You might meditate before inviting the family to sit down to dinner, or you might perform the "Kitchen Blessing" first.
- One excellent and Earthy way of blessing a home is with laughter. You can ask everyone who will participate to bring a new joke to share. After the toast (Step 7 in the spell), everyone can tell a joke during dinner. The laughter becomes part of the blessing.[46]

APPROPRIATE DEITIES:
Lakshmi, Lares Domestici, Hestia, Frigg, Gardsvor. You might also, or instead, invoke elementals of Earth (gnomes) to reside in your home.

THE SPELL:
1. You can begin by performing the "Kitchen Blessing," or you can choose to bless your kitchen once and not repeat it for each spell.
2. Make sure the kitchen or dining room is very clean and attractive. Use a good tablecloth or nice placemats, the good china, and so on. A vase of flowers on the table can serve as a subtle invocation of the presence of the Goddess if you choose or can be seen as an offering and brings beauty to the home.

---

46 I first heard of a joke-telling ritual from the late Patricia Monaghan. The ritual here is very different, but Pat still deserves credit for inspiration.

3. Before serving dinner, set a little of each dish (a small spoonful will do) onto a plate. Add a small cup of beverage. This isn't put on the table but is set aside.
4. Serve dinner. Allow yourselves to appreciate the sight and aroma of the meal you will eat. You can remark on how lovely it is, and how wonderful it is to have a meal like this in your new (if it's new) home. Don't eat yet.
5. Join hands. Ground, center, and merge. The following "light" reading can aid this process without sounding too much like magic:

Let's take a deep breath and calm ourselves. Let's forget about the day and our worries and just notice that we're here. Let's take a deep breath and find ourselves here, in our chairs, around our table, together.

6. If you're performing an invocation, do so here. If you wish, you can silently invoke the aid of a deity or you can perform a simple invocation aloud. You might make the invocation partly or entirely nondenominational, using the following as an example:

I'd like to invite any and all gods who are meaningful to those of us here. I'd like to invite Lakshmi, a goddess who blesses homes and is meaningful to me. Maybe others here would like to offer an invitation as well…?

Now, each person can have a chance to briefly speak.

7. Lift your glasses in toast and say:

May our (new) home be blessed (by those we've invited) with good feeling, good times, security, safety, and happiness. May our (new) home be the right home for us.

You might have a song to sing together. It can be a prayer or blessing that you all know or something you found for the occasion. After the song, or after the blessing if there is no song, say:

So be it.

8. Enjoy your meal! As you eat, insert into the conversation affirmative language about how great the new place is, how positive you feel about your future here, and so on. Now is also when you can tell jokes, as already described.
9. At the end of the meal, thank any deities invoked.
10. When the meal is over, set the dish and cup you prepared in Step 3 outside your front door as an offering to household spirits. If it's still there after a day, you can dispose of it by pouring the beverage directly onto the earth and burying or scattering the food. Animals eating the food or drinking the beverage act as agents of the spirits to whom you made the offering.

BURIAL AND PLANTING MAGIC

It stands to reason that whenever you bury something in the earth, you use Earth energies.

There are three main things that are buried in life, and burial of any kind almost always relates to one or more of them, and they relate to each other. These three things are seeds, treasure, and corpses.

Wicca, commonly called an earth religion, is intrinsically concerned with Earth mysteries, and the connection of birth to death to rebirth is central to Wiccan mysticism. The God of Grain, John Barleycorn, is cut down; he dies as harvested wheat and is reborn twice—reborn as the seeds that will grow again in the spring, and reborn in the people whom his body nourishes.

The burial of bodies is connected to the burial of treasure because death is connected to treasure. The name *Pluto* doesn't refer to a Lord of the Dead but to a treasure-keeper. The Lord of Death in Greek and Roman Paganism was referred to euphemistically as a Lord of Treasure because certain names are unwise to utter.

Folk legends of buried treasure often involve gravesites, and this is logical since, in many cultures, the dead were buried with whatever wealth they had, be it a simple piece of jewelry or the fabulous wealth of the pyramids.

What is treasure? It is wealth, surely, and Earth as well. It is connected to the things that Earth and wealth bring us; with treasure, we can buy a home, food, and other things that support and nourish us. Thus, treasure is a sort of a seed; it provides food as surely as the crops we plant do.

When we bury a corpse, we give it to the Lord of the Dead, who is a treasure-keeper. We return it to the earth with the hope that the soul it held will be reborn; hence, metaphysically, it is a kind of seed, the promise of new life.

A fourth thing that is buried is the foundation of a home or other building. This can be seen as a form of planting; the building grows from the foundation. It can also be seen as a form of buried treasure; it brings a form of wealth by staying in the earth. Finally, it is often associated with burying the dead. Mausoleums are buildings that house the dead, and basements often figure in horror stories as places from which ghostly creatures or zombies emerge. In the famous Edgar Allan Poe story, *The Cask of Amontillado,* a human being is walled up in a basement/foundation to die—a burial within a buried place.

We can look at burial another way: what happens to the buried item once it is in the earth? When we bury treasure in the ground, it stays there until dug up again. When we bury corpses, they rot—they decompose to become part of the earth (they compost); and when we bury seeds, they grow and emerge into the light. When we use burial in magic, we must first decide what our intention is for the item buried: to remain, to rot, or to grow and emerge.

Decomposition is usually a disposal method. Spells can be finished in the earth via burial. As you'll recall from Chapter 2, disposing of a spell's remains is part of the spell, and burial is an Earth method of disposal. This can add Earth to a spell that is not otherwise an elemental spell. It can also add the Earth qualities of patience and longevity: when you bury something in the earth, it stays there a long time, dissipating only very slowly. Hence, you can burn something in fire to add speed and urgency to a spell, dissolve something in water to add unpredictable movement, or bury something in earth to add a quality of slow settlement (like a foundation settling).

In Chapter 2, we talked about that Very Important Spell: Making Deborah Wealthy. If you did a spell that involved, say, a piece of paper that said "Deborah is wealthy" on it, you might burn that piece of paper at the end of the spell, and that might be consistent with an intent that I receive a flash of money all at once—that would be Fiery. If you buried the piece of paper, that would convey something like my money growing over time, gradually, nurtured by the earth.

Rotting can also be used to symbolically lay something to rest: burial-as-funeral. Whenever a funeral is held for someone whose body is not available (for example, a soldier missing in action), a little bit of magical symbolism is used; the coffin and some treasured objects (there's treasure again!) represent the body. You can ritually bury someone who isn't there, and when some*one* becomes some*thing*, the ritual becomes more of a spell. You can "funeralize" an object, an idea, or even a lifestyle. For example, if you've decided to give up your wandering ways and finally settle down, you can hold a funeral for your hiking boots and bury them, symbolizing that that part of your life is dead. Funeral-burial is a pretty dramatic step; most people put things aside without declaring them dead, but there are times it is called for and burial is a way of using magic to reinforce this declaration.

Things left in the ground permanently, like treasure or a foundation, are often protective; they serve as permanent guardians of the ground in which they reside. Sometimes they are deflectors or decoys; just as a decoy might draw fire in a gun battle, a magical decoy might draw negative energy in a psychic attack. Magical decoys are buried at the borders of a home to attract negative energy that might otherwise reach the home. Another version of this sort of protection is a buried magical "trap"; just as an animal trap prevents animals from passing it, this magical device prevents those who intend harm from passing it, thereby protecting a home, business, or other location.

Sometimes we magically bury treasure as a blessing or offering. Most offerings (such as food) are allowed to rot and thereby enter the earth, but a piece of jewelry or other baubles can be buried as a gift to the local ground, nature spirits, or deities.

Finally, we come to planting. Planting is inherently magical. I am in touch with the magic of nature every time I plant a little seedling and end up with an eggplant a few weeks later. Planting makes us a part of the circle of life; it is a powerful connection to earth, to rebirth, and to the Goddess. Wicca and many other Pagan religions use planting and its mystical, life-affirming cycles as a potent metaphor for everything in life that waits, grows, and reaches fruition. The Wiccan Wheel of the Year, as well as many other Pagan celebratory cycles, are based, in large part, on agricultural tradition.

From the beginning of agriculture, folk magic arose in connection to planting. Our ancestors did magic for the benefit of plants, and a little research can turn up a great many magical customs from all over the globe related to plowing, planting, and harvesting. We can also reverse this: instead of doing magic for plants, we can plant for magic. The simple act of planting, of placing something into the earth, tending to it, and discovering something new and wonderful arising from the earth, has enormous potential for spellwork. Normally, this is done by attaching magical energy to the seed or seedling. In addition, we gain whatever properties are already associated with the particular herb, flower, or food we grow. Tulips, for example, are associated with protection and good luck. You might plant tulip bulbs for protection, or you might do a planting spell for protection, *or* you might combine the two; use tulip bulbs as the focal object of your spell and then plant them, thereby doubling up the connecting energies.

Aromatherapy can be brought into play as well. (Unfortunately, tulips don't have much of a scent.) When tending a magical garden, inhale the aromas of the plants. Aromatic plants like rosemary are very potent, but allow *any* plant, and indeed the scent of soil and the outdoors, to fill your lungs. Visualize protection coming into your aura as you inhale while weeding protective plants, or energy filling your body as you inhale while watering energizing plants, or whatever is appropriate to the spell. Earth is patient and bides its time, so performing magical acts in incremental steps is an important way of staying in touch with that part of Earth energy.

To Protect a Location: A Burial Spell[47]

Goal:
To prevent negative influences from entering a piece of property, be it a home, business, or other location. This spell drives away physical, psychic, and emotional dangers—keeping away, for example, both theft and psychic attack.

Note: Should you do the house blessing spell or the location protection spell? Possibly both. The house blessing is something you could always do, whenever you move to a new location. You can never have too many blessings! The location protection spell is something you might routinely do as well, or you might reserve it for when you feel there is an actual threat.

Target:
The piece of property. The target is a shield or aura that is being created around the property.

Needed Tools:
- Four small mirrors
- A small hand shovel or spade
- A compass to confirm the four directions
- Your athame

Other:
- This spell can be done solitary, jointly by co-owners/co-residents, or as a battery operation. For a battery, cast a circle in the center of the location (inside the house if you're working the four corners of the property; use the psychic/emotional center, not the physical center point). Have everyone send power into the mirrors, and then

---

[47] At Starwood 2004, I was giving a talk on spellcasting and discussed burial spells for protection. Someone attending that class said she used buried mirrors to protect her property, an idea I thought was pretty neat (and I said so). I thank that anonymous woman for sharing her idea, and I hope she is pleased to see it in print.

everyone but the battery (who is the homeowner/resident) stays in the circle sending power while the battery goes out and does the burial and spell. In this case, you probably should dig the holes before you begin to maintain a better rhythm and timing.
- Perform the spell during the dark of the moon.
- Because the holes being dug are quite small, you can probably do the spell without trouble on a rental property.
- However, for the sake of privacy, if you have neighbors, you should probably do the work in the wee hours of the morning.
- Before you begin, determine the four directions, and then walk the perimeter to figure out exactly where you'll dig. It is not helpful to discover in the middle of a spell that the exact eastern corner of the property is paved in concrete or has a tree on it. Moving over a bit is fine, of course, but it's best if you know in advance.

APPROPRIATE DEITIES:
Thor, Gaia, Athena, Shango. Or you can invoke a deity or guardian spirit of each of the four directions.

THE SPELL:
1. Ground and center. Merge, if working as a group.
2. If you're performing an invocation, do so here.
3. Point your athame at the four mirrors, and say:

Bad, go away! Good, come on in!

NOTE: You can modify the words to suit your intention. For example, to emphasize privacy, you might say *Uninvited, go away!* But keep in mind that there are many wonderful things out there that you'd never think to invite.

4. Raise power and send it into the mirrors.
5. Take the mirrors and shovel outside. Normally, you would start in the east, but if you want to start in the north to emphasize Earth, that works too.

6. Dig the first hole. Looking into the first mirror, again say:

Bad, go away! Good, come on in!

Spit into the center of the mirror, and say:

If bad comes looking for me, here I am!

Bury the mirror so that it faces out. The reflection should face anyone approaching the property from outside.
7. Repeat Step 6 in the remaining three quarters. Some people will choose to do this spell deosil to wind protection around the house (this is my preference). Some people will choose to do this spell widdershins to drive ill away.
8. Return to the quarter where you began and say:

The circle is sealed and safe. No harm can cross it. So mote it be.

9. Thank any deities you have invoked and let them know the work is done.

To Bring Money: A Planting Spell

GOAL:
To bring money into your life.

TARGET:
You are sending abundance energy into the plants. Your target is the plants, which are being filled with this energy. Your secondary target is yourself; you are establishing a connection between yourself and the plant and receiving abundance through that connection.

NEEDED TOOLS:
- Peas for planting in a bowl or dish, enough for each participant to have one
- Potting soil, enough for all, in a large bowl or cauldron
- A transplant pot for each pea

- A pitcher of water, enough to water each new plant.
- A small trowel or large spoon to help with planting.
- Your athame or other power-directing tool, if desired.

Note: Sometimes you can find peas in self-planters—individual seedlings in organic pots that are planted directly into the earth. These are convenient and probably better for the plant, and you can easily modify the spell to accommodate them.

OTHER:
- This spell is written for a group but can easily be done solitary. If done with a group, you can easily accommodate people who aren't necessarily Witchy by skipping the use of an athame and just using your hand for consecrating. Or perhaps your group has its own traditional tool.
- Decide in advance where you're going to plant your pea. Peas are an early spring plant, making this ritual ideal for the spring equinox in a temperate zone. In New Jersey, where I live, I'd plant peas in late March; they are ready for harvest by the time the rest of the garden is planted in late May. You'll have to look up the ideal planting conditions for your own region. The soil for peas should not be allowed to dry out.

APPROPRIATE DEITIES:
Demeter, Habondia, Amalthea, Freyr.

THE SPELL:
1. Ground, center, and merge. Do an opening chant or "Om" while holding hands (touching is very Earthy).
2. Plunge your power-directing tool or hand into the soil, saying:

O, earth, be consecrated!
O, earth, be a fertile ground where abundance grows.
Be the soil where our hopes become reality! So be it!

All respond:

So be it!

3. Plunge your power-directing tool or hand into the dish of peas, saying:

   O, seeds, be consecrated!
   O, seeds, as you grow, bring us wealth.
   Be the seed of hope that grows into the plant of fulfillment.
   Nurture us with abundance! So be it!

   All respond:

   So be it!

4. Each person, one by one, comes to the altar and plants a pea in the transplant pot, using the consecrated soil. Use the pitcher of water to immediately water the seed. As you plant your pea, say:

   Money in the earth, money rising up, money coming into me.
   So be it!

   All respond:

   So be it!

5. Leave each little pot on or near the altar in the center of the circle. The plants will form an inner circle, as shown in Figure 24.

   Each person will be behind their own plant but will have enough room for power raising.

6. When all the peas have been planted, use chant and rhythm to raise power—while drumming, chant:

   Money in the earth, money rising up, money coming into me!

7. When the power reaches a peak, someone calls *Now!* and all throw power into the plants, concentrating on money growing out of the peas, and coming into themselves.
8. Thank any deities you have invoked.

9. Bring the peas home and transplant them into a permanent spot. Every day, water, weed, or otherwise tend to your plant and say:

Money in the earth, money rising up, money coming into me!

10. When the first peas are ready for harvest, join together with your group and eat the peas in a ritual setting. If you invoked any deities the first time you were in circle, invoke the same one(s) now.

    Sit in circle, and one by one, lift your pea pod and say:

This is the fruit of my labor. This is my abundance and my wealth. Wealth flows into me. So be it!

All respond:

So be it!

When everyone has eaten, celebrate!
11. Thank any deities you have invoked and let them know the work is done.

Figure 26: Altar Setup—Plants in a Circle

STONE AND GEM MAGIC

It would be impossible to write about Earth magic without including a little something about stones and gems. Whether or not a spell has an Earth purpose, all magic that uses stones is considered to be Earth magic. This is true even if the stones are not associated with Earth. This is something we've seen many times already: that within an element we can find subsets for all four elements. In this case, within stones/Earth, there are Air, Fire, Water, and Earth stones with Air, Fire, Water, and Earth meanings and associations.

I'll tell you a secret about gem and mineral lore—a lot of it is color magic! While it's true that stones have particular properties and that meditation and experimentation can reveal a good bit about the energies and uses of different sorts of minerals, it's also true that a lot of magical gem lore is no different from any other color lore. For example, green stones tend to be Earth, pink stones tend to be Water, and red stones tend to be Fire. When you have a stone about which you cannot find information, start with the color. Color is not merely visual, and qualities associated with color are not random. Psychologists have documented extensively the impact of color on mood. Color has vibration; some psychics can even detect color through their fingertips, blindfolded. Therefore, judging the properties of a stone by its color makes perfect sense.

Of course, that's not all there is to it. In a calm, meditative state, hold a stone in your more receptive hand and ask what its nature is. I like to move a stone from hand to hand and to hold it over my chakras: Does my third eye respond to this stone? Does my throat? My heart?

I use reference materials to check myself. A good reference book will have folklore from various places where this sort of stone or gem is found, as well as, in many cases, the author's own psychic impressions and experiences (the bibliography has a few good choices).

In addition to various gems and stones, do not forget that ordinary stones—plain old *rocks*—are also Earth. The many combinations of granite, shale, and other surface minerals that you find in your garden, on your stoop, and as you go about your day are Earth. Concrete is Earth as well, and I find broken concrete exceptionally Earthy, as it bespeaks the passage of time that wears away even the firmest structures and shows us the upheavals beneath our feet that are capable of breaking a sidewalk or causing a pothole to appear in the road. The earth lives and grows even when we pave over it.

You can use stone magic whenever your magic should be permanent or long-term. Stones can be carried or left places with some assurance that they won't go anywhere under their own steam. For example, a magically charged stone can be left on a plot of land, in a room, in a car, or under a bed. *Don't* leave a stone in a baby's crib or anywhere else a child might swallow it. Stones can also be buried, combining two forms of Earth magic.

TO MAKE A GARDEN GROW: A STONE SPELL

GOAL:
To make a garden grow. This spell stimulates the health and growth of plants in your garden on an ongoing basis. You might wish to renew this spell every year, but the spell is designed to bring permanent fertility and health to the area in which the stone is placed.

TARGET:
There are two targets: the garden and the stone. When you charge an object for a long-term, ongoing purpose, such as protection or abundance, one way to visualize the target clearly is to visualize the object emanating that purpose. You create an energy field of the right sort around the object. I have found that such objects remain effective when moved from place to place. For example, my car-protecting mojo bag has been moved from car to car without diminished effect.

NEEDED TOOLS:
- A piece of moss agate
- Your athame (optional)

OTHER:
- This spell is done in three phases, each of which uses a different sort of magic. You can do all three phases as written, or you can do any combination of one or two phases. Personally, I would always do the first (charging) phase, but you might feel it is redundant.

- Phase 1 involves charging the stone with energy and purpose. The technique is typical of this sort of spell: point a magical tool or your hand at an object, state your purpose, raise energy, and pour it into the object. This phase can be done solitary, as a group, or in a battery fashion (see Chapter 2).
- Phase 2 is a form of sex magic. You can skip this part if it makes you uncomfortable. If you choose to do it, you can work solitary or as a couple.
- Phase 3 is a form of imitative magic, in which you will "teach" the stone to imitate garden-growing energies. Since you will be carrying the stone with you during this phase, it would normally be done solitary.
- Begin the spell during a waxing moon.

APPROPRIATE DEITIES:
Abundita, Osiris, Demeter, Azaka-Tonnerre.

THE SPELL:
1. Ground and center. If in a group, merge.
2. If you're performing an invocation, do so here.
3. Point your athame (or fingers) at the moss agate stone, saying:

> *Stone will make the garden grow,*
> *Healthy plants, green and tall,*
> *Stone will make the garden grow,*
> *Strength and power, one and all.*

4. Now raise power however you have chosen to do so (drumming, clapping, and dancing are all good for Earth power), and send it into the stone. Say:

> *So mote it be!*

5. Thank any deities you have invoked.

THIS COMPLETES PHASE 1.

6. This step involves anointing the stone with sexual fluids, which is to say, vaginal fluids and/or semen. You can use fluids produced when performing sex magic, as discussed in Chapter 7. Usable quantities of semen are available only after orgasm. Vaginal fluids are available at other times, but they do have the greatest magical power right after orgasm.[48] The simple thing to do here is to perform sex magic focused on *plant* fertility[49] and then rub the fluids all over the stone. You can have the stone under the mattress or a pillow during sex. You could, alternately, simply insert a finger or the stone itself (if it is clean) into your vagina and acquire anointing fluids that way.

    Sexual fluids bring potent fertility energy to the spell. This is true whether or not the person or people providing the fluids are physically fertile or want to have children. Your garden is an object of your magical fertility every bit as much as your children are objects of your physical (and magical) fertility.

THIS COMPLETES PHASE 2.

7. You now have a charged stone. Hold the stone in a position such that you can talk to it; for example, hold it up before your eyes. Tell the stone:

    Now you are going to learn to make a garden grow.

    While preparing your garden in the spring, you will almost certainly need to make a trip to a garden store to buy seeds, seedlings, fertilizer, etc. In a good garden store, there will be

---

[48] The first edition of this book referred to "male" and "female" sexual fluids. This is not accurate terminology, as men sometimes have vaginas, women sometimes have penises, and non-binary people might have either.

[49] If you don't want the fertility energy to spread farther than that, be assiduous about birth control!

plenty of areas where you can find lush, plentiful, abundant plants—the kind of plants you want to grow. Take your stone to such a spot, and place it among those plants, saying:

This is how a garden grows. This is what you do!

You can also take your stone to similarly lush spots in parks or in nature and do the same thing. You might also take the stone to a vegetable stand or to the vegetable section of your supermarket (provided, that is, that you are growing vegetables; use a flower market or herb store as appropriate). Take the stone to a section of wonderful, healthy, delicious-looking plants, and say:

This is what you're going to create. Isn't it wonderful? Don't you just love it? This is what you do. You have this power.

Obviously, all these "scripts" can be (and are meant to be) improvised.

THIS COMPLETES PHASE 3.

8. Put the stone in your garden.

MAGIC IN CLAY AND SCULPTURE

Sculpture is one of the earthiest of Earth techniques. First and foremost, the use of clay is the use of earth itself in one of its most direct forms. Clay not only *is* earth, but it *feels like* Earth, connecting us to the element in a tactile and experiential way.

Using clay is also an Earthy experience. Because it involves touch, and because you create something directly with your hands, it is Earthy. Because it is dirty and messy, it is, again, Earthy. The dirtiness is, I think, an important Earth quality that too many of us avoid. It pushes us face to face with nature and helps release the inhibitions that distance us from our authentic selves.

Finally, sculpture as part of a spell is Earth magic because it involves producing a *thing* from earth.

Don't shy away from this wonderful form of magic because you're not an experienced or gifted artist! Sculpture can be amazingly simple. Examples include:

- Simple spheres, cubes, and pyramids
- Flat plates, disks, or tiles inscribed with symbols
- One or more long tubes twisted into a symbolic shape, such as a pentagram or ankh, or into a freeform shape
- Simple body-part shapes, such as a phallus or yoni

Sculpting in clay is an inexpensive, accessible, creative, and fun way of putting Earth into your magic. Anyone can pick up clay at a craft store and a single purchase can serve for multiple spells. Sculpting is also an excellent substitution technique. For example, if you want to do the previous gardening spell, but have no moss agate, you can sculpt an appropriate object to place in your garden and proceed with the spell as written.

When using clay for the first time, you'll find a number of options available. Water-based clay is often called self-hardening clay. It has several advantages, including the fact that you don't need a kiln. It is fairly easy to work; you add the amount of water you desire to get the texture that feels comfortable to you. The disadvantage is that it *does* harden by itself, which means you have to store it properly and keep it moist while working.

Oil-based clay is sometimes called modeling clay. It stays moist and often feels nicer when working it in your hands, which certainly helps. However, it does have to be baked. Check different brand labels for baking temperatures; many require a professional kiln. Polymer clay is my least-favorite option, though many people love this stuff. It is sold under a number of brand names, the most popular of which is Sculpey. It is easy to work and is baked at a low temperature, which makes it very convenient. It comes in a variety of interesting colors and finishes. The problem is that a polymer is a chemical compound—not earth at all! Save polymer clay for your fun hobby projects and use earth clay for Earth magic.

To Bring Fertility:
A Sculpture Spell

Goal:
Physical fertility, i.e., pregnancy.

Target:
The birthing person's body. You can visualize their womb (uterus) or the ovum being fertilized, or both.

Needed Tools:
- Your preferred clay and tools you use to sculpt. Plastic knives and toothpicks, for example, are very handy
- Your white-handled knife or whatever magical tool (if any) you use for forming magical objects
- A hair from each person in the couple
- Patchouli incense (optional).

Other:
- This spell can be performed solitary or as a couple. You might do the spell solitary if your partner is not a practitioner of magic, but it is essential that you have your partner's consent, not just to do magic but to seek after pregnancy. To work this spell without your partner's knowledge would be a huge violation. The spell here assumes a couple.
- The spell is written with the assumption of a heterosexual couple. It can easily be modified for any couple in which a person with a uterus is seeking to become pregnant, or a single person with a uterus who is seeking pregnancy via artificial insemination. The goal is physical pregnancy. The spell isn't designed for those seeking to adopt.
- The spell should be performed during a waxing moon.

Appropriate Deities:
Anahita, Boann, Taouris, Nona, Mother Eingana.

THE SPELL:
1. Your first step is to make the sculpture. I suggest a pregnant belly, but you can choose something else if you prefer. The belly has several advantages: it is easy for an inexperienced sculptor to create, it is evocative, and it is very Earthy. When working as a couple, you will prefer a simple sculpture even if one of you has some skill in the art form.

    Set up your sculpting materials. Either prepare your altar by covering it in newsprint or a sheet or set up your handcraft area with whatever altar stuff you'll use (idols, incense, a vase of flowers, etc.). Also, have on hand a white-handled knife if you are using one and hand wipes of some kind.
2. Ground, center, and merge.
3. If you're performing an invocation, do so here.
4. Begin with a handful of clay that is comfortable to hold. Mold an egg shape to begin with. Pass the clay back and forth, maintaining eye contact, as you soften this first bit of clay. Your final product can be anywhere from one to five inches in height, whatever is comfortable. Use that to guide your selection of the first piece of clay.
5. Allow this passing-back-and-forth process to raise power. You can hum or "Om" as you do so. (If you're working alone, use a hand-to-hand movement as you hum or Om.)
6. Now take each other's strand of hair. You may have plucked or snipped the hair in advance, or you can reach over and pluck or snip (with scissors) one of your partner's hairs while they do the same.
7. With the clay in your hands, add your partner's hair to the egg shape. As you do so, pour the power you have raised into the clay, visualizing its fertility. Visualize a baby beginning to take shape inside a pregnant belly. Say:

You and me and baby makes three.

NOTE: This is, I admit, a very dumb chant. You can replace it with something better, but some-times I like the corny ones; they really stick in your head!

8. Your partner repeats Step 7 with your hair, using the same visualization, and saying:

   You and me and baby makes three.

9. Continue to mold the clay, passing it back and forth, and repeating your phrase each time you pass it. As it goes back and forth, begin to shape it more consciously, so it looks more like a belly (Figure 27).

   You might want to flatten out one side, to represent where the belly attaches to the rest of the torso, or you might want to leave it egg-shaped to represent the shape holding the baby inside. Note that a pregnant belly gets a vertical stripe in the second or third trimester, creating a distinctive feature not found on a belly that is merely large. Add the stripe with a strip of clay or with color.

   A pregnant person's belly button also pops out around that time, even if the person previously had the most sunken of "innies." Use another dot of clay to add this feature to your sculpture.

   Later on, you'll be carrying the sculpture around with you. If you want, you can add a loop to the top of the sculpture so that it can be strung (Figure 28).

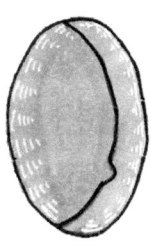

Figure 27: A stylized pregnant belly sculpture

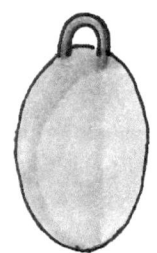

Figure 28: A loop of clay attached to the back of the sculpture

10. By now, you've been passing this thing back and forth and saying your phrase for some time. If you're using the white-handled knife, the last bit of work should be done

with it, adding a detail, your initials, or the initials of your future child. Say:

So mote it be.

When you're finished, pause for a moment to really look at your sculpture and see it as a pregnancy.
11. Clean your hands and raise power once again (you'll have more options now, with your hands free). Send the power into the sculpture.
12. If you've invoked any deities, thank them now.
13. Allow the sculpture to dry, baking if needed.
14. The person who intends to become pregnant will carry the completed sculpture with them at all times. When you make love, have the sculpture under the pillow, under the bed, or in your hands.

Appendix A

The Spells

Here is a list of all the spells in this book, sorted by subject.

Balancing the Elements: A Spell of Self-Empowerment... 87
Balancing the Elements: A Spell of Group Empowerment. 92
To Bring Air into Yourself: A Feather Spell.......... 96
To Bring Fire into Yourself: A Body-Painting Spell..... 100
To Bring Water into Yourself: A Bath Spell.......... 103
To Bring Earth into Yourself: A Cookie Spell......... 107
To Bring About Travel: A Simple Aromatherapy Spell... 123
To Increase Understanding: A Scent/Memory Spell..... 125
To Improve Memory: An Affirmation Spell.......... 133
To Improve School Performance: A Writing Spell...... 135
To Bring Justice: A Writing Spell 139
To Restore Libido: A Candle Spell 151
To Aid a Cause: A Candle Spell................... 155
For Courage: A Spell of Offering.................. 165
To Make a Decision: Releasing into the Fire 167
To Gain Freedom from Obsession: A Spell of Burning .. 168
To Release Rage: A Spell of Destruction 172
To Create a Beacon: A Sex Magic Spell.............. 191
To Cleanse an Object of Negativity: A Soaking Spell.... 191
To Drive Away Bad Dreams: A Bathing Spell 194

To Keep Something Hidden: An Invisibility Spell 197
To Improve Health during Pregnancy: A Magical Tea . . . 203
Finding Love: A Cup Spell 205
To Bring a Dream: A Sleep Spell. 214
To Gain Psychic Ability: A Tarot Spell 219
Kitchen Blessing: A Home Spell 226
To Gain Strength: A Magical Bread. 228
House Blessing: A "Grace" Spell 230
To Protect a Location: A Burial Spell 237
To Bring Money: A Planting Spell. 239
To Make a Garden Grow: A Stone Spell 244
To Bring Fertility: A Sculpture Spell 249

Appendix B

Going Shopping

It occurred to me that something I've never seen in a book on magic, and something that might be really useful, is a shopping list.[50]

I've compiled lists here, sorted alphabetically by the type of product/type of store you'll buy the items in. These lists comprise every single item suggested for use in the spells in this book with a few exceptions. Some spells call for things you already have in the house. For example, in Chapter 6, the spell "To Bring Justice" calls for an article of clothing. Some spells call for fresh ingredients, like fresh flowers, as in "Finding Love" in Chapter 8. These are things you'll have to go out and get that day, so having them on a master list in this appendix is of no value.

Because you will probably not use every spell in this book, I've noted what spell each ingredient is for, so you can easily omit it from your purchase plan.

---

50 In *Magical Power for Beginners*, I expanded on this concept by creating a generic magical shopping list, meant for stocking your shelves so that magical practice is easier. I've still never seen a list like this one—with exactly what you need to perform the specific spells in the book.

CANDLES

- *Candle snuffer:* For general use. Used for "To Bring a Dream."
- *Candle shaver:* Use this, if necessary, to shave the bottom of a candle to fit into a holder; keep in your magic box.
- *Any color taper (3):* Keep one in your magic box for use in lighting other candles. You'll need one for "To Bring a Dream" and one for "To Improve School Performance."
- *Red pillar candle:* Used for "To Bring Fire into Yourself."
- *Red tapers (10):* Used for "To Create a Beacon" (7), "To Restore Libido" (2), and "To Aid a Cause" (1).
- *One pink or white votive or taper:* Used for "To Drive Away Bad Dreams."
- *Seven pink or blue votives or tapers:* Used for "To Bring Water into Yourself."

CRAFT STORE

Big craft stores like A.C. Moore or Michael's have a full range of hobby/art supplies and can be incredibly helpful for magical projects.

- *Bag of feathers:* Used for "To Bring Air into Yourself."
- *A cloth bag or white, light-blue, yellow, or gray cloth and sewing supplies:* Used for "To Bring Air into Yourself."
- *Clay and sculpting tools:* Used for "To Bring Fertility."
- *Mirrors (6):* Used for "To Protect a Location" (4), "To Keep Something Hidden" (1), and "To Improve Memory" (1).

GROCERY STORE/SUPERMARKET

- *Kosher/coarse/sea salt:* Used to represent Earth in many spells.
- *Corkscrew:* Used anytime you use wine in ritual. Used for "Finding Love."
- *Cotton ball/swab:* Used for "To Improve School Performance."
- *Olive oil:* Used for "To Bring Water into Yourself," "To Restore Libido," and "To Aid a Cause."
- *Tea:* Used for "For Courage."

- *Hand wipes:* Used for "To Bring Fertility."
- *Plastic sealed box:* Used to keep incense, herbs, and charcoal briquettes dry.
- *Cookie ingredients:* Used for "To Bring Earth into Yourself."
- *Bread ingredients:* Used for "To Gain Strength."

HARDWARE/GARDEN STORE

Many practical supplies are readily available at hardware stores, garden/outdoor stores, or stores like Home Depot.

- *Fire extinguisher:* Always have one for any spells involving candles or fire.
- *Potting soil:* Used for "To Bring Money."
- *Peas for planting:* Used for "To Bring Money."
- *Transplant pots:* Used for "To Bring Money."
- *Small trowel/hand spade:* Used for "To Bring Money" and "To Protect a Location."
- *Heavy-duty broom:* Used for "To Release Rage."
- *Dustpan:* Used for "To Release Rage."
- *Heavy-duty garbage bags:* Used for "To Release Rage."
- *Outdoor or indoor firepit setup:* Used for "For Courage," "To Make a Decision," and "To Gain Freedom from Obsession."
- *Wooden matches:* Wooden matches are nicer and easier to work with than paper matches, and (in my opinion) are Witchier than a lighter. Used for most spells.
- *Keys and/or locks:* Used for "To Keep Something Hidden."

HERBS AND INCENSES

You can easily make your own loose incense by mixing herbs with a pestle and mortar or in a food processor or coffee mill. Frankincense is an excellent all-purpose incense that, with benzoin, is commonly used to moisten dry herb mixtures so that they burn better. Loose incense is burned on a charcoal briquette (not the kind for your backyard grill; they make special charcoals for incense). Fill your burner about halfway with sand, soil, or clean kitty litter, put the lit briquette on top of the sand, and sprinkle the incense on that. Keep your burner on a fireproof surface.

- *Pestle and mortar:* Used to blend your own incense.
- *Charcoal briquettes:* Used to burn loose incense.
- *Incense burner/holder:* Used with any incense.
- *Fireproof tile or trivet:* Put the incense burner on this.
- *Stick/rope incense:* Have on hand as a spare in case your charcoal briquettes all go blooey.
- *Apple blossom:* Used for "Finding Love."
- *Benzoin:* All-purpose, for adding resin to dry or powdery mixtures.
- *Carnation:* Used for "To Aid a Cause."
- *Cinnamon:* Used for lots of Fire purposes, including "To Bring Fire into Yourself," "To Gain Strength," "To Create a Beacon," "To Aid a Cause," and "To Restore Libido."
- *Cinquefoil:* Used for "To Bring Justice."
- *Clove:* Used for "To Bring Fire into Yourself" and "To Gain Strength."
- *Frankincense:* All-purpose, for adding resin to dry or powdery mixtures. Also used for "To Bring Fire into Yourself," "To Drive Away Bad Dreams," and "To Create a Beacon."
- *Freesia:* Used for "Finding Love."
- *Geranium:* Used for "Finding Love."
- *Ginger:* Used for "To Restore Libido."
- *Lavender:* Used for "To Bring Air into Yourself."
- *Mugwort:* Used for "To Bring a Dream."
- *Myrrh:* Used for "To Drive Away Bad Dreams."
- *Patchouli:* Used for "To Bring Fertility."
- *Raspberry leaves:* Used for "To Improve Health During Pregnancy."
- *Rosemary:* Used for "To Gain Strength."
- *Sage:* All-purpose smoke cleansing; for purifying Air objects. Also used for "To Bring Air into Yourself" and "To Gain Strength."
- *Thyme:* Used for "Finding Love."
- *Violet:* Used for "Finding Love."
- *Woodruff:* Used for "To Aid a Cause."

HOUSEWARES STORE

Furnishings, dishes, and home decor can be purchased at ordinary housewares stores like Bed Bath & Beyond or T.J. Maxx.

- *Altar:* This can be a small table, chest, or trunk. Used for most spells.
- *Candle holders:* "To Bring Water into Yourself" and "To Create a Beacon" both call for seven candles, necessitating seven candle holders. You'll probably want a variety of holders for votives, tapers, and pillars.
- *Pitcher or ewer:* Used for "To Bring Water into Yourself," "To Keep Something Hidden," and "To Bring Money."
- *Water dish:* Try something about 4–6 inches in diameter. Used for every spell that calls for Water to be represented.
- *Salt dish:* Used for every spell that calls for Earth to be represented.
- *Medium-sized bowl:* Try something about 10–12 inches in diameter. Used for "To Bring Air into Yourself," and "To Cleanse an Object of Negativity."
- *Small dish:* Get one that is safe for paint, oil, etc. Used for numerous spells; use for dressing oils, anointing, etc.
- *Lidded dish:* You might try a Japanese soup dish. Used for "To Bring About Travel."
- *Large bowl or cauldron:* Used for "To Bring Money."
- *Lidded jars (4):* Used for "To Bring Justice," "To Restore Libido," "To Aid a Cause," and "To Keep Something Hidden."
- *Cup:* Ceramic, silver, and pewter goblets are usually preferred. Used in many spells that call for Water to be represented.
- *Broom:* This is a magical broom, not a household broom. You might want something fancy, pretty, or handcrafted for this. General-purpose uses.
- *Apron:* Used for "To Bring Earth into Yourself" and "Kitchen Blessing."
- *Blankets:* You'll need these to sit on outdoors. Used for "To Gain Freedom from Obsession" and "To Release Rage."

- *Ashtray:* Get a nice one at a housewares store since you'll be using it in ritual. Used for most spells.
- *Nice box:* Maybe a jewelry box? Get one to use as your "magic box."
- *Soft bathrobe or towels:* Used for "To Bring Water into Yourself."

OILS

These are usually essential oils, but sometimes oil infusions or absolutes. Use one or more of each oil suggested for a spell.

Avoid those marked with an asterisk (*) if you are pregnant.
Avoid those marked with a double asterisk (**) if you have epilepsy.

- *Sandalwood:* Used for "To Bring Water into Yourself."
- *Myrrh*:* Used for "To Bring Water into Yourself."
- *Vanilla:* Used for "To Bring Water into Yourself."
- *Sage**:* Used for "To Improve Memory" and "To Improve School Performance."
- *Caraway:* Used for "To Improve School Performance."
- *Clary sage*:* Used for "To Improve School Performance."
- *Lavender*:* Used for "To Improve School Performance."
- *Spearmint:* Used for "To Improve School Performance."
- *Anise/star anise:* Used for "To Improve School Performance."
- *Ginger:* Used for "To Restore Libido."
- *Carnation:* Used for "To Aid a Cause."
- *Cinnamon:* Used for "To Aid a Cause."
- *Marigold:* Used for "To Bring Justice."

RECIPES

- *Bread:* Used for "To Gain Strength."
- *Cookies:* Used for "To Bring Earth into Yourself."

SPECIALTY STORES

- *Red body paint:* Try a cosmetics or sex-toy shop. Used for "To Bring Fire into Yourself."
- *Paintbrush for body paint:* Used for "To Bring Fire into Yourself."
- *Compass:*[51] Try a camping gear store. Used anytime you are working with direction, especially in a new place. Used for "To Protect a Location."
- *Athame:* A double-bladed knife can be purchased in knife specialty shops and in camping gear stores, as well as in occult stores. Used for most spells.
- *White-Hilt Knife:* Used for "To Bring Fertility," "To Restore Libido," and "To Aid a Cause."
- *Bell:* Can be used during any invocation. Used for "To Bring a Dream."
- *Drum(s); rattle(s):* Used as a power-raising tool during many spells. Used for "To Gain Freedom from Obsession."
- *Tarot deck:* Used for "To Gain Psychic Ability."
- *Piece of moss agate:* Used for "To Make a Garden Grow."
- *Piece/bead of rose quartz:* Used for "Finding Love."
- *May wine; strawberry-flavored wine; strawberry-flavored beverage:* Used for "Finding Love."
- *Breakable dishes:* Don't get these at a housewares store; get cheap ones at a thrift store like Goodwill. Used for "To Release Rage."
- *Wand:* Find or make a wand or purchase one at an occult store. Used in numerous spells.
- *Rosary:* This can be a beaded necklace or strand and can be homemade. Used for "To Improve Memory."

---

51 There were no smartphones when I wrote this in 2006. Today, you could use a compass app. Of course, a real compass is still handy if you're choosing to keep your phone off for magical purposes or if you're in the woods, removed from wireless connectivity.

- **Seashells:** Used for "To Bring Water into Yourself."
- **Hand-held fan:** Used for "To Bring Travel" and "To Increase Understanding."
- **Stick or twig of bamboo or birch or a bamboo chopstick:** Used for "To Keep Something Hidden."

STATIONERY STORE/OFFICE SUPPLY STORE

- **Sealing wax:** Used for "To Improve School Performance."
- **Ritual pen:** Used for "To Improve School Performance."
- **Parchment/ritual paper:** Used for "To Improve School Performance" and "To Make a Decision."
- **Envelope:** Used for "To Improve School Performance."
- **Writing instrument that you can use with water:** Used for "To Bring Justice."
- **Labels for jars:** Used for "To Bring Justice," "To Restore Libido," "To Aid a Cause," and "To Keep Something Hidden."
- **Dream journal:** Used for "To Bring a Dream."
- **Dream journal pen:** You can use an ordinary pen, your ritual pen, or a special pen set aside for dream journaling. Used for "To Bring a Dream."
- **Grease pens/laundry markers:** Used for "To Release Rage."

Appendix C

Gods and Goddesses

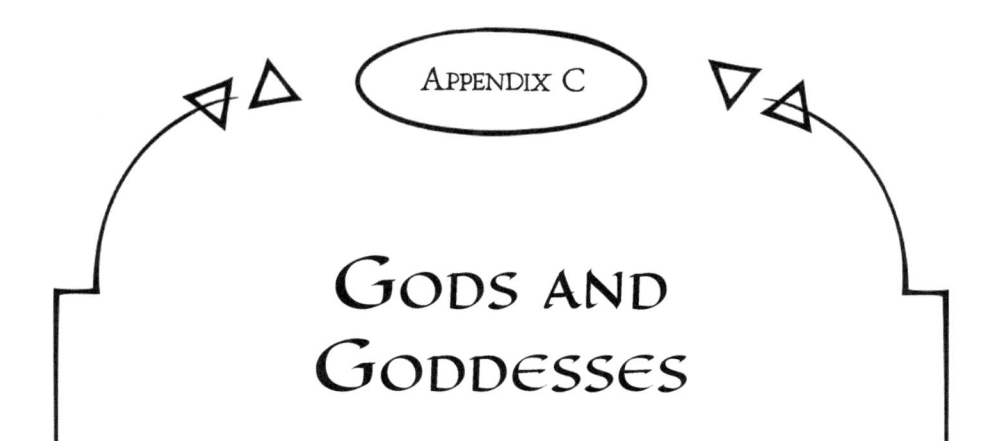

Throughout this book, I've offered names of appropriate gods and goddesses to invoke during a spell. However, I've also cautioned you not to invoke anyone with whom you are unfamiliar. To make your research easier, I've compiled a list here of all deities named in these pages; they are sorted alphabetically within each category.

CELTIC

- Boann
- Brigid
- Cerridwen
- Dagda
- Danu
- Epona
- Lugh
- Mannanan
- Nuada
- Ogma
- Rhiannon

EGYPTIAN

- Ermutu
- Geb
- Hathor
- Isis
- Ma'at
- Nuit
- Osiris
- Ra
- Sekhmet
- Taouris
- Thoth

GREEK

- Amalthea
- Aphrodite
- Ares
- Artemis
- Athena
- Demeter
- Dionysus
- Eileithyia
- Eros
- Gaia
- Hecate
- Hera
- Hermes
- Hestia
- Hypnos
- Mneme
- Morpheus
- Nyx
- Orpheus
- Poseidon
- Rhea
- Selene
- Themis
- Zeus

HINDU

- Agni
- Anna Purna
- Bhavani
- Durga
- Garuda
- Kali
- Kama
- Lakshmi
- Mahalakshmi
- Parvati
- Sarasvati
- Shiva
- Vishnu

NORSE

- Baldar
- Freya
- Freyr
- Frigg
- Frigga
- Gardsvor
- Hod
- Huginn
- Muninn
- Odin
- Thor

OTHER

- Ameratsu
- Anahita
- Azaka-Tonnerre
- Dream of the Endless
- Dugnai
- Enki
- Evaki
- Habondia
- Inanna
- Ishtar
- John Barleycorn
- Kojin
- Kwan Yin
- Mother Eingana
- Tara
- Zao-jun

ROMAN

- Abundita
- Carmenta
- Fornax
- Janus
- Juno
- Lares Domestici
- Mars
- Mercury
- Nona
- Pluto
- Somnus

YORUBAN

- Erzuli
- Nana Buukun
- Obatala
- Oshun
- Oya
- Papa Legba
- Shango
- Yemaya

Appendix D

Invoking and Banishing Pentagrams

An *invoking pentagram* is a pentagram (five-pointed star) drawn to bring in a specific sort of energy or to aid in an invocation or consecration. A *banishing pentagram* reverses this process, driving energy away or finishing, closing, or saying farewell to something.

There are invoking and banishing pentagrams for each of the four elements, as well as for Spirit if you're working a five-element system. For general-purpose invocations, the invoking pentagram of Earth is used. Because this pentagram is considered "all-purpose," Earth invoking and Earth banishing pentagrams can be used to invoke and banish other elements.

When banishing, always use the banishing pentagram that corresponds to the invoking pentagram you used to invoke. If you invoked with Earth, banish with Earth, and so on.

The type of pentagram you draw is determined by the beginning and end points. These symbols are drawn over or on an object or in the air with the fingers, athame, wand, or other tool. To consecrate an element, you can make the pentagram *in* the element (i.e., by putting the tip of your athame into the salt and drawing) or just *above* the element. I prefer to touch anything that is safe to touch (not hot coals), but it's not strictly required.

Invoking and Banishing Pentagrams

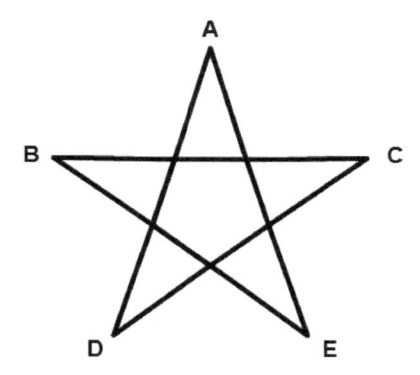

Figure 29: Pentagram for Invoking and Banishing

NOTE: When drawing a pentagram, visualize it clearly, seeing each line form as if drawn in neon. After you've finished drawing it, continue to see it in the spot where you placed it.

- An *Earth invoking* pentagram begins at point A, then goes to point D. You just finish the pentagram from there: A-D-C-B-E-A. Always return to your starting point; otherwise, the symbol isn't whole.
- With a banishing pentagram, you reverse the direction of the first line drawn. An *Earth banishing* pentagram is D-A-E-B-C-D.
- An *Air invoking* pentagram is C-B-E-A-D-C
- An *Air banishing* pentagram is therefore B-C-D-A-E-B
- *Fire invoking* pentagram: A-E-B-C-D-A
- *Fire banishing* pentagram: E-A-D-C-B-E
- *Water invoking* pentagram: B-C-D-A-E-B (the same as an Air banishing pentagram—your *intent* makes the difference)
- *Water banishing* pentagram: C-B-E-A-D-C (the same as an Air invoking pentagram)
- *Spirit invoking* pentagram: E-B-C-D-A-E
- *Spirit banishing* pentagram: B-E-A-D-C-B

Appendix E

Correspondence Charts

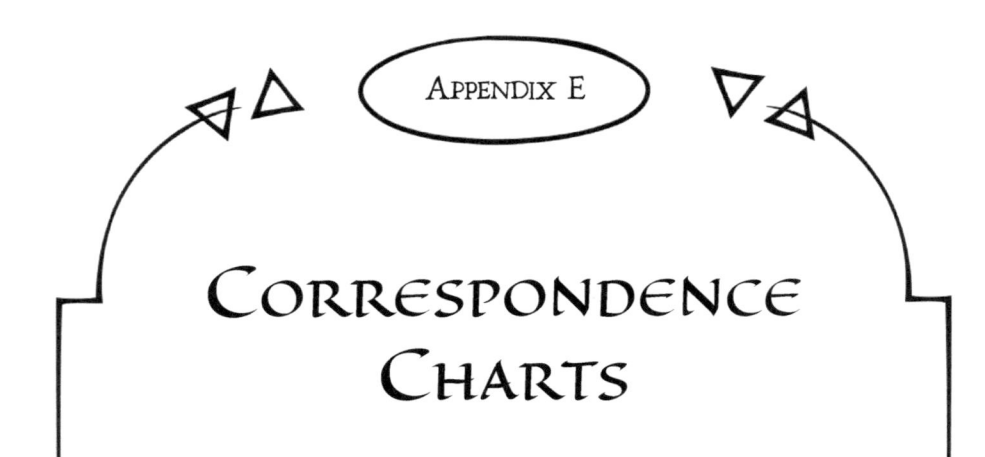

These charts provide useful information for constructing your own spells or for adding appropriate ingredients to the spells in this book.

ELEMENTAL HERBS, FLOWERS, AND OTHER PLANTS

Since this is a sampling and not a comprehensive list, I tried to select only those plants that are readily available in perfumes, teas, tinctures, or in the wild. I also looked for unusual relationships between the elements and the planets, as this can sometimes be very handy when working magic.

Certain planet/element relationships are obvious and expected: Air to Mercury, Fire to the Sun or Mars, Water to Venus or the Moon, etc. In cases where something is more properly a food (like grapefruit) or less readily available, I have included it if the unusual relationship makes it worthwhile.

Herbs of Air

Planet	Herb
Jupiter	Anise, dandelion, endive, maple, sage, star anise
Mars	Hops, pine
Mercury	Almond, caraway, clary sage, clover, lavender, lemongrass, lemon verbena, lily of the valley, mace, marjoram, mint, spearmint
Sun	Chicory, honey
Venus	Goldenrod

Herbs of Fire

Planet	Herb
Jupiter	Clove, nutmeg, sassafras
Mars	Basil, coriander, cumin, garlic, ginger, hawthorn, pepper (black pepper), pimento (red pepper), tobacco, woodruff, yucca
Mercury	Celery, dill, fennel, peppermint, pomegranate
Moon	Camelia
Sun	Angelica, bay, bergamot, carnation, cedar, cinnamon, goldenseal, heliotrope, juniper, lime, marigold, neroli (orange blossom), peony, rosemary, sesame, sunflower

Herbs of Water

Planet	Herb
Mars	Cranberry
Moon	Camphor, gardenia, jasmine, lemon, lily, myrrh, rosewood, sandalwood, willow, wintergreen
Sun	Chamomile, grapefruit
Venus	Apple blossom, cardamon, freesia, geranium, heather, hyacinth, iris, jonquil, lilac, narcissus, orchid, orris, plumeria (a.k.a. frangipani), rose, thyme, tuberose, vanilla, violet, yarrow, ylang-ylang

HERBS OF EARTH

Planet	Herb
Jupiter	Honeysuckle, oakmoss, tonka beans
Moon	Honesty
Saturn	Cypress, horsetail, mimosa, oleander, patchouli
Venus	Magnolia, mugwort, primrose, tulip, vervain, vetiver (a.k.a. vetivert), wood sorrel

ELEMENTAL GEMS AND STONES

Most gems are minerals, but such organic items as pearl and coral are included. Highly ambiguous stones have been omitted, as they require more in-depth study than a simple chart can afford. For example, you'll notice that quartz crystal is not included. This may seem strange given its near ubiquity in magical work. However, quartz crystal has been associated with the Sun and Fire, the Moon and Water, Air because of its clarity, the Goddess, and the God, and is often used to symbolize Spirit by people using a five-element system. Now *that's* what I call ambiguous!

STONES OF AIR

Planet	Stone
Jupiter	Fluorite
Mercury	Aventurine, jasper (mottled), mica, pumice
Saturn	Sphene (a.k.a. titanate)

STONES OF FIRE

Planet	Stone
Mars	Bloodstone, flint, garnet, jasper (red), lava, onyx (also Saturn), rhodochrosite, rhodonite, ruby, sard, sardonyx, tourmaline (red), tourmaline (watermelon—also Venus)
Mercury	Agate (banded, black, brown, or red)
Pluto	Spinel

Planet	Stone
Saturn	Apache tear, obsidian, onyx (also Mars), serpentine
Sun	Amber, carnelian, citrine, diamond, pipestone (also Mars), sulphur, sunstone, tiger's-eye, topaz, zircon
Venus	Tourmaline (watermelon—also Mars)

Stones of Water

Planet	Stone
Jupiter	Amethyst (also Neptune), sugilite
Mercury	Agate (blue lace)
Moon	Aquamarine, beryl, chalcedony, moonstone, mother of pearl (also Neptune), pearl, sapphire, selenite
Neptune	Amethyst (also Jupiter), lapidolite (also Jupiter), mother of pearl (also Moon)
Venus	Azurite, calcite (blue or pink), chrysocolla, coral, jade, lapis lazuli, rose quartz, sodalite, tourmaline (blue, green, and pink)

Stones of Earth

Planet	Stone
Earth	Granite and ordinary found stones can be assumed to be associated with both the planet and the element of Earth
Mercury	Agate (green and moss)
Neptune	Turquoise (also Venus)
Pluto	Kunzite (also Venus)
Saturn	Alum, coal, hematite, jasper (brown), jet, salt, tourmaline (black)
Venus	Calcite (green), cat's-eye,[52] chrysoprase, emerald, jasper (green), kunzite (also Pluto), malachite, olivine, peridot, tourmaline (green), turquoise (also Neptune)

---

52 This is the natural stone sometimes known as "hawk's-eye." The iridescent "stone" with the iris-like center stripe that is sold as cat's-eye is a kind of optical glass.

BIBLIOGRAPHY

Aftel, Mandy. *Essence and Alchemy: A Book of Perfume*. New York: North Point Press, 2001.

Bittman, Mark. *How to Cook Everything: 2,000 Simple Recipes for Great Food*. Hoboken, NJ: John Wiley & Sons, Inc., 1998, 2008.

Bonewits, (Philip Emmons) Isaac. *Real Magic: An Introductory Treatise on the Basic Principles of Yellow Magic*. Revised edition. York Beach, ME: Weiser Books, 1989.

———. *Rites of Worship: A Neopagan Approach*. Miami, FL: Earth Religions Press, 2003.

Brau, Jean-Louis, Helen Weaver, and Allan Edmands. *Larousse Encyclopedia of Astrology*. New York: New American Library, 1977.

Campbell, Joseph. *The Hero with a Thousand Faces: Bolllingen Series XVII Third Edition*. Novato, California: New World Library, 2008.

Crowley, Aleister. *Magick Without Tears*. Tempe, AZ: New Falcon Publications, 1994.

Cunningham, Scott. *The Complete Book of Incense, Oils & Brews*. St. Paul, MN: Llewellyn Publications, 2004.

———. *Cunningham's Encyclopedia of Crystal, Gem & Metal Magic*. St. Paul, MN: Llewellyn Publications, 2001.

———. *Cunningham's Encyclopedia of Magical Herbs*. St. Paul, MN: Llewellyn Publications, 1985.

———. *The Magic of Food: Legends, Lore & Spellwork*. St. Paul, MN: Llewellyn Publications, 1996.

———. *Magical Aromatherapy*. St. Paul, MN: Llewellyn Publications, 1989.

Dey, Charmaine. *The Magic Candle: Facts and Fundamentals of Ritual Candle-Burning*. Plainview, NY: Original Publications, 1982.

Dorsey, Lillith. *Voodoo and Afro-Caribbean Paganism*. New York: Citadel Press, 2005.

Bibliography

Ellwood, Taylor. *Pop Culture Magick.* Staffordshire, UK: Immanion Press, 2004.

Farrar, Janet and Stewart. *Spells and How They Work.* Custer, WA: Phoenix Publishing, 1990.

———. *The Witches' Way: Principles, Rituals and Beliefs of Modern Witchcraft.* London: Robert Hale, 1984.

Gamache, Henry. *The Master Book of Candle Burning: How to Burn Candles for Every Purpose.* Highland Falls, NY: Sheldon Publications, 1942.

Goodman, Linda. *Linda Goodman's Sun Signs.* New York: Bantam, 1985.

Harary, Keith, Ph.D., and Pamela Weintraub. *Lucid Dreams in 30 Days: The Creative Sleep Program.* New York: St. Martin's Griffin, 1989.

Johnson, Robert A. *Inner Work: Using Dreams and Active Imagination for Personal Growth.* San Francisco, CA: Harper & Row, 1986.

Kozminsky, Isidore. *The Magic and Science of Jewels and Stones.* Volume 1. San Rafael, CA: Cassandra Press, 1988.

Kraig, Donald Michael. *Modern Sex Magick.* St. Paul, MN: Llewellyn Publications, 1988.

LaBerge, Stephen. *Lucid Dreaming: The Power of Being Awake & Aware in Your Dreams.* Los Angeles, CA: J. P. Tarcher, 1985.

LaBerge, Stephen, and Howard Rheingold. *Exploring the World of Lucid Dreaming.* New York: Ballantine Books, 1991.

Lipp, Deborah. *The Elements of Ritual: Air, Fire, Water, and Earth in the Wiccan Circle.* St. Paul, MN: Llewellyn Publications, 2003

———. *Magical Power for Beginners: How to Raise & Send Energy for Spells That Work.* Woodbury, MN: Llewellyn Publications, 2017.

———. *Merry Meet Again: Lessons, Life & Love on the Path of a Wiccan High Priestess.* Woodbury, MN: Llewellyn Publications, 2013.

———. *Tarot Interactions: Become More Intuitive, Psychic & Skilled at Reading Cards.* Woodbury, MN: Llewellyn Publications, 2015.

———. *The Way of Four: Create Elemental Balance in Your Life.* St. Paul, MN: Llewellyn Publications, 2004.

Liungman, Carl G. *Dictionary of Symbols.* Santa Barbara, CA: ABC-CLIO, 1991.

MacGregor, Trish. *The Everything Astrology Book: Discover Your True Self Among the Stars!* Holbrook, MA: Adams Media Corp., 1999.

Mathers, S. Liddell MacGregor, trans. and ed. *The Key of Solomon the King (Clavicula Salomonis).* Translated and edited from manuscripts in the British Museum. York Beach, ME: Weiser Books, 2002.

Mella, Dorothee L. *Stone Power*. New York: Warner Books, 1986.

Monaghan, Patricia. *The Book of Goddesses & Heroines*. St. Paul, MN: Llewellyn Publications, 1990.

Morrison, Dorothy. *Everyday Tarot Magic: Meditation & Spells*. St. Paul, MN: Llewellyn Publications, 2002.

Mumford, Jonn. *Ecstasy Through Tantra*. St. Paul, MN: Llewellyn Publications, 1988.

Renée, Janina. *Tarot Spells*. St. Paul, MN: Llewellyn Publications, 2000.

Regardie, Israel. *The Golden Dawn. Sixth Edition*. St. Paul, MN: Llewellyn Publications, 1989

Todd, Jude C. *Jude's Herbal Home Remedies*. St. Paul, MN: Llewellyn Publications, 1992.

Weed, Susun S. *Wise Woman Herbal for the Childbearing Years*. Woodstock, NY: Ash Tree Publishing, 1985.

Index

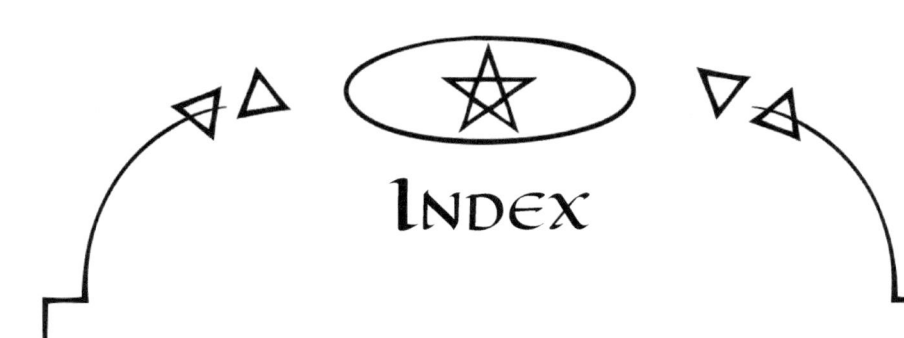

A

addiction, 164, 168–169
affirmations, 129–133
AIDS, 194, 228
alchemical, 10, 13, 16, 18, 99, 102, 106, 109
alchemical symbol, 18, 99, 102, 106, 109
alphabet, 128, 139–140
altar, 14, 16–17, 19, 71, 75, 84, 88, 91, 107, 128, 133, 136, 138, 143, 148–150, 182–183, 185–187, 192, 206, 216, 241–242, 250, 259
Angelic, 139, 141, 175
Angelic (script), 141, 175
anxiety, 194–195
apathy, 100
appetite, 107, 119, 223, 228
Aquarius, 10, 147
Aries, 13, 147, 225
Aristotle, 12, 14, 16–17
aromatherapy, x, 67, 121–124, 202, 236, 253, 272
asthma, 118, 133
athame, 12, 37, 73–74, 76–77, 79–81, 103, 105–106, 108–109, 121, 124, 126, 133–134, 139, 141–142, 145, 149, 151–152, 156–157, 181, 184–185, 192–193, 205, 207, 214, 216, 229, 237–238, 240, 244–245, 261, 266

B

Bath, 67–68, 103–105, 194–196, 202, 253, 259
bath, 67–68, 103–105, 194–196, 202, 253, 259
battery, 31, 58–60, 179–180, 182, 186, 228, 237–238, 245
beacon, 181–182, 185–186, 216, 253, 256, 258–259
bell, 12, 52, 73, 81–82, 97–98, 115, 121, 214, 216–217, 261
between the worlds, 30, 60
bind rune, 198–199
blood, 12, 14–15, 27, 86, 103, 118, 148, 188
Bonewits, Isaac, xiii, 2, 41, 45, 55, 140, 272
brews, 202, 272
Buffy the Vampire Slayer, 25
burning as, 160, 163

C

Campbell, Joseph, 15, 272

Cancer, 16, 132, 147, 228
Capricorn, 16–17, 147
central nervous system, 122
Ceremonial Magic, 175–176
chakras, 33, 67, 88, 243
childbirth, 15, 118, 163, 188, 203–204
choleric, 14
clay, x, 224, 247–251, 256
color, 10, 12–13, 16–17, 29, 47, 55, 71–72, 99, 101, 104, 117, 145–149, 225, 243, 248, 251, 256
compass, 18, 67, 75, 237, 261
compassion, 104–106, 148, 227
courage, 118, 144, 148, 165–166, 253, 256–257
coven, 42, 58, 71, 181–183, 192
Crowley, Aleister, 11, 26, 272

D

death, 15, 148, 163, 233
decision, 42, 118, 139, 144–145, 167, 188, 210, 212, 253, 257, 262
decoy, 235
destruction, 145, 160, 163–164, 171–172, 253
disorder, iv, 103, 118, 144, 188
divination, x, 116, 146, 189, 209, 217–218
drumming, 37–38, 41, 94–95, 140, 158, 170–171, 225, 228, 241, 245

E

east, 10, 18–19, 67, 81, 185, 187, 193, 227, 238

ecology, 119, 223
elemental, ix, xi–xii, 1, 4, 9–13, 17, 19–24, 29, 36, 53, 68, 74, 76, 78–79, 86–87, 94, 110–111, 113, 115–117, 119, 132, 146, 148, 175, 182, 231, 234, 268, 270, 273
Elements of Ritual, The, 28, 273
ethics, 45, 47

F

Farrar, Janet and Stewart, 273
fear, 63, 97
feathers, 12, 97–99, 256
fertility, 17, 119, 148, 181, 207, 223, 244, 246, 249–250, 254, 256–258, 261
flowers, xi, 36, 54, 122, 194–195, 202, 205–206, 230–231, 250, 255, 268
for courage, 118, 144, 165–166, 253, 256–257
Fortune, Dion, 26
Friday, 152, 206
funeral, 235

G

Gaia, 16, 108, 238, 264
garden, xi, 119, 220, 223, 236, 240, 243–248, 254, 257, 261
Gardnerian, ii, 11, 27
Gemini, 10, 147
gnome, 17, 20, 22–24, 108–109, 231
Golden Dawn, 1, 9–11, 274

H

Healing, v, 13, 30, 35, 43, 47–51, 53–54, 56, 62, 111–112, 118, 121, 125, 127, 132, 148, 150, 164, 166, 203, 210–213, 228, 230
health, 35, 41, 48–49, 51, 59, 62–63, 148, 202–203, 228, 244, 254, 258
hero's journey, 15
Hippocrates, 12, 14, 17
Holy Grail, 16

I

imitative magic, 53, 245
immunological, 118, 144
insomnia, 23, 103
inspiration, xii, 9–10, 15, 18, 78, 83, 89, 97, 116–117, 120, 231
interconnection, 27–28, 49
intuition, 12, 16, 18, 22, 53, 85, 89, 103–105, 116, 118, 148, 188, 212–213
invisible, 36, 39, 139, 141, 143, 191, 196–197, 200
invoking and banishing, xi, 266–267

J

job, 5, 43–44, 46–47, 56–57, 62, 110, 117, 119, 123, 132, 150, 164, 167, 223
joke, 231, 233
Jung, Carl, 12, 14, 17
Jupiter, 135, 269–271

justice, 46–47, 53, 61, 118, 120, 139–142, 148, 157, 166, 196, 253, 255, 258–260, 262

K

King, Francis X, 11, 274
kitchen, 22–23, 48, 73, 108, 123, 225–231, 254, 259
Kitchen Witch, 73
Kraig, Donald Michael, xiii, 2, 175, 180, 273

L

lactation, 118, 188
Leo, 13, 147
libido, 100, 118, 144, 150–151, 253, 256, 258–262
Libra, 10, 147
love spells, 45, 116, 206, 225
lucid dreaming, 208–209, 214, 273
lymphatic, 118, 188

M

magic box, 75, 256, 260
Magical Alphabet, 128, 139–140
Magical Power for Beginners, v, 5, 25, 55–56, 255, 273
Maharishi Effect, 1, 55
mandala, 34, 162
marriage, 27, 119, 163–164, 167, 190, 192, 223
meditation, 31–33, 35, 37–38, 55, 69–70, 84, 86, 105, 116, 128, 211, 243, 274

melancholic, 17
memory, 14, 29, 121–123, 125–127, 129, 133–134, 190, 253, 256, 260–261
menstrual cramps, 203–204
Mercury, 124, 126, 135, 162, 265, 268–271
mirror, 34, 39, 73, 88–91, 133–134, 189, 197–199, 202, 237–239, 256
mojo bag, 113, 128, 244
Monaghan, Patricia, 231, 274
money, 11, 17, 49–50, 57, 107, 110, 117, 148, 150, 224, 235, 239, 241–242, 254, 257, 259
Monkey's Paw, The, 57

N

National Library of Ireland, 11
neurological, 118, 144
north, 17–19, 67, 81, 174, 184, 193, 227, 238, 272

O

obsession, 24, 168–170, 253, 257, 259, 261
offering, 54, 160–162, 164–166, 231, 233, 235, 253
orgasm, 35, 40–41, 176–180, 182, 186, 246
overload, ix, 23–24

P

Paganism, 8, 18, 169, 233, 273
pain, 37, 118, 188, 203

Paracelsus, 20–21
past life, 30
pentacle, 11, 17, 36, 224
pentagram, xi, 17–19, 33, 81, 185, 187, 248, 266–267
phlegmatic, 16
Pictorial Key to the Tarot, The, 10
Pisces, 16, 147
political action, 118, 144, 148, 155–156
poppet, 8, 34, 111, 128
pregnancy, 17, 48, 163, 203–204, 249, 252, 254, 258
protection, v, 47, 54, 60, 113, 148, 180, 183, 196, 235–237, 239, 244
psychic, v, 36, 71, 73, 110, 116–118, 122, 144, 176, 188–190, 195, 213, 218–219, 222, 235, 237, 243, 254, 261, 273

R

rage, 164, 171–174, 253, 257, 259, 261–262
Regardie, Israel, 12, 274
relatives, 27
Respiratory, 97, 118, 120
rhyming, 216
rhythm, 37–38, 78, 95, 229, 238, 241
rule of silence, 61
runes, 72, 138, 198–199, 217
Runic, 128, 139–140

S

Sagittarius, 14, 147
salamander, 12–13, 20–24, 101–102, 160

sanguine, 12
school, 117, 119–120, 132–133, 135–138, 253, 256, 260, 262
Scorpio, 16, 147
Sculpey, 248
sex magic, x, xiii, 38, 145, 175–183, 187, 212, 245–246, 253
Smith, 10, 12, 129–130
solitary, 38–39, 42, 64, 67, 88, 92, 98, 103, 108, 123, 127, 133, 140, 152, 156, 165, 167, 177, 182, 186, 192, 194, 198, 204, 215, 226, 228, 237, 240, 245, 249
south, 13, 17–19, 67, 81, 174, 193, 227
spells of, 119, 145, 161, 171
spirit, 4, 18–20, 24, 33, 36, 45, 116, 145, 160, 163, 166, 175, 233, 235, 238, 266–267, 270
spring, 10, 17–18, 67, 233, 240, 246
stamina, 41, 118, 144
studying, 56, 96, 113
Styx, 15
summer, 13
Sunday, 101, 156
sword, 10–12, 14, 21, 181, 192
sylph, 10, 12, 20–21, 23, 98–99
Sympathetic Magic, 8–9, 28, 30
sympathetic objects, 9, 31, 34, 38, 50, 53, 71

T

Tantra, 175–176, 274
Tarot, ii, v, 10, 12, 14–17, 36–37, 217–220, 222, 254, 261, 273–274
Taurus, 16–17, 27, 29, 147–149
thaumaturgy, 86

Theban, 128, 139–140, 175, 198
trance, 15, 34, 37–38, 73, 128, 146, 229
Transcendental Meditation, 55
transformation, 13, 15, 127, 160, 163–164, 171
transportation, 110
transubstantiation, 86
travel, 21, 28, 73, 118, 120, 122–126, 160, 202, 253, 259, 262
treasure, 14, 17, 196, 199, 233–235
turquoise, 113–114, 147, 271

U

undine, 16, 20, 22–24, 104, 107, 190

V

Venus, 104, 205, 207, 268–271
Virgo, 17, 147
Voodoo doll, 8

W

Waite, Arthur Edward, 10–12, 222
wand, 11–12, 14, 73–74, 76, 80–81, 121, 123–126, 133–134, 139, 145, 151, 156, 185, 261, 266
waning moon, 149, 192, 198
waxing moon, 98, 134, 136, 149, 152, 156, 192, 206, 229, 245, 249
Way of Four, The, v, 1, 3–5, 86–87, 96, 132, 150, 273
west, vii, 15, 18–19, 67, 81, 193, 227
Western occultism, 8, 10, 16, 18
white-hilt knife, 74, 149, 151, 156, 261

Wicca, ii, v, 8, 17–18, 23, 73–74, 113–114, 149, 183, 233, 236
Wiccan, v, 5, 9, 14, 16, 18–19, 30, 35, 44, 60, 71, 74, 93, 156, 183, 187, 228, 233, 236, 273
Wiccan Rede, 44
winter, 17–18
Witches' Pyramid, 9, 13, 16–17, 197
writer's block, 103

Y

Yeats, William Butler, 11–12

MORE FROM CROSSED CROW BOOKS

The Way of Four by Deborah Lipp
Witchcraft on a Shoestring by Deborah Blake
Circle, Coven, & Grove by Deborah Blake
Aislings by Jeremy Schewe
Merlin: Master of Magick by Gordon Strong
The Bones Fall in a Spiral by Mortellus
Your Star Sign by Per Henrik Gullfoss
The Complete Book of Spiritual Astrology by Per Henrik Gullfoss
Icelandic Plant Magic by Albert Bjorn
The Black Book of Johnathan Knotbristle by Chris Allaun
A Witch's Book of Terribles by Wycke Malliway
In the Shadow of Thirteen Moons by Kimberly Sherman-Cook
Witchcraft Unchained by Craig Spencer
Wiccan Mysteries by Raven Grimassi
Wiccan Magick by Raven Grimassi
A Victorian Grimoire by Patricia Telesco
Celtic Tree Mysteries by Steve Blamires
Star Magic by Sandra Kynes
Witches' Sabbats and Esbats by Sandra Kynes
A Spirit Work Primer by Naag Loki Shivanaath
A Witch's Shadow Magick Compendium by Raven Digitalis
Flight of the Firebird by Kenneth Johnson
Witchcraft and the Shamanic Journey by Kenneth Johnson
Travels Through Middle Earth by Alaric Albertsson
Be Careful What You Wish For by Laetitia Latham-Jones
Death's Head by Blake Malliway
The Wildwood Way by Cliff Seruntine

Learn more at
www.CrossedCrowBooks.com